SHILOH—*in Hell before Night*

"Fill your canteens boys!
Some of you will be in hell before night
and you'll need water!"

—A UNION COLONEL'S CRY TO HIS
REINFORCEMENTS DURING THE
BATTLE OF SHILOH

SHILOH

–in Hell before Night

JAMES LEE McDONOUGH

THE UNIVERSITY OF TENNESSEE PRESS

Manufactured in the United States of America.

This book is printed on acid-free paper.

Cloth: 1st printing, 1977; 2nd printing, 1979;
3rd printing, 1980; 4th printing, 1987;
5th printing, 1991.

Paper: 1st printing, 1977; 2nd printing, 1982;
3rd printing, 1985; 4th printing, 1987;
5th printing, 1991; 6th printing, 1997;
7th printing, 2003.

Library of Congress Cataloging in Publication Data

McDonough, James L., 1934–
    Shiloh—in hell before night.
    Bibliography: p.
    Includes index.
    1. Shiloh, Battle of, 1862. I. Title
E473.54.M22   973.7'32   76-18864
ISBN 0-87049-199-7 (cl.: alk. paper)
ISBN 0-87049-232-2 (pbk.: alk. paper)

Preface

Confederate General Basil Duke, who fought at Shiloh, acknowledged a particular mystique associated with the battle as he recalled the struggle a number of years later. "Two great battles of the Civil War," he said, "seem to command an especial interest denied the others. . . . There yet lingers a wish to hear all that may be told of Shiloh and Gettysburg. . . ." Civil War scholar, Otto Eisenschiml, after extensive study and visits to many of the battlefields of America, wrote of Shiloh: "No novelist could have packed into a space of two days more action, romance and surprises than history did on that occasion. Of all the battlefields . . . I thought Shiloh the most intriguing."

There is something special about Shiloh. Many people have recognized this fact, but that special something is hard to define, probably because it reaches beyond the strategic significance of the battle, even as significant as the engagement undoubtedly was. I would not claim that I have either fully grasped this elusive mystique or told "all that may be told" of Shiloh, but I hope the reader may leave this book with a better understanding of the tragic struggle.

The engagement was, up to its time, the biggest battle of the American Civil War and of American history. It was a colorful, dramatic, blundering, and confused fight in which several of the most important commanders of the war participated, such as Grant, Sherman, Johnston, Beauregard, Bragg, and Forrest. The first day at Shiloh was possibly, relative to the number of men engaged, as bloody as any day of the entire war. The battle was one of the major engagements, along with Fort Donelson and Vicksburg, that determined the ultimate outcome of the most significant campaign in the Western theater of war, the campaign to control the Mississippi Valley. Without the Mississippi Valley the Confederacy was cut in half and had no realistic hope of succeeding. Shiloh was a battle in which the Confederates made an all-out, determined, desperate effort to throw back the Blue army. They almost succeeded. But when the gods of war ceased to smile upon them and the Rebels went trudging back to Corinth in the mud and rain on the night of April 7, 1862, one of the best opportunities they ever knew had slipped from their grasp. The late Robert Selph Henry in *The Story of the Confederacy* succinctly stated the meaning of Shiloh: "The issues of Shiloh . . . were the defeat of major armies and the possession of the Mississippi. The stake was immense."

The battle of Shiloh probably has more hard questions associated with it than any battle of the war. Grant himself later wrote of the engagement that it "has been perhaps less understood or more persistently misunderstood" than any other battle. The questions raised by Shiloh do seem almost endless.

Why was the Union army situated with a river at its back? Why was Grant absent when his army was attacked? Why were Grant and Sherman so confident the Confederates would not advance, ignoring evidence of such advance and neglecting ordinary precautions against attack? Would the Union force have been destroyed if Buell had not arrived when he did? What happened to Lew Wallace that he never got his division into the fight on the first day of the battle? Why did it take the Rebels so long to get from Corinth to the battlefield? How much difference, if any, did this loss of time make in the outcome of the battle? Could the Rebels have won the battle of Shiloh, or were they doomed from the start? Were Johnston and Beauregard working at cross-purposes in planning the strategy and making the attack? Did Beauregard throw away the victory when he called off the attack Sunday evening? Why was virtually no effort made to reorganize the Confederates and get ready for the next day's battle?

These are some of the research questions that make a study of Shiloh difficult, fascinating, and controversial.

A study of Shiloh is also significant and intriguing because of its importance to the careers of certain officers who fought there. If the Confederates had won at Shiloh, Grant and Sherman, the two men who eventually emerged to lead the Union to victory, would probably have been ruined. On the Confederate side the battle saw the death of Johnston, whom some considered the Western Confederacy's greatest general, and it also became, to a great extent, the undoing of Beauregard, in whom Jefferson Davis never again seemed willing to place his trust.

The battle is fascinating too because of the human interest stories associated with it. Some of the most unusual, pathetic, and heartrending occurrences conceivable took place there.

Less important battles have sometimes been the subject of several books. Yet even though Shiloh has always been recognized as one of the most important engagements of the war and a wealth of source material has been available, I discovered that the only books to treat the subject had been sketchy and impressionistic in nature, obviously not, and in most cases never intended to be, full historical treatments of the battle. One novel had appeared—Shelby Foote's *Shiloh*—which is interesting and well written, but a novel cannot take the place of a full, documented work when a reader desires to separate fact from fiction.

Thus I long thought that my book would be the first comprehensive historical treatment of the battle. Several months after my manuscript had been accepted for publication by the University of Tennessee Press, I was surprised to learn of the imminent appearance of Wiley Sword's *Shiloh: Bloody April*. Having now read his book, I think it appropriate to point out that I agree with Sword on the significance of the battle, but differ with him on several major points of interpretation, such as Johnston's leadership and the impact of his death, and the Rebel chances of a successful attack in the late afternoon of the first day of the battle. In fact, my analysis of the campaign is contrary to Sword's on several other questions as well. Readers of both books should find the disagreements thought-provoking.

Finally, I would add that it has been an enjoyable experience to do the research and to write about Shiloh. Even as a boy, I was impressed by Shiloh when other battlefields that my father took me to visit were then of no particular concern. When I later came to have more than a passing interest in the war, the battle of Shiloh increasingly loomed intriguing and decisive in the total conflict. It seemed strange, in view of the battle's importance and the vast number of books published about the Civil War, that I could find no modern, documented monograph on Shiloh. I decided to write one.

ACKNOWLEDGMENTS

Many people assisted me in the completion of this book. I am especially grateful to David Lipscomb College for the Faculty Fellowship Grant which provided an uninterrupted block of time to work when I needed it the most. Mrs. Josephine Buffington and the staff of the Crisman Memorial Library of David Lipscomb College deserve much credit for assisting me in locating materials. Mr. Alvoid Rector, former Superintendent of the Shiloh National Military Park, was always gracious and helpful when I was visiting the battlefield. Mr. Rudy Sanders is to be acknowledged for his work in preparing the preliminary maps for the book. To all others who may have assisted in any way I wish to say "thank you."

Nashville, Tennessee   JAMES LEE MCDONOUGH

Contents

Illustrations

MAPS

PHOTOGRAPHS

SHILOH—*in Hell before Night*

1. *A Gathering of "Armies"*

ABOUT ONE HUNDRED MILES east of Memphis the Tennessee River winds northward from Alabama on a lazy, meandering course across the Volunteer State toward the Kentucky line. The countryside is serene and resplendent on a warm sunny day in early April. The banks of the river are alive with the fresh sights and sounds of spring. Wildlife and flora are in abundance. Birds sing and squirrels, rabbits, and occasionally a deer scamper about the forest. Violets are in bloom, and the redbuds, dogwoods, and tall white oaks are budding. A sparkle of color is everywhere, and perhaps nothing is more delicately beautiful than the peach trees' soft pink blossoms.

The Tennessee Valley does not seem a likely setting for a bloody struggle among a hundred thousand men. Such carnage ought to be on the dry hot sands of a North Africa, or the bitter cold and snow of a Stalingrad. Those are sites fitting for war. But sometimes hellish scenes occur in the midst of picturesque surroundings and at inappropriate, even, many would say, sacrilegious times—such as on Sunday. Thus it was along the western bank of the Tennessee River on Sunday, April 6, 1862.

The place, of no apparent significance to the casual observer, was called Pittsburg Landing, a steamboat docking point on the west bank of the river, only a few miles from the junction of Mississippi and Alabama to the south. The landing's name came from Pitts Tucker, a man who built a rustic log cabin on the site and traded in hard liquor with the rivermen, who quickly discovered his place of business. By the time of the Civil War several cabins stood on the bluff which ascended 80 to 100 feet high, and roads ran west to Purdy, Tennessee, and southeast to Hamburg, Tennessee, and

southwest to Corinth, Mississippi. A few farmers worked the
surrounding fields which now and then alternated with vast
tracts of heavily wooded land. Pittsburg Landing was about
nine miles upstream, on the opposite bank of the river, from
the little town of Savannah, Tennessee. It would come to be
better known as Shiloh, a Biblical word meaning, ironically, "a
place of peace," a name given to the Methodist meetinghouse
which had been erected about two and a half miles southwest
of the landing.

The Civil War had already gone on for nearly a year, but
nothing to compare with what was now about to happen had
yet occurred. The carnage at Manassas, Wilson's Creek, Fort
Donelson, Pea Ridge—the "big" battles thus far in the war and
household words to many—would soon pale into relative
insignificance when contrasted with the bloodletting at
Shiloh. The killed and wounded of all those battles put together would fall far short of the number of killed and
wounded at the "place of peace." Soldiers who had been eager
to "see the Elephant," as they commonly referred to combat,
would never feel so anxious for a fight again.[1]

Sam Watkins, private in the First Tennessee Infantry,
would one day write that Shiloh was "the first big battle in
which our regiment had ever been engaged. . . . I had heard
and read of battlefields . . . but I confess that I never realized
the 'pomp and circumstance' of the thing called glorious war
until I saw this. Men . . . lying in every conceivable position;
the dead . . . with their eyes wide open, the wounded begging

[1] Thomas L. Livermore, *Numbers and Losses in the Civil War in America,
1861–1865* (Boston, 1900), 77–80. The killed and wounded at Shiloh numbered 19,897 compared to 11,953 for the combined killed and wounded at
Manassas, Wilson's Creek, Fort Donelson, and Pea Ridge. Total casualties at
Shiloh are placed at 23,741 by Livermore. See Lloyd Lewis, "Rivers of
Blood," *American Mercury* (May 1931), 73, who argues convincingly that
probably no battle of the war saw *both* sides lose so heavily in relation to the
number engaged as at Shiloh. Also see Samuel M. Howard, *The Illustrated
Comprehensive History of the Great Battle of Shiloh* (Gettysburg, S. D., 1921),
105–15, 120, 121. Jacob Ammen, "Diary of the March to and Battle at
Pittsburg Landing," *War of the Rebellion: A Compilation of the Official Records of
the Union and Confederate Armies,* 129 vols. (Washington, D. C., 1880–1901),
serial 1, vol. x, part 1, 333. Hereafter cited as *OR.* All references are to serial
1 unless otherwise noted. John K. Duke, *History of the 53rd Ohio Volunteer
Infantry* (Portsmouth, Ohio, 1900), 48.

piteously for help. . . . It all seemed to me a dream; I seemed
. . . in a sort of daze. . . ."[2] It was with the impressions of Shiloh
fresh in his mind that William T. Sherman, who had earlier
fought at Manassas or Bull Run, wrote his wife of the scenes
he had just witnessed, describing the "horrid nature of this
war," the wounded and maimed, "the piles of dead soldiers'
mangled bodies . . . without heads and legs," and concluding
that he did not expect to survive the war.[3]

Many would remember Shiloh as the most horrible, san-
guinary struggle in all their four years of fighting. R. F.
Learned, of the Tenth Mississippi Infantry Regiment, wrote
of Shiloh: "Since then I have been in many pitched battles
including Perryville, Murfreesboro, Chickamauga, and
Franklin, but none ever made the same impression upon me."
A soldier of the Twelfth Michigan Infantry by the name of
Franklin Bailey, writing to his parents from Savannah on the
day after the battle, said that the engagement made him
shudder to think about it; that the sight was simply terrible
beyond description. "Let a dark veil be drawn over the scene"
was the one-sentence entry made in his diary by Oliphant M.
Todd of the Seventy-Eighth Ohio Infantry after he had
walked the battlefield on the day following Shiloh. "From that
hour," said L. B. Crooker, captain in the Fifty-fifth Illinois, as
he evaluated the impact of Shiloh, "all sentimental talk of an
easy conquest ceased upon both sides." Ulysses S. Grant, in his
memoirs, wrote that "Shiloh was the severest battle fought at
the West during the war. . . ."[4]

People like Grant, who had thought that one great battle
would bring the war to a conclusion, would now sense that

[2] Samuel R. Watkins, *"Co. Aytch," Maury Grays, 1st Tennessee Regiment*
(Jackson, Tenn., 1952), 64–66.
[3] M. A. DeWolfe Howe, ed. *Home Letters of General Sherman* (New York,
1909), 222, 223.
[4] R. F. Learned to D. W. Reed, Mar. 22, 1904, Miscellaneous MSS Collec-
tion, Shiloh National Military Park Library. The library is hereafter cited as
SNMP. Franklin Bailey to parents, Apr. 8, 1862, Personal Accounts, Federal,
SNMP. Oliphant M. Todd, Diary, MSS Division, Library of Congress. L. B.
Crooker, "Battle of Shiloh," *Manual of the Panorama of the Battle of Shiloh*
(Chicago, 1885), 8. See also *Confederate Veteran*, 40 vols. (Nashville, 1893–
1932), XVIII, 471. Ulysses S. Grant, *Personal Memoirs of U. S. Grant*, 2 vols.
(New York, 1885), I, 355–56.

such was not to be, that the war must go on, draining the nation of men, money, and resources, and changing the very fiber of the nation's existence, until either the Confederacy was finally smashed or the Union was divided.[5] And considering all of its ramifications, Shiloh would be one of the most strategically significant engagements of the Western theater of war.

The prelude to Shiloh began in the winter of 1862—a disastrous winter for the Confederates. Union General Ambrose Burnside captured Roanoke Island on February 8. Union General Samuel R. Curtis defeated Confederate General Earl Van Dorn at Pea Ridge, Arkansas, in early March. About the same time the *Monitor* came forth to successfully check the Confederate breakthrough in the development of ironclad warships, battling the Rebel *Virginia* to a standoff at Hampton Roads. But these Union achievements were minor compared to what was happening in Tennessee.

In early February a combination land-water Union invasion force under Grant and Andrew H. Foote breached the Confederate defensive perimeter across southern Kentucky. Driving south up the Tennessee and Cumberland rivers, they captured the supposed bastions protecting those vital waterways, Fort Henry and Fort Donelson. Fort Henry fell to the Federals first, with ludicrous, almost unbelievable ease, when one-third of its fortifications were underwater and the single 10-inch Columbiad with sufficient range to contest the Union gunboats was accidentally spiked, while a rifled 24-pounder burst; Fort Donelson collapsed after some hard fighting, amply mingled with Confederate bungling, disunity of command, and vacillation, climaxed by a brief siege—all occurring in cold weather punctuated with snow and sleet. The very heart of Tennessee was thereby laid open to the Union forces.

The Confederates in the center of the line at Bowling Green, Kentucky, led by Albert Sidney Johnston, who had been hailed by many as the savior of the Confederacy when he took command back in September, found themselves

[5] Clarence C. Buell and Robert U. Johnson, eds., *Battles and Leaders of the Civil War*, 4 vols. (New York, 1887–88), I, 485–86. Hereafter cited as *Battles and Leaders*.

outflanked and fell back rapidly. Newspapers around the country, such as the Chicago *Times*, the Richmond *Enquirer*, and the New Orleans *Daily Picayune*, were reporting that the Rebels would make a stand at Nashville and that Nashville would be held "at all hazards."[6] But Johnston led his army on through Tennessee's capital city without attempting to defend it and also left to the Federals much of the enormous military supplies which had been stored there. Only the strenuous efforts of Nathan Bedford Forrest and his rear guard enabled the Rebels to carry off some of the provisions. Then rumors circulated that Johnston would make a stand at Murfreesboro. However, the Confederates continued to fall back through Murfreesboro and Fayetteville, all the way to Alabama. The Rebel forces on the western flank of the line, commanded by the Louisiana Episcopal Bishop, General Leonidas Polk, evacuated Columbus, Kentucky, and marched south. Two hundred miles to the east of Nashville, Knoxville was left in a perilous position after the East Tennessee wing of Johnston's defensive line was destroyed in Kentucky at the battle of Mill Springs, otherwise known as Logan's Cross Roads.

A Union army under Don Carlos Buell advanced, virtually unopposed, into the capital of Tennessee, the first Confederate state capital to be occupied by Union forces, while the army that had taken Fort Donelson continued up the Tennessee River all the way past Savannah to Pittsburg Landing. And still farther to the west the grand advance continued as Federal General John Pope applied pressure on the Mississippi. When Polk evacuated Columbus the Rebels attempted to hold the great river farther south, in the vicinity of the Kentucky-Tennessee-Missouri boundary. The key points were Island Number Ten, a strong fortification in the southern end of a big loop of the river, and New Madrid, an old Missouri town farther downstream on the west bank of the Mississippi. Pope could not approach New Madrid by river because of the batteries on Island Number Ten, but he was able to reach it overland from the north and west. By March 14 the town was

[6] Chicago *Times*, Feb. 20, 1862. Richmond *Enquirer*, Feb. 19, 1862. New Orleans *Daily Picayune*, Feb. 20, 1862.

in Union hands, leaving Island Number Ten almost isolated as the Federals then controlled the west bank of the river both above and below the island. It appeared the Confederates would soon be falling back again, perhaps all the way to Fort Pillow, 50 river miles north of Memphis. Mrs Braxton Bragg, characteristically alternating between giving her husband advice and criticizing the Confederate war effort, wrote the general, who had left Pensacola and Mobile to help reinforce the retiring Confederates: "In truth we can not retreat much more without coming upon the enemy on the Gulf." If the Southern soldiers "continue to behave so disgracefully we women had better take the field and send them home to raise chickens . . . ." As for derelict commanders, she wondered if Bragg could not "hang or shoot them?"[7]

Indeed the events of February had produced a Confederate disaster of unequaled proportions. The suddenness with which it all happened, together with the timing—occurring when Rebel self-confidence and optimism, reveling in the intoxication of the early triumphs of the war, were still at a zenith—made the losses seem all the more appalling.

The situation was so desperate that some Southern newspapers, in an effort to bolster Confederate morale, were resorting to the dubious expedient of finding something positive in the reverses suffered. "They were for our own good!" proclaimed one of the Richmond papers, while the New Orleans *Daily Picayune* consoled: "In the economy of Providence apparent evil sometimes becomes the prolific source of good. . . . So in every just cause, true faith and unshrinking courage will make disaster itself the means of making a way to victory." A few weeks later a paradoxical editorial in the same paper was expressing its "sincere belief" that "the fall of Fort Donelson secures the independence of the Confederate States."[8] It was as if Divine Providence, disturbed and angered by Southern overconfidence, were somehow teaching the Confederates an indispensable lesson through their defeats.

[7] Mrs. Braxton Bragg to Bragg, Mar. 26, Apr. 2, 1862, William P. Palmer Collection, Braxton Bragg Papers, Western Reserve Historical Society, Cleveland.

[8] Richmond *Enquirer*, Feb. 18, 1862. New Orleans *Daily Picayune*, Feb. 16, 1862, Mar. 2, 1862.

No doubt some must have thought that Divine Providence was being rather harsh in conveying the lesson.

The heart of Tennessee with its growing industrial complex and great war potential was gone. The state was the Confederacy's largest producer of such essential war materials as pig iron and bar, sheet, and railroad iron. The furnaces, forges, and bloomeries were concentrated in the fifty-mile-wide area from about Fort Donelson to Nashville and south—the area the Union army had just penetrated. Nashville had been the greatest storehouse and arsenal center in the Western Confederacy for such items as gunpowder, ammunition, small arms, and artillery, as well as for huge stores of a general variety of military provisions from tents, clothing, saddles, and sabers to flour and bacon.[9]

Now the Union army was approaching dangerously close to what had become the most strategically important town west of Chattanooga: Corinth, Mississippi, a railroad junction only twenty miles from a major river, where the north-south Mobile and Ohio Railroad crossed the east-west Memphis and Charleston line. If the Union army captured Corinth, not only would Memphis be untenable and thus the Mississippi River soon be opened to Federal forces for several hundred more miles, but most significantly, the Union army would smash what former Confederate Secretary of War General Leroy P. Walker appropriately described as "the vertebrae of the Confederacy"—the Memphis and Charleston Railroad.[10]

This railroad was a lifeline which Secretary of War Judah P. Benjamin told Robert E. Lee "must be defended at all hazards." The Confederate cabinet even discussed the possibility of abandoning Richmond in order to protect it.[11] With this line broken, Rebel east-west communications would be forced to drop south all the way to Vicksburg and Meridian, Mississippi, to Mobile, Alabama, and then proceed north by a

---

[9] J. P. Lesley, *Iron Manufacturer's Guide to the Furnaces, Forges and Rolling Mills of the United States* (New York, 1859), 130–36. J. B. Killebrew, *Middle Tennessee as an Iron Centre* (Nashville, 1879), 9–15. Allan Nevins, *The War for the Union*, 4 vols. (New York, 1960), II, 74. Thomas L. Connelly, *Army of the Heartland* (Baton Rouge, 1967), 8–10.

[10] *OR*, VII, 889.

[11] *OR*, VI, 398, 828. Nevins, *War*, II, 74.

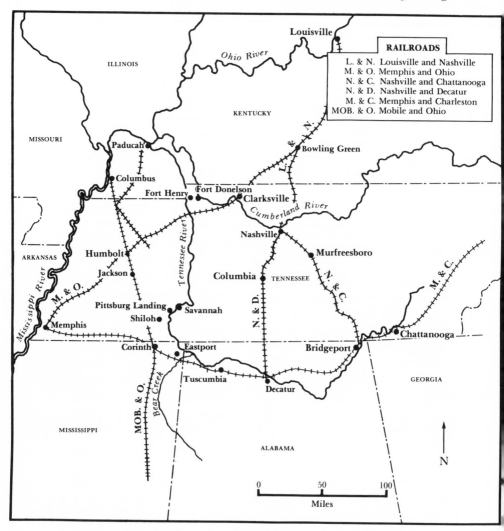

Map 1. Western Theater, Spring 1862.

circuitous route through Alabama and Georgia back up to
Chattanooga, before proceeding northeast to Virginia. A
more damaging blow to the Confederacy in the West is
difficult to conceive.

But now the Rebels, shocked, shamed, and reeling from the
Federal successes, were gathering in force around Corinth.
They were coming from all over the South—Mobile, Pensacola, New Orleans, Nashville, Memphis—hoping and determined to muster enough strength to arrest and roll back the
onrushing Blue juggernaut and reverse the tide of war in the
Western theater before it would forever be too late. The New
Orleans *Daily Picayune* was approvingly quoting a proclama-
tion of the Nashville *Banner of Peace* that the people of the
South "can not be too much penetrated with the momentous-
ness of the hour. The coming struggle should know no retreat . . . , nothing but a victor's palm, or a soldier's grave."[12]

A victorious campaign was a "must" for the Confederates.
They had to protect the Memphis and Charleston Railroad;
they had to recover the central and western portions of Middle Tennessee; they had to regain control of the Cumberland
and Tennessee rivers. If the Rebels were going to win the war
they had to do it early, before the Yankees could fully marshal
and bring to bear their admittedly overwhelming resources.
Time was already running short for the South. Thus the
Confederates at Corinth were gathering for a battle that they
had to win—or be irrevocably doomed, in the face of ever-
increasing Union strength, to continue the struggle like a
disabled man fighting for his life against a whole man; to
continue the conflict from a drastically altered and critically
weakened position, psychologically as well as physically.
P. G. T. Beauregard, recently arrived from the Eastern theater, graphically summarized the gravity of the Confederate
plight when he wrote Earl Van Dorn: "We must do something
or die in the attempt, otherwise all will shortly be lost."[13]

Many diverse elements composed the Southern army.
From New Orleans came the heralded "Crescent Regiment,"

[12] Nashville *Banner of Peace*, Feb. 1, 1862, quoted in the New Orleans
Daily Picayune, Feb. 23, 1862.
[13] Nevins, *War*, II, 75.

composed of men eighteen to thirty-five years of age, many of whom regarded themselves as the blue bloods of Louisiana. Nicknamed the "Kid Glove" regiment, the unit was a colorful, well-drilled outfit, including many members equipped with "servants," and enamored with the glory of war. The command impressed a resident of Corinth as one of the finest regiments he ever saw. The Crescents would fight gallantly and be badly cut up at Shiloh.[14] On the other hand, there were units like the Sixth Mississippi, which, to judge from the picture of some of its members, was a ragtag regiment whose men were dressed and equipped with little or no regard for uniformity.

Some of the Southerners who assembled at Corinth were very young. Nineteen-year-old Henry Morton Stanley of the Sixth Arkansas Infantry, the "Dixie Grays," recalled going into battle at Shiloh beside Henry Parker, a boy of seventeen. W. E. Yeatman, who fought at Shiloh with the "Cumberland Rifles," Company C, Second Tennessee Infantry (a regiment organized at Nashville that claimed to be the first to reenlist for the duration of the war), wrote that his company "mustered with a roll of 80 men, or boys rather, as much the largest number were youths from 16 to 18 years of age."[15]

Willie Forrest, the son of Nathan Bedford Forrest, fought at Shiloh although he was only fifteen years old. His father spent part of the night of April 6 searching for Willie among the casualties. The boy later turned up safe, along with two companions and some Yankee stragglers the three had captured.[16] Brigadier General James R. Chalmers commended two seventeen-year-old boys, in his official report of the battle, who acted as staff officers for him. He wrote that one of them, Sergeant Major William A. Rains, deserved special notice for

[14] *Confederate Veteran*, V, 10; XIX, 211. New Orleans *Daily Picayune*, Mar. 1, 1862.

[15] Henry Morton Stanley, *The Autobiography of Henry Morton Stanley*, ed. by his wife Dorothy Stanley (New York, 1937), 187. W. E. Yeatman, Memoirs, Confederate Collection, Tennessee State Library and Archives, Nashville. Hereafter cited as TSLA.

[16] Bell I. Wiley, "Johnny Reb and Billy Yank at Shiloh," *West Tennessee Historical Society Papers*, 26 (1972), 7.

carrying an order on Sunday evening "under the heaviest fire that occurred during the whole engagement." Major General B. Franklin Cheatham told of "a noble boy," John Campbell, who "while acting as my aide-de-camp, fell dead, his entire head having been carried away by a cannon shot."[17]

A colonel of the Fifth Tennessee Infantry was amazed at the "coolness and bravery throughout the entire Shiloh fight" of a Private John Roberts who, although knocked down twice by spent balls, and his gun shattered to pieces, continued to push on with his advancing company. He was fifteen years old.[18]

Not all of them were young, or even middle-aged, however. One man of about sixty, who lived near Corinth, came to see his two sons who were in the army. He happened to arrive on the very day their unit was moving out to attack the enemy at Pittsburg Landing. The father could not resist shouldering his musket and marching into the fight with his sons. He paid for his rashness with the loss of a leg.[19]

A father and son, John C. Thompson, seventy, and Flem, thirteen, enlisted in a north Mississippi company that fought at Shiloh. The old gentleman was a lawyer, who, when asked why he joined up, replied that he had talked and voted for secession and now felt that he ought to fight for the cause. Though wounded, he survived Shiloh only to fall at Chickamauga in the midst of a charge on Snodgrass Hill.[20]

The Southerners were coming to fight for many reasons. Some were romantics. A Tennessean of Patrick Cleburne's command, George T. Blakemore, wrote that he "volunteered to fight in defense of the sunny South, the land of roses, . . . and for my Melissa, Ma and Sister, and all other fair women . . . ."[21] Henry M. Doak described himself as a "soldier of fortune—eager for the fray . . . ." When he heard a great battle was expected near Corinth, so anxious was he for a fight that he arose from a sick bed and headed west on the first train

---

[17] *OR*, x, part 1, 552, 443.
[18] *Confederate Veteran*, xxv, 222.
[19] Katharine M. Jones, ed., *Heroines of Dixie* (New York, 1955), 110.
[20] *Confederate Veteran*, xvi, 585.
[21] George T. Blakemore, Diary, Confederate Collection, TSLA.

in order not to miss it. He got to Shiloh in time—in time, after six years instruction on the violin with German and French masters, for a rifle ball to shatter his left hand.[22]

J. M. Lashlee came from Camden, Tennessee, to join the Confederates. He was a man opposed to slavery and to secession, who enlisted with the Rebels, as did many others, only because the Union army had invaded his state. For Lashlee the memory of the second day of the battle would hold an unlikely nostalgia—one all its own. For there on the battlefield, wounded, he would meet a young girl from near Iuka, Mississippi, by the name of Emma Dudley. And he would marry her.[23]

Another soldier who reached Corinth in time to hear the guns of Shiloh but too late to take part in the fight was brief about his reasons for joining the Confederates. He said simply: "Our liberties are threatened, our rights endangered." He was perhaps echoing the Memphis *Daily Avalanche* which was calling forth every armed, able-bodied man to the "scenes of a great and decisive battle" in the struggle for "Southern Independence." The New Orleans *Daily Picayune* was likewise sounding the theme of a great "struggle for independence" without which there would be "nothing left . . . for which a free man would desire to live." The New Orleans paper was in fact running a series of articles under the heading "Chronicle of the Second American Revolution." Its editorials were also fervently declaring that the situation now facing the South was the "crisis of the Confederate cause." Governor John J. Pettus of Mississippi proclaimed that the decision to be faced was "liberty or death."[24]

Many Southerners, of course, fought to protect the "peculiar institution." As previously noted, some Confederates even took selected blacks along with them as personal body servants when they went to war. A man who fought at Shiloh later recounted a gory but impressive occurrence he witnessed

[22] Henry M. Doak, Memoirs, Confederate Collection, TSLA.

[23] Interview with Dr. Lewis Maiden, grandson of J. M. Lashlee, July 1972.

[24] Garrett Turman Overby, Diary, in possession of Mrs. Ann Beasley Johnson, Franklin, Tenn. Memphis *Daily Avalanche*, Mar. 18, 24, Apr. 5, 1862. New Orleans *Daily Picayune*, Feb. 18, 19, 20, 1862.

involving a young Rebel officer and his slave. As the officer rode into battle on the first day of the fight, a cannon shot completely decapitated the young man. The Negro servant almost immediately caught his master's horse, and put the lifeless body on it. Then the black man moved off the battlefield, going slowly to the rear with the remains in the saddle and he behind on the horse, steadying the animal while they made their way back toward Corinth. The witness was convinced that the slave was taking his dead master's body back home for burial.[25]

Every type of man seemed to be represented among the soldiers gathering at Corinth. Like all armies the Confederates had their gamblers. Some had a mania for cockfighting, scouring the country for fighting cocks and, whenever the opportunity offered, staging a contest and betting on the outcome. "There were five or six men, mostly officers, who were ring leaders in this sport," remembered James I. Hall, who was convinced that the Almighty took a dim view of their activities. "In the Battle of Shiloh," he wrote, "they were all killed and although I remained in the army three years after this, I do not remember ever seeing or hearing of another cock fight in our regiment. . . ."[26]

Some of those who were coming to join the Rebels were in love. Confederate Captain Benjamin Vickers of Memphis was no doubt thinking much of the time about his fiancée, Sallie Houston, also of Memphis, as he marched to the defense of the South at the battle of Shiloh. There in the midst of one of the many Rebel charges he suffered a mortal wound. The young lady, even though she knew he was about to die, insisted upon their marriage, which was solemnized ten days after the battle and a few days before his death.[27]

[25] Mary B. Chestnut, *A Diary from Dixie*, ed. Ben Ames Williams (Boston, 1905), 54. *Confederate Veteran*, XIX, 211. Clement Eaton, *A History of the Southern Confederacy* (New York, 1954), 84. W. P. Conner in the McNairy County *Independent*, Oct. 20, 1933, in SNMP. Frank L. Richardson, "Shiloh," July 1877, Albert Sidney Johnston and William Preston Johnston Papers, Mrs. Mason Barrett Collection, MSS Division, Howard-Tilton Memorial Library, Tulane Univ., New Orleans. Hereafter cited as Johnston Papers.
[26] James I. Hall, "Notes on the War," Southern Historical Collection, Univ. of North Carolina, Chapel Hill. Hereafter cited as SHC,UNC.
[27] New Orleans *Daily Picayune*, Apr. 19, 1862.

There were men who came to pillage and plunder. Major General Braxton Bragg, commanding the Confederate "Second Corps," was particularly disturbed by "the mobs we have, miscalled soldiers." He complained to General Beauregard that while there was "some discipline left" in those troops from the Gulf (Bragg's own command), there was "none whatever" in the rest of the army. He further stated that "the unrestrained habits of pillage and plunder" by Confederate soldiers about Corinth were making it difficult to get supplies, and, worse yet, reconciling the people to the approach of the Federals "who certainly do them less harm." The troops were even "monopolizing or plundering the eating and sleeping houses" on the railroads. The forty-five-year-old Bragg, with his lowering brow, and haggard, austere, no-nonsense appearance, was determined to do something about the pillaging, and he quickly gave substance to his growing reputation as a severe disciplinarian. One of the Rebel soldiers wrote that Bragg's name became a "terror to deserters and evil doers," claiming that "men were shot by scores." Another said he hanged sixteen men on a single tree.[28]

The last two statements were, of course, wild exaggerations, but it was soon after the Shiloh campaign, on the retreat from Corinth, that an incident occurred which did much to stamp Bragg as stern and unreasoning. Bragg gave orders that no gun be discharged lest the retreat route be given away, and set the penalty of death for disobedience. Subsequently a drunken soldier fired at a chicken and wounded a small black child. The soldier was tried by court martial, was sentenced to be shot, and was executed. Some of the facts of the event were soon twisted, or ignored, however, and the story circulated that because a Confederate soldier shot at a chicken, Bragg had the soldier shot—a soldier for a chicken. Although he was falsely maligned as a result of this incident, there is no denying that many of the soldiers thought he was unreasonably strict. Even in the earlier Mexican War, where Zachary Taylor's

[28] *OR*, x, part 1, 12; part 2, 340. Watkins, *"Co. Aytch,"* 67. Glenn Tucker, *Chickamauga: Bloody Battle in the West* (Indianapolis, 1961), 76. There were no regularly constituted corps in the Confederate army at Shiloh. The "corps" organization was an idea effected by P.G.T. Beauregard.

statement at the battle of Buena Vista had helped make Bragg famous ("Double-shot your guns and give 'em hell, Bragg"), somebody hated Bragg enough to attempt his destruction by planting a bomb under his tent. Bragg was undoubtedly right, however, that the Rebel army at Corinth was in need of more discipline.[29]

Some of those gathering at Corinth were despondent. Chief Engineer Jeremy Gilmer wrote of the "confusion and discomfort—dirty hotels, close rooms, hot weather—and many other disagreeable things."[30] And no doubt many were thinking of the possibility of death. One man confided to his diary: "E'er I again write on these pages, I may be sleeping in the cold ground . . . as a battle is daily . . . anticipated."[31]

Although they were a mixed lot, one quality was shared by nearly everyone in the Confederate army and a sizable part of the Union army also: they had little if any experience as soldiers. It has been stated that "probably 80 percent of each army had never heard a gun fired in hatred."[32] The estimate may be about right for the Rebel army at Shiloh but not for the Union force. Three and one-half of the nine Federal divisions which fought at Shiloh had also seen action at Forts Henry and Donelson. There was a smattering of men in the Confederate ranks who thought of themselves as veterans, usually because they had been in one battle or heavy skirmish, but most had not seen combat. General Leonidas Polk, in his official report, stated that one company of artillery, because of "the scarcity of ammunition, had never heard the report of their own guns."[33]

Many of the officers, elected by their soldiers or appointed by state governors, were no better prepared than the men in the ranks. A Confederate brigadier general said later that

[29] Tucker, *Chickamauga*, 75, 76. Don C. Seitz, *Braxton Bragg: General of the Confederacy* (Columbia, S.C., 1924), 9.

[30] Jeremy F. Gilmer to Mrs. Gilmer, Mar. 29, 1862, Gilmer Papers, SHC,UNC.

[31] George T. Blakemore, Diary, Confederate Collection, TSLA.

[32] Lloyd Lewis, *Sherman: Fighting Prophet* (New York, 1932), 217.

[33] Charles W. Wright, *A Corporal's Story: Experiences in the Ranks of Company C, 81st Ohio Volunteer Infantry* (Philadelphia, 1887), 33, Shelby Foote, *The Civil War: A Narrative* (New York, 1958), I, 324, estimates two-thirds of Grant's men had been in battle. *OR*, x, part 1, 411.

before Shiloh he had never heard a lecture or read a book on the science of war, nor seen a gun fired.[34] At least he could appreciate the necessity to learn, whereas among the enlisted men were many who could see no need for drill; after all, they thought, they already knew how to walk!

The top Rebel commanders were attempting to bring organization and discipline out of the chaos, but the necessity for haste in attacking the enemy came to seem imperative, finally overriding all other considerations.

Meanwhile, in the Union camp, although the new recruits and even some of the commands that fought at Forts Henry and Donelson were in need of better organization and discipline, most of those gathering in the Blue ranks at Pittsburg Landing were not short on confidence. Excited by the recent victory at Fort Donelson, which had been climaxed with the surrender of nearly 15,000 soldiers in Gray, some of the Federals believed they were moving in for the *coup de grâce*. A feeling of victory was in the air. That some of the Union soldiers coming up the Tennessee River to Pittsburg Landing had not fought at Fort Donelson made little difference. The sense of pride in that triumph was contagious, and now the Union army "from private to commanding general" knew, in the words of a soldier in the Sixth Iowa Infantry, that a great battle was shaping up "for the mastery and military supremacy in the Mississippi Valley." With new Springfield rifled-muskets, good clothing, fine camp equipage, and wholesome rations, and inspired by music from "splendid bands and drum corps," the troops in his regiment were "happy and supremely confident," he said.[35]

A Northerner in the Fifteenth Illinois agreed. "The weather was delightful," he wrote. "Spring had just begun to open. . . . We all knew that a battle was imminent," but the victory at Fort Donelson "had given us great confidence in ourselves. . . ." Alexander Downing of the Eleventh Iowa recorded in his diary: "The boys are getting anxious for a fight."

---

[34] Bruce Catton, *This Hallowed Ground* (New York, 1956), 134.

[35] Henry H. Wright, *History of the Sixth Iowa Infantry* (Iowa City, 1923), 66, 67. Louisville *Journal*, Apr. 3, 1863.

Division Commander Major General Lew Wallace told his wife in a letter that the enemy was disorganized and demoralized and that the war, if pushed, could not last long. General Grant, writing to his wife and obviously misinterpreting the Southern will to resist, said the " 'Sesesch' is . . . about on its last legs in Tennessee. A big fight" would soon occur which, "it appears to me, will be the last in the west." Many a man in the ranks, like William Skinner, was echoing the same sentiment. Skinner wrote his sister and brother on March 27, 1862: "I think the rebellion is getting nearly played out, and I expect we will be home soon." The same theme was found in the letters of some people who were writing to the soldiers. Mrs. James A. Garfield, wife of the thirty-two-year-old man then serving in Buell's army who would become the twentieth President of the United States, was telling her husband: "If our army accomplishes as much this month as during the past month it seems as though there will not be much left of the rebellion."[36]

Some Union men were so confident that the Confederates were demoralized and giving up that they seemed to be looking for a sizable number of Southerners to swell their ranks. A correspondent traveling with the army in Tennessee wrote, with evident satisfaction, of an alleged 150 or so men from Hardin County who joined the Federal army at Savannah. This does not seem particularly hard to believe since there was much Union sentiment in that county.[37]

If the soldiers read the Northern newspapers, and many of them did (Chicago and Cincinnati papers were available at the landing about a week after publication), they would have found it difficult to escape the conclusion that the war was about over. Through the latter part of February and March

---

[36] Lucius W. Barber, *Army Memoirs of Co. "D" 15th Illinois Volunteer Infantry* (Chicago, 1894), 48. Alexander Downing, *Downing's War Diary* (Des Moines, 1916), 38. Wiley Sword, *Shiloh: Bloody April* (New York, 1974), 7. Catton, *Hallowed Ground*, 131. William Skinner to sister and brother, Mar. 27, 1862, SNMP. Mrs. James A. Garfield to Garfield, Mar. 2, 1862, James A. Garfield Papers, LC.

[37] Chicago *Times*, Mar. 26, 1862. *OR*, x, part 2, 39. Isabel Wallace, *Life and Letters of General W. H. L. Wallace* (Chicago, 1909), 175.

the headlines were continually recounting dramatic Union successes, and some of the editorials were fervent in implying, and occasionally actually stating, that the war could not last much longer. A correspondent of the Chicago *Times* who interviewed Confederate prisoners from Fort Donelson at Camp Douglas reported that many of the Confederates were weary of war, that they declared the cause of the Confederacy was lost, and that it was useless to fight any longer. A few days later the same paper was reporting that the administration of Jefferson Davis was being bitterly denounced by the Richmond newspapers.[38]

The Cincinnati *Gazette*, on April 3, reported a great dissatisfaction in the Rebel ranks. Many Confederates, coming in from Corinth, were deserting to the Union army assembled at Pittsburg Landing, the *Gazette* observed, and many more would desert if they could. Day after day, the New York *Times* in big headlines heralded the triumphs of Union armies, noting that in London the capture of Fort Donelson had caused a change in British opinion and a rise in United States securities. Even the pro-Southern London *Times*, anticipating the demise of the Confederacy, was quoted as saying, " 'There are symptoms that the Civil War can not be very long protracted.' "[39]

Although Northern papers occasionally carried warnings that some signs indicated that the Confederate will to resist was still alive, such articles were often buried in the corner of a second or third page or else virtually obscured by the general optimism exuding from the continual accounting and recounting of Union triumphs.

Not only were some of the Union soldiers overconfident; there were also men gathering at Pittsburg Landing who were so inexperienced and naïve about war that they seemed to be enjoying a holiday. They banged away at flocks of wild geese from the steamboat decks as they came up the Tennessee River. It was all like "a gigantic picnic," one wrote. And some of them were getting wild, such as those men in the Twenty-first Missouri Infantry who were firing from the decks of their

[38] Chicago *Times*, Feb. 22, 27, 1862.
[39] Chicago *Times*, Apr. 8, 1862. New York *Times*, Mar. 12, 13, 15, 1862.

steamer as it moved up the river, aiming their guns at citizens on the riverbanks. Grant labeled the conduct "infamous" and preferred charges against the colonel of the regiment.[40]

A correspondent from the Chicago *Times* traveling with the army thought that some of the soldiers had no respect for anything. He was appalled by their morbid curiosity, when debarking at Pittsburg Landing and finding some fresh and rather shallow graves—the evidence of a small skirmish in mid-March—some of the troops, with pointed sticks and now and then a spade, removed the scanty covering of earth, which in most cases was less than a foot deep, exposing the bodies of the dead, with remarks such as: "He keeps pretty well" and "By golly! What a red moustache this fellow had!"[41]

The Union army, like the Confederate, had some very young soldiers in their ranks. A sixteen-year-old boy in the Union army would remember, sometime during the battle of Shiloh, passing the corpse of a handsome Confederate, blond hair scattered about his face, with a hat lying beside him bearing the number of a Georgia regiment. Seeing the boy was about his own age, he said he broke down and cried.[42]

A fourteen-year-old Yankee, Private David W. Camp, of Battery G, First Ohio Light Artillery, was said by his captain to deserve particular mention, having served "with the skill and bravery of an old soldier during the entire engagement." The captain further added, "I did not for a moment see him flinch."[43]

Years later, Charles W. Hadley of the Fourteenth Iowa recalled one of the most affecting events of his war experience, which occurred in the area of prolonged and fierce fighting that became known as the "Hornets' Nest." He watched as a small boy, mounted on a fine horse, was suddenly lifted from the saddle by an exploding shell and dropped lifeless to the ground.[44]

[40] *OR*, x, part 2, 74; see also p. 42 for further information on the misconduct of Union troops.

[41] Chicago *Times*, Mar. 26, 1862.

[42] John A. Cockerill, "A Boy at Shiloh," *Under Both Flags* (Chicago, 1896), 372.

[43] *OR*, x, part 1, 376.

[44] Charles W. Hadley, "The Hornets' Nest," Washington, D. C., *National Tribune*, Apr. 11, 1935.

The youngest of all usually were the drummer boys, among whom was Johnny Clem, ten years old, who went along with the Twenty-second Wisconsin Infantry, and whose drum was smashed at Shiloh, the exploit winning him the name "Johnny Shiloh"; he later became still more famous as the drummer boy of Chickamauga and retired from the army in 1916 as a major general.[45]

With the rapid concentration of so many men at Pittsburg Landing it was inevitable that accidents would occur, some of them fatal. A soldier in the Fourteenth Iowa who had just come up the river on the steamer *Autocrat* watched as a soldier on the *Hiawatha* fell into the Tennessee close to Pittsburg Landing and drowned before anyone could reach him. He was not the only one to suffer such a fate, for several drownings have been recorded.[46] Major General Charles F. Smith, a crusty, square-shouldered old officer who played a leading role at Fort Donelson as a division commander, and for a while afterward replaced Grant as the army's commander, slipped and fell while getting into a rowboat and skinned his shin. Infection set in which forced him to relinquish his command while the buildup at Pittsburg Landing was in process, and in about a month he was dead.

Many of the men in Blue who left records in letters, diaries, and memoirs revealing why they fought said they did so for the Union. But of course, again like the Confederates, the Federals had their share of soldiers seeking glory, adventure, and plunder. Clement Eaton has suggested that it is "highly probable that the typical soldier, Northern or Southern, had no clear idea why he was fighting."[47] It must have seemed to him, especially when he left for war as many did, with the hometown looking on, bands playing, girls waving, and small boys watching with awe and envy, that he fought for something splendid and glorious. The cheers told him so. That realization assured him of his own individual worth and greatness; but at the same time he fought for something,

[45] Wiley, "Johnny Reb," 7.
[46] B. F. Thomas, *14th Iowa Volunteer Infantry* (n.p., 1907), ch. III (pages are not numbered).
[47] Eaton, *Confederacy*, 83.

whether "Southern Rights" or "the Union," that must also at times have seemed vague and intangible. Perhaps the most concrete thing for which the soldier fought, mentioned time and again by the warriors on both sides, was "his country."

Regardless of why they were in the army, many of the Union troops, despite the recent successes and their confidence that more would soon follow, found that army life on the whole was dull, monotonous, and unpleasant. When the exhilarating but all too brief periods of camaraderie through card playing, gambling, wrestling, joking, and singing were over, the soldier still brooded, worried, got sick, and thought of loved ones back home. There was too much drill and routine, rain and mud. Sanitation was bad, with logs serving as latrines, and sickness and diarrhea (a correspondent remarked that no person could really claim to be a soldier who had not experienced the latter[48]) were rampant at times.

Perhaps above all there was loneliness. An unknown soldier of "Co. C." of an unknown regiment was keeping a small, pocket-size diary, pathetic in its brief entries revealing utter boredom. Again and again, he set down such comments as: "Weather cold and unpleasant. Nothing of any importance"; "In camp . . . no drill. Nothing new"; "Drill today . . . boys sitting by fires." Toward the latter part of March, entries begin referring to "Beautiful morning," "Beautiful spring day," and "Weather pleasant," but the evidences of loneliness and boredom are still present. The pages are blank after March 29, except for one. There appears a final entry—in a different hand: "Killed in the evening by the exploding of a boom-shell from the enemies battery." The entry appears on the page for April 6.[49]

Some of the soldiers found army life unpleasant because they simply did not care for their companions. "One thing that makes me tired of the army is that the people in the army don't suit me," wrote John Ruckerman of the Fifty-seventh Ohio. "I believe I am safe in saying one half of the talk we hear is swearing. In fact I have heard so much of it that every time I

[48] Chicago *Times*, Mar. 26, 1862.
[49] SHC,UNC.

hear a man swear it seems he has a rotten place about him somewhere. . . ."[50]

Many of the soldiers who opposed each other at Shiloh were indeed a crude and profane people who wrote and talked in base terms and with few inhibitions. Even a well-educated man like James A. Garfield, an accomplished orator, whose letters evidence an obvious facility with words, could be quite earthy about elemental functions of nature as he complained in letters to both his wife and his mother of such things as a "violent attack of Bloody Dysentery . . . accompanied by an incipied attack of Piles." He then set forth details of his suffering and regularly capitalized "Bloody Dysentery."[51] The soldiers were generally a poorly educated group, often spelling "cat" as "kat," "get" as "git," "leg" as "laig," and "where" as "whar." Such examples could be multiplied almost endlessly as one reads their correspondence.

A lot of these men were fiercely independent, and it is not surprising that discipline was a problem in both armies. Sometimes privates "sassed" officers, and occasionally the matter was settled by a fistfight. Farm boys who had been trained to be self-reliant did not always fit easily into the scheme of organization as conceived by the West Point minds of trained officers.

The mixture of uniforms in each army gave the forces a curious appearance. Some Confederates were dressed in blue in fact, and some Federals in gray. There were soldiers who wore homemade imitations of fancy foreign uniforms, and a few Union men clanked about in steel vests ("shields for cowards' hearts" a New Orleans newspaper mockingly labeled them), which could be purchased for about $7.50 back in Missouri or Kentucky. In general, however, the Union army exhibited a more "regular" appearance than did the Confederate force, simply because throughout the war period the Union was able to outproduce the Confederacy and therefore do a better job of clothing its soldiers.

It has sometimes been alleged that the inferior weapons

[50] John Ruckerman to John Kinsel, Mar. 6, 1862, SNMP.
[51] Garfield to Mrs. Garfield, Apr. 21, 1862, May 1, 1862; Garfield to mother, May 8, 1862, Garfield Papers.

with which the Confederates were equipped placed them at a great disadvantage during the battle of Shiloh.[52] The statement is not fully supported by the evidence. True, some Southerners depended upon shotguns and carried Bowie knives in their belts because of a shortage of rifled-muskets; of the available muskets some were outmoded flintlocks; and certain regiments were handicapped by a mixture of weapons, each type requiring a different caliber of ammunition. Other Rebels, however, still profiting from the Southern takeover of Federal arsenals at the start of the war, carried .58-caliber Springfield rifled-muskets—as good as anything the Union troops possessed. The Springfields were the most common equipment of the Federal soldiers, although some Union men at Shiloh, especially the Iowa troops, had new and equally good .577-caliber Enfield rifled-muskets imported from Great Britain. But the Rebels too had Enfields; in fact, thousands of them were available in the Southern army. Six thousand Enfields had arrived in the Confederacy through the Union blockade in early February, and more than half had been ordered to the West. A little later another steamer ran the blockade at New Orleans with 15,000 guns, and the Secretary of War approved all these for distribution to the troops in the West. Enfields were still being received at Corinth right up to the night of April 3. Also, many Federal units were armed only with caliber .69 muskets converted to percussion, and with substandard Belgium and Austrian rifled-muskets. It is a debatable question whether the Union soldiers' small-arms were superior to the Confederates at Shiloh. Indeed the Confederates may have had the advantage in this respect. Furthermore, the Rebels were not alone in confronting logistics problems. One of the Union divisions—Sherman's, which would be in the heart of the fight from its very inception—required six different kinds of ammunition. The Union had an overall edge, but the degree of Union superiority in weaponry and logistics at Shiloh has been exaggerated in Confederate legend.[53]

[52] Braxton Bragg, "General A S J and the Battle of Shiloh," Johnston Papers. Sword, *Shiloh*, 86, 87. John J. Hollister, *Shiloh on Your Own* (n.p., 1973), 37.
[53] Claude E. Fuller and Richard D. Steuart, *Firearms of the Confederacy*

And so in late March 1862, the armies were gathering—a large, curious, sometimes weird looking, and not very well prepared lot—gathering for what both sides expected to be the biggest battle of the war. It was a battle that would settle the question of who would dominate the Mississippi Valley and a battle that would reclaim what the Confederates had lost along the Tennessee-Kentucky line. This was the battle that the South desperately needed to win.

(Huntington, W.Va., 1944), 218. *OR*, vii, 863, 872, 883, 886. *OR*, x, part 2, 379. E. Porter Thompson, *History of the First Kentucky Brigade* (Cincinnati, 1868), 87. Duke, *53rd Ohio Infantry*, 49.

2. *Napoleon Is Not among Them*

JEFFERSON DAVIS remembered him as "the great pillar of the Confederacy" and in the spring of 1862 said that "If he is not a general . . . we have no general." Mrs. William M. Inge, at whose home he made his headquarters in Corinth, recalled him as "handsome, chivalrous, impressive," and "determined." An aide-de-camp who observed him while standing beside a campfire the night before Shiloh wrote of his "straight form standing out like a specter against the dim sky." A Rebel private remembered that he was tall and muscular, a rugged-looking man. And one who saw him in the heat of battle at Shiloh said his "massive figure seemed to enlarge," becoming the "embodiment of the fiery essence of war."[1]

When allowance is made for romantic notions of war and the embellishments of time and imagination, there is still abundant evidence that Albert Sidney Johnston's appearance was impressive. The general had blue-gray eyes, his hair was streaked with gray, and he sported a large moustache. At fifty-nine years of age, he stood over six feet tall and was still solidly built, and wearing his well-fitted gray cloak the Confederate general seemed to look like a commanding officer.

The Union commander, on the other hand, impressed some people as looking and acting like anything but a commanding general. "How profoundly surprised Mrs. Grant

---

[1] Hudson Strode, *Jefferson Davis: Confederate President* (New York, 1959), 221. Otto Eisenschiml, *The Story of Shiloh* (Chicago, 1946), 59. *Thirteen Months in the Rebel Army: By an Impressed New Yorker* (New York, 1862), 146. John Johnston, Diary, Confederate Collection, TSLA, 23. I. W. Avery in the Cincinnati *Daily Enquirer*, n.d., in the Johnston Papers.

must have been," observed one journalist, "when she woke up and learned that her husband was a great man."[2]

Thirty-nine-year-old Ulysses S. Grant was a short man, but there any resemblance to Napoleon seemed to end. He said very little to anybody and went about, much of the time, wearing an old slouch hat and a plain, faded blue coat with nothing to indicate his rank, and was eternally chomping on the butt of a cigar. He did wear a sword at Shiloh. There was nothing about his appearance that caused the average person to remember him. When he arrived at Pittsburg Landing on April 6, in the fury of battle, and gave an order to the colonel of the Fifteenth Iowa Infantry, that officer just stared blankly at him. The colonel did not know who Grant was, and Grant was compelled to identify himself before the man would take action. Later on in the day at Shiloh, Grant inadvertently wandered into the line of vision of a signal corpsman who was sending messages across the river relative to the disposition of William Nelson's troops from Buell's army. A young lieutenant, who had been assigned to keep the corpsman's view unobstructed, likewise did not recognize Grant and yelled out at the general: "Git out of the way there! Ain't you got no sense?"[3]

Regardless of his unlikely appearance, and his past which was a history of hardship with many failures, Grant, with his victories at Forts Henry and Donelson, had emerged as the most successful Union general of the war. The acclaim that naturally followed from such triumphs was embellished by the cryptic message that he sent Rebel Brigadier General Simon B. Buckner at Fort Donelson informing him that there would be "no terms except unconditional surrender. I propose to move immediately upon your works." "Unconditional Surrender" Grant, as he was known after Fort Donelson, was the hero of the North. But Grant was not without problems. In fact, the Union and Confederate commanders shared at

[2] Otto Eisenschiml and Ralph Newman, eds., *Eyewitness: The Civil War as We Lived It* (New York, 1956), 276.

[3] W. W. Belknap, *History of the 15th Iowa Veteran Infantry* (Keokuk, Iowa, 1887), 189. John D. Billings, *Hardtack and Coffee or The Unwritten Story of Army Life* (Boston, 1887), 405, 406.

His army surprised and almost beaten by the Confederate attack at Shiloh, General Ulysses S. Grant wrote in his memoirs that "Shiloh was the severest battle at the West during the war."

least one cross in common—they both had been under heavy criticism shortly before Shiloh—though from different sources and for different reasons.

When Albert Sidney Johnston came east from California in 1861 to take command of the vast Confederate Department Number Two—an area stretching from the Appalachian Mountains westward to the Indian territory, embracing the states of Tennessee, Arkansas and part of Mississippi; a command which also included control of military operations in Kentucky, Missouri, Kansas and the Indian country immediately west of Missouri and Arkansas—lavish praise was heaped upon him. Stanley Horn has written: "If there was any one thing on which everybody seemed agreed in 1861 it was that Albert Sidney Johnston was the Number One soldier of the Continent."[4] The reputation he had to uphold was indeed awesome. By spring 1862 all that had changed. After the abandonment of the Kentucky line and the retreat into Alabama, venomous criticism of Johnston poured forth from Southerners generally and Tennesseans in particular: Johnston had been outgeneraled; Johnston was incompetent; Johnston had been drunk when Fort Donelson fell. Some even charged him with treason.

In the Confederate Congress, members of the Tennessee delegation presented a petition demanding that Johnston be relieved of command. Soldiers were writing home that Johnston's men had lost confidence in him as a leader. New Confederate recruits sometimes made it a condition of enlistment that they not be required to serve under Johnston. A congressman from Kentucky wrote President Davis that Johnston's "errors" had been "greater than [those of] any general who ever preceded him in any country." The President himself should take command in the field, he said, or if that was impossible, then "for God's sake" he must give immediate command to Beauregard, Bragg, or Breckinridge before all was lost. Newspapers had joined the "hate Johnston" campaign, and even when a newspaper editor wrote in defense of Johnston, he might do so in a curious manner. The

---

[4] *OR*, IV, 405. Stanley F. Horn, *The Army of Tennessee: A Military History* (New York, 1941), 52.

Memphis *Daily Avalanche* suggested "a suspension of judgment" upon Johnston's military conduct "until all the facts and circumstances be fully known," and then, perhaps with unthinking prejudgment, added that it was difficult to believe that Johnston had been "so deficient and derelict" as the results "seem to indicate." When referring to the Southern generals thereafter the *Avalanche* habitually placed Johnston's name last (if indeed it was mentioned at all), following Beauregard, Bragg, and Polk, in spite of Johnston's position as the ranking commander.[5]

Even Johnston's own officers were criticizing him. William J. Hardee said Johnston's military ability had been greatly overrated, and W. W. Mackall, Johnston's adjutant general, agreed. Braxton Bragg was writing Secretary of War Judah P. Benjamin: "Confidence is lost on all hands, from the private to the major general, and nothing but a change can restore it." P. G. T. Beauregard was acting as if he expected to assume command from Johnston. And Johnston's chief engineer Jeremy F. Gilmer, in a letter to his wife, revealed a lack of confidence in all of the generals, of which he seemed to think there were too many anyway. "We have here now Generals A. S. Johnston and Beauregard—Major Generals Bragg and Polk and Hardee—and Brigadier Generals too numerous to name," he said. "Among them all, I fear, there is not a Napoleon."[6]

A careful study of Johnston's performance through the fall and winter of 1861–62 reveals that he was something less than Napoleonic in his new role as commander of Department Number Two, although, in all fairness, Napoleon himself probably could not have measured up to the image of Johnston held by some people in the South when he took command

---

[5] William Preston Johnston, *The Life of General Albert Sidney Johnston* (New York, 1878), 496–500, 512. Alvin Buck to father, Mar. 2, 1862, Irvin A. Buck Papers, SHC,UNC. Horn, *Army*, 104, 105. Charles P. Roland, *Albert Sidney Johnston: Soldier of Three Republics* (Austin, Tex., 1964), 299. Memphis *Daily Avalanche*, Mar. 6, 10, 11, 31, Apr. 3, 1862.

[6] *The Southern Bivouac*, 5 vols. (Louisville, 1882–87), I, 530. *Confederate Veteran*, II, 137. Bragg to Benjamin, Feb. 27, 1862, Bragg Papers, Palmer Collection. Connelly, *Army*, 129–32. Gilmer to wife, Mar. 29, 1862, Gilmer Papers.

in September 1861. It is somewhat strange that such an image ever developed in the first place, because Johnston's previous life had not given evidence of any particularly outstanding military ability. Johnston's life in fact had been a series of setbacks, disappointments, financial difficulties, and even tragedies.

Born in Washington, Kentucky, he had yearned as a young man to go to sea. His family discouraged the idea and sent him instead, when he was fifteen, to study medicine at Transylvania College in Lexington, Kentucky. Jefferson Davis was also a student at Transylvania, and the two became friends. Probably Johnston was never really interested in the study of medicine because a few years later he obtained an appointment to the United States Military Academy at West Point in spite of the efforts of his family to dissuade him from a military career. Cadet life on the banks of the Hudson River was satisfying to Johnston and also brought a renewal and strengthening of his friendship with Davis who enrolled at the academy two years after Johnston. Following graduation Johnston experienced a rather dull brand of frontier duty at Jefferson Barracks near St. Louis which was broken only by his service with the Sixth U.S. Infantry in the Black Hawk War and his marriage to Henrietta Preston, but Henrietta died soon after the birth of their second child.

For a time after her death the despondent Johnston, who had resigned from the army to be with her upon learning that she had tuberculosis, kept to himself on a farm near St. Louis, caring for his two small children. At last the Texas Revolution in 1836 attracted his interest, and he headed for the Lone Star State to become a leader of the Republic's army. He took great pride in the cause of Texas and eventually came to think of himself as a Texan rather than a Kentuckian. For a brief time it must have seemed that Providence was smiling upon him as he rose to senior brigadier general in the Texas army. His success, however, led to a quarrel with a jealous subordinate and the fighting of a duel. Severely wounded in the duel, he returned to Kentucky for awhile but could not seem to stabilize his life and was soon back in Texas. Drifting in and out of Texas several times, he engaged in politics, planting,

Confederate General Albert Sidney Johnston, the only Rebel army commander to be killed in action during the Civil War, rode into the battle that claimed his life with the words, "We must this day conquer or perish!"

and real estate, never achieving marked success in any of his ventures. He married again, taking Eliza Griffin, a cousin of his first wife, as his new bride.

The coming of the Mexican War filled Johnston with excitement and anticipation. Here was the chance to strike at the hated Mexicans whom he held in contempt as an inferior people and yearned to chastise for their brutality toward Texas. Perhaps the war would also provide the path to advancement and success. Vowing to his wife, who was naturally alarmed and concerned for his safety, that he would enlist for no more than a six-month period without her consent, he led a regiment of Texas Volunteers into Mexico. He fought with some distinction at the battle of Monterrey, but soon after, the war began to go sour for Johnston. Above all, he was unable to obtain the rank he thought he deserved, and he left the army in disappointment.

Following his service in the Mexican War, Johnston went back to his plantation at China Grove in Texas, where his efforts to succeed as a planter ended in bankruptcy. His dire financial condition compelled him to board his two older children for a time with relatives in Kentucky. Then Jefferson Davis became secretary of war, remembered his old friend, and made Johnston colonel of the Second Cavalry. In 1857 Johnston led the famous expedition into Utah against the Mormons, but he saw no action, suffering instead through severe winter blizzards before peacefully reestablishing government authority in the summer. In 1860 he became commander of the Department of the Pacific and was a strong advocate of the Union when the secession crisis broke upon the nation. He decided not to resign his command unless Texas left the Union. Upon learning of Texas' secession, and after much deliberation Johnston sadly sent his resignation to Washington and made his way eastward, traveling through the dangerous Apache country, in order to serve the Confederacy.[7]

Certainly Johnston had never held a command with anything like the responsibilities that he faced in the fall of 1861.

[7] See Roland, *Johnston*, for a modern account of the general's life.

In addition to being responsible for Rebel operations in Missouri, Arkansas, and the Indian territory, he had to defend a line east of the Mississippi River which stretched more than three hundred miles from Columbus, Kentucky, on the river, to Cumberland Gap in the east. Commanding his left flank at Columbus was Bishop Leonidas Polk, while Major General George B. Crittenden anchored the right in front of the mountain gap. Forts Henry and Donelson were being constructed just south of the Kentucky line to block the Tennessee and Cumberland rivers, and Johnston placed his center at Bowling Green, where William J. Hardee, with 10,000 men, was to command the line of the Louisville and Nashville Railroad. With only 30,000 inadequately equipped men to maintain the whole Kentucky line against approximately twice as many Federals, Johnston desperately determined to put up a bold front, sending out raiding parties from the Bowling Green sector and acting like a man about to assume the offensive in a drive to the Ohio River. If he could pull off the big bluff, perhaps he could frighten the Union badly enough that any plans for a Federal invasion would be delayed until spring. By then, the Confederates hoped, they could be strengthened sufficiently to throw it back. Initially Johnston was quite successful, and Sherman, commanding at Louisville, was panicked into believing an overpowering Rebel army was about to descend upon the city.

In the long run, however, Johnston seemed unable to grasp the total command picture of his department, becoming preoccupied with the defense of Bowling Green where he established his headquarters. The grave danger the Tennessee and Cumberland rivers represented as avenues for a rapid Yankee thrust into the South could not have been adequately appreciated by Johnston, or he would have been more concerned about the lack of preparations at Fort Henry and Fort Donelson. Also he developed no overall departmental strategy; consequently, there was no coordinated defensive effort among his district commanders. He was of such personality, gentle and patient, that he did not properly control and discipline strong-willed subordinates such as Leonidas Polk and Gideon Pillow. Furthermore, he did not provide for an adequate means of checking on subordinates to whom he had entrusted difficult tasks.

Johnston's tendency to place too much trust in unproved subordinates explains, to no small degree, why Fort Henry, Fort Donelson, and Nashville were in such poor defensive condition when Grant made his drive up the rivers in February 1862. Johnston had sent his chief engineer, Jeremy F. Gilmer, to oversee the task of establishing adequate defenses, and Gilmer had not pushed the work. Gilmer was unhappy with his assignment in the Kentucky-Tennessee area. He had hoped to be assigned to strengthen the defenses at Savannah, Georgia, where his wife and many friends lived; and he much preferred the warmer climate of south Georgia. Furthermore, Gilmer supposed that the Union army would strike down the Mississippi against Polk at Columbus, Kentucky, and through central Kentucky against Johnston at Bowling Green. In his opinion, then, there was nothing too serious to worry about on the Tennessee and Cumberland rivers. He did not think the Federals would attempt to advance before spring anyway. Consequently he not only procrastinated at Nashville, but also virtually ignored Fort Henry and Fort Donelson. Albert Sidney Johnston appeared to be content with Gilmer's reports that all was going well.

After Grant suddenly came up the Tennessee and took Fort Henry, Johnston was apparently surprised that the Federals then turned east toward Fort Donelson instead of going west toward Columbus. The general's preconceived ideas of how a Union offensive might unfold must have left his mind inflexible. Until it was too late, he seemed to believe that the main threat to Donelson was from the river rather than the land side of the fort. Once Donelson fell and the Cumberland River was open to Nashville, which had no adequate defensive position prepared, the whole center of Johnston's line caved in. It is not difficult to understand why there was criticism of the Rebel commander.[8]

[8] This evaluation of Johnston's leadership is well documented by Connelly, *Army*, 62–77, 80–85, 103–18. The writer's examination of the papers of Johnston, Gilmer, Bragg, Breckinridge, Beauregard, and Polk, as well as the wealth of orders and correspondence in the *OR*, has only reinforced

As for Grant, the immediate source of his difficulties was his superior, Henry Wager Halleck, forty-seven-year-old commander of the Department of the Missouri—a man whom some of the soldiers knew best as "Old Brains" because of his scholarly background and authoritative writings on military science. Halleck's department, headquartered at St. Louis, formed one-half of a faulty Union command structure in the West, the other part being the Department of the Ohio with headquarters at Louisville, under Don Carlos Buell, a West Point graduate and veteran of the Seminole and Mexican wars. The Cumberland River was the boundary separating the two departments. By its very nature the arrangement encouraged Halleck and Buell to compete with one another rather than cooperate in trying to pierce the Western Confederacy's defensive line. The arrangement made command conflict almost inevitable, as both men were jealous of their prerogative, a not uncommon fault among officers on both sides in the Civil War.

The tragedy of the tension between Halleck and Buell was that Grant unwittingly found himself in the middle of their struggle; the wrath of Halleck then descended upon Grant, and the Union offensive in the West ground to a halt. The trouble began about the first of the year 1862. Washington had been encouraging a cooperative offensive between Halleck and Buell. Halleck, who was never noted for being overly aggressive, wrote Washington that he had never received a word from Buell, was not ready to cooperate with him, and concluded "too much haste will ruin everything." Two days later Buell was telegraphing Halleck that "whatever is done should be done speedily, within a few days"—strange words from a man who, if anything, was even more carefully deliberate in his movements than Halleck. But when Grant, more than a month later and with Halleck's reluctant approval, was moving on Fort Henry, Buell changed his tune about the need for haste and returned to a more characteristic theme. Obviously irritated, he charged in a letter to General-in-Chief George B. McClellan that while the move up the rivers was

---

Connelly's conclusions about Johnston's leadership. See also Connelly, "The Johnston Mystique," *Civil War Times Illustrated* (Feb. 1967), 15–23.

right in its strategical bearing, it had been begun by General Halleck without adequate appreciation of the problems involved or preparations to cope with them. The result, he said, was to place his own army in a "hazardous" position if he now tried to support Grant. The truth was that since Grant's movement had been initiated independent of Buell, the latter's personality simply would not allow him to evaluate it with an open mind.[9]

Halleck had been trying to get the command situation corrected, to his own advantage of course. He was asking Washington preferably to transfer Buell's army to him, or at least place it under his command. Then, he promised, a unified offensive would follow.[10]

Before General Halleck received a reply to his request for departmental consolidation, however, Grant was marching against Fort Donelson on the Cumberland. He had sent a wire to Halleck announcing his victory at Fort Henry, laconically adding that he would move over and take Fort Donelson in a couple of days. After the fall of Donelson, Grant showed an inclination to cooperate with Buell, sending General Charles F. Smith's division over to Clarksville, which was in Buell's department; worse yet, from Halleck's viewpoint, Grant had even gone to Nashville "without authority," where he had been consulting with Buell in person! When Halleck did not receive Grant's messages, because of a breakdown in communications, he too hastily assumed Grant was not sending them. Overly impressed with his own importance in the whole campaign and jealous of Grant's recent glory and publicity, Halleck acted irresponsibly.[11]

He ordered that Smith's division be withdrawn from Clarksville. He dashed off an intemperate communication to Washington reporting Grant's supposed faults, which seemed to be legion: Grant sent him "no returns, no reports, no information of any kind," he had "left his command without . . . authority," his army was as much "demoralized" by the victory at Fort Donelson as was the Army of the Potomac by

[9] *OR*, vii, 526, 529, 587–88.
[10] *Ibid.*, 590–91, 594, 595.
[11] *Ibid.*, 682; x, part 2, 15.

the defeat at Manassas but, Grant was "sitting down and enjoying" his victory at Fort Donelson "without any regard to the future." Grant "richly deserved" to be censured, for Halleck was "worn out and tired" of Grant's "neglect and inefficiency."[12]

The next day Halleck was again writing Washington about Grant: a rumor had reached him that since taking Fort Donelson, General Grant had "resumed his former bad habits"—a statement which Halleck knew, in view of Grant's reputation before the war, would be taken to mean that Grant was drinking to excess. Halleck went on to say that perhaps this problem accounted for Grant's neglect of orders. He was not going to arrest Grant "at present," he concluded, but he was placing General Smith in command in Grant's stead. Smith was a tall, slim, blue-eyed man who had been in the military service for more than forty years. He had been commandant of cadets when Grant was attending West Point.[13]

The first that Grant knew about Halleck's villification campaign was when he received a telegram of two short sentences suspending him from command, detailing General Smith to take his place, and ordering him back to Fort Henry to await instruction. Smith was ordered to proceed up the Tennessee River and attempt to break the Confederate line on the Memphis and Charleston Railroad.[14]

Excuses may be offered for Halleck's actions—for example, he was irritable due to overwork, was deeply troubled about the situation in Missouri where Rebel partisan activities were a continual menace, and had been turned down on February 22 on his proposal for Western command consolidation—but in the final analysis he had done Grant a serious injustice. (When Grant learned, after the war, about Halleck's dispatches, he apparently never forgave the general.) There was little truth to any of the charges, and when Washington finally challenged Halleck to make his allegations against Grant more precise and specific, he had to back down. Halleck lamely explained that Grant had satisfactorily accounted for every-

[12] *OR*, VII, 679–80.
[13] *Ibid.*, 682.
[14] *OR*, X, part 2, 3, 6; VII, 674.

thing. Any irregularities in his command had taken place while Grant was absent, and his trip to Nashville had been made with the best of intentions and for the good of the service![15]

Although Halleck's actions put Grant under eclipse for a while (Grant even considered leaving the army and sent a letter to Halleck asking to be relieved of his command), the most serious result was to stymie the Union offensive. It is true that Halleck, like Grant, had the strategic concept of breaking the Rebel line between Bowling Green and Columbus by striking through the Tennessee and Cumberland rivers. Possibly, as suggested in a recent study,[16] Halleck thought of the plan before Grant, but if the Union had waited for Halleck to carry out the idea the southern Kentucky area would still have been in Confederate hands long after Grant had captured Forts Henry and Donelson. When Halleck approved Grant's movement up the Tennessee against Fort Henry, he told General-in-Chief McClellan that he did not believe much could be accomplished.[17] Grant had been trying to push on. After the capture of the forts he seemed to sense, perhaps more clearly than any other person in authority in the West, that the Confederates were reeling from the Henry-Donelson disaster. Johnston was falling back with only about 15,000 to 17,000 men, which were widely separated from Polk's forces retreating from Columbus, Kentucky. The Union army could marshal forces numerically superior to both of the Confederate armies, even if they were joined. Had Halleck been willing to allow Grant a free hand, the Union army might have captured Corinth because they had a straight shot at it and had the opportunity to reach it before the Confederates arrived in force. Instead, Halleck's major contribution was to slow down the Union advance and permit the Confederates more time to assemble a large army and make a formidable attempt to recover what had been lost in the West.

By the middle of March, Halleck had finally received the command he wanted. The Department of the Missouri and

[15] *OR*, VII, 532, 533, 652, 683, 684; x, part 2, 62–63.
[16] Sword, *Shiloh*, 4.
[17] Catton, *Hallowed Ground*, 113.

the Department of Kansas together with the western portion of the Department of the Ohio had been consolidated into the Department of the Mississippi, dating from March 11, with Halleck assigned to command both armies then operating in Tennessee. Meanwhile, unwilling to further embarrass the only general in the Union army who had won a major victory, Halleck decided to restore Grant to duty until he himself could come up the Tennessee and assume personal direction of the army.[18] But more blundering seemed to be in order— this time Grant himself contributing to it.

Grant arrived at Savannah, Tennessee, on March 17 and found the army divided, part of it deployed on each side of the Tennessee River and the separate forces ten to twelve miles apart. The Tennessee River in this area near the Tennessee-Mississippi line was a sparsely settled country of small riverboat communities and "landings" where steamboats tied up to load and unload their cargoes. Savannah, where Grant landed, was the largest of the towns and the only important one on the east bank of the river. Across the river and aligned along the west bank as one traveled south toward the Mississippi line were Crump's Landing, Pittsburg Landing, and Hamburg, in that order. Next came Tyler's Landing, barely across the line in Mississippi, and then Eastport, the latter located almost due east of the larger inland town of Corinth.

Ferry crossings to Savannah were provided at both Crump's and Pittsburg, but of more importance to Grant's troops were the roads on the west side. From Crump's, about four miles upstream from Savannah, a road ran due west through Adamsville and Purdy to Bethel Station on the Mobile and Ohio Railroad. Another road from the landing paralleled the river to connect with Pittsburg, some five miles farther upstream. Continuing on to Hamburg, the river road (also known as the Hamburg-Savannah road) provided one of two basic approaches to Pittsburg Landing from the south. The other approach was by way of the main road that angled off in a southwesterly direction to connect Pittsburg directly with Corinth.

[18] *OR*, viii, 605; x, part 2, 22, 24, 25, 28, 29, 32, 36.

The Union forces were indeed widely dispersed. Major General John A. McClernand's division, composed largely of Illinois soldiers who had fought at Fort Donelson, was encamped at Savannah. Across and up the river at Crump's was Major General Lew Wallace's division, also including many troops who were engaged at Donelson. Farther south, Brigadier General William Tecumseh Sherman, with basically raw soldiers, had stationed his division at and near Pittsburg Landing. Sherman placed the bulk of his troops about 2½ miles southwest of the landing, pitching his tents on both sides of the one-room log church known as the Shiloh Meeting House, where he encamped to guard the main road from Corinth. The remainder of Sherman's command, Colonel David Stuart's brigade, was placed close to the river, about two miles south of Pittsburg Landing and well over a mile away from the rest of the division. Stuart was in position to cover the Hamburg-Savannah road, the first of the two basic approaches to Pittsburg Landing from the south. Major General Charles F. Smith's division disembarked at Pittsburg and encamped close to the landing. The great majority of Brigadier General Stephen A. Hurlbut's division was on the transports anchored at the landing. Other steamers loaded with troops were at Savannah, and still more were coming up the river.

The widespread division of Union forces was primarily the responsibility of General Smith, influenced in part by Sherman. When Smith had first reached the town of Savannah, he decided to make that point his base of operations and there landed the troops that had accompanied him. Savannah was peopled with a number of Union sympathizers, was on the opposite side of the river from the Rebels assembling to the southwest at Corinth, and would be a convenient site for joining with General Buell's army as it approached from Nashville. Knowing that the Confederates were building up their strength at Corinth, Smith decided to break their rail communications on both sides of the town. The task was entrusted to Sherman and Lew Wallace.

Smith ordered Sherman, with a new division of troops organized at Paducah, to steam up the river to about Eastport, Mississippi, disembark, and try to break the Memphis and

Severe fighting raged around the church building sketched here, which gave the battle of Shiloh its name. The present-day Shiloh Methodist Church now occupies the site.

Charleston Railroad near Burnsville, a few miles southwest of Eastport and about halfway to Corinth. While on his way up the river Sherman observed Pittsburg Landing and learned of the good road that ran from Pittsburg to Corinth. Fearing that a large Confederate force reported encamped in the vicinity of Pittsburg might occupy the landing, and troubled by the rising Tennessee, so swollen from the recent rains that Pittsburg was then one of the few elevated points where troops could be disembarked, Sherman requested Smith to occupy the landing in force while he proceeded with the attempt to break the railroad.

Disembarking a few miles down river from Eastport, Sherman rapidly bogged down in the mud and rising water of the low country. He discovered that the tiny creeks cutting across his line of march had become surging, swirling torrents from the heavy rains. Some of the troopers who were spearheading the advance were unhorsed and nearly drowned while trying to swim their mounts across one of the rampaging creeks. An attempt to build a bridge was thwarted by water rising so rapidly that it covered the timbers which had just been emplaced to support the bridge. The pouring rain continued, and even some snow began to mix with it. The Tennessee, at one period, rose 15 feet in less than twenty-four hours. The disgusted Sherman, realizing that to continue would necessitate bridging every stream between the Tennessee and the railroad, a distance of nineteen miles, ordered the men back to the boats. When Sherman returned from his unsuccessful "mud march," he found that Smith, complying with his request, had ordered Stephen A. Hurlbut's division to disembark at Pittsburg. Smith instructed Sherman to go ashore with his division there also, and position them far enough back from the river that other divisions might encamp there.[19]

Lew Wallace's expedition fared better than Sherman's. His soldiers at Crump's Landing faced an objective that lay almost due west—the Mobile and Ohio Railroad, which came down from the north through Jackson, Tennessee, into Corinth. Wallace sent the Fifth Ohio Cavalry, under Major Charles S.

[19] *OR*, x, part 1, 22; part 2, 34–36, 42, 43, 45.

Hayes, striking for the railroad. The cavalry succeeded in damaging it at a trestle across Beach Creek, tearing up track for a distance of about 150 feet, bending the rails and throwing them into the water. General Smith was pleased to hear the news, but it was of little significance because the Confederates repaired the damage the very next day.[20]

Moving from Savannah to Pittsburg Landing, Grant found himself in the midst of troops going ashore from the steamers, along with their camping equipment, guns, wagons, and animals. The scene must have been spectacular. Nothing like this river-borne Federal advance occurred at any other time in the Civil War. The Union command had assembled 173 steamboats for use as transports, and these were convoyed by several gunboats. The transports advanced, not all at once, but in divisions. One day there were forty. On another day there were sixty-three.[21]

After landing at Pittsburg, Grant reported at once to Halleck—Grant was unusually careful now to keep his commander informed—telling the general the precise conditions of the army. Knowing that the army's ultimate objective was to destroy the railroad connections at Corinth, and freshly reminded of this goal in a communication from Halleck, Grant decided to transfer the remainder of the army, except for a small garrison at Savannah, to the Shiloh side of the river. Other than Lew Wallace's command at Crump's Landing all the Union divisions were to be stationed at Pittsburg. Grant was probably impressed by a report from Sherman. After Grant and Smith, Sherman was the ranking regular army officer on the field, a West Pointer who had served as superintendent of the Louisiana Military Academy that was to become Louisiana State University, and he had fought at Manassas. The forty-two-year-old Sherman was a lean, red-haired native of Ohio who wore a grizzled, short-cropped beard. He had a penetrating expression about his eyes and appeared to be somewhat nervous. "Cump" Sherman was a man in whom

[20] *Ibid.*, 10, 11.
[21] Donald Davidson, *The Tennessee: The New River, Civil War to TVA* (New York, 1948), 28.

Grant had developed confidence, and Sherman had reported that the site of Pittsburg was a good one for camping and drilling, as well as a military point of great strength. Commanding high ground and with the Owl, Snake, and Lick creeks to protect the army's flanks, as well as the Tennessee River to provide gunboat cover, the position would have been formidable had it been properly developed.[22]

Sherman, however, was not recommending, as has often been assumed, that the entire army be placed at Pittsburg Landing. In another report of the same day he suggested that the Federal forces should be stationed not only at Pittsburg Landing, but also at Hamburg and Tyler's Landing to the south as well as at Crump's Landing to the north. Then the Union forces, Sherman said, could move "concentrically on any . . . point along the [Memphis and Charleston] railroad." It was Grant, not Sherman, who decided to concentrate all the Union troops, except the Third Division, at Pittsburg Landing. And certainly the decision was Grant's responsibility.[23]

When the buildup was completed, the Army of the Tennessee, as it was designated, consisted of six divisions. The First Division was commanded by forty-nine-year-old Major General John A. McClernand, a "political general" from Illinois. His military experience before the Civil War was limited to the Black Hawk Indian War, but after Fort Sumter he became a leader in rousing many Illinois soldiers to the Union cause. The Lincoln administration needed such help from Democratic congressmen, and McClernand's star, for a while, was in rapid ascent. He commanded a brigade at the battle of Belmont in November 1861 and then a division at Fort Donelson, after which he was promoted to major general. McClernand was a gangling, loose-jointed man, possessing a hot temper and a rapidly expanding ego. He particularly disliked West Pointers and generally had difficulty in his associations with fellow officers. Nevertheless, he would conduct his command well during the fight at Shiloh, and Sherman complimented

[22] *OR*, x, part 2, 45–46; part 1, 27. William T. Sherman *Memoirs of General W. T. Sherman*, 2 vols. (Bloomington, Ind., 1957), I, 232–33.

[23] Basil Henry Liddell-Hart, *Sherman, Soldier, Realist, American* (New York, 1929), 121.

him in his official report for acting in perfect concert with him as they struggled to maintain their lines. Soon after the battle of Shiloh, McClernand would write Abraham Lincoln that his division "as usual" had borne the brunt of the fight, that the Confederate commander had been killed "within 30 yards of [his] tent" (a gross inaccuracy), and that "a great mistake" had been made in not pursuing the Rebels after the battle. He closed by thanking the President for the favor of his recent promotion.[24] The ambitious McClernand would eventually scheme, unsuccessfully, to gain control of the Vicksburg campaign, arousing the wrath of Grant, Sherman, and other officers. His high-handed action in violating one of Grant's orders finally led to his removal from corps command.

Major General Lew Wallace, the leader of the Third Division, was a thirty-five-year-old native of Indiana who had served in the Mexican War and was practicing law in Crawfordsville, Indiana, when the Civil War broke out. He had a background in politics, his father having served as governor of Indiana, while he himself had been elected to the state senate. He appeared slight in figure, with black hair and a full beard and moustache. Wallace moved about rather quickly and did not seem to talk a great deal, but he was popular with his men. They prided themselves, after Fort Donelson, on belonging to "Lew Wallace's fighting crowd."[25] Shiloh was to bring him much publicity and much sorrow. Before his life was ended, however, he would be known, above all, as a writer.

Brigadier General Stephen A. Hurlbut, commanding the Fourth Division, was born in Charleston, South Carolina, the son of a Unitarian minister. He became a lawyer, served in the Seminole War, and then migrated to Illinois. He was twice elected as a Republican to the Illinois General Assembly, where he was serving when the war came. Commissioned a brigadier general, he was in northern Missouri in 1861 before becoming a division commander under Grant. He would handle his unit with bravery and skill at Shiloh, helping to

---

[24] *OR*, x, part 1, 114.
[25] Description taken in part from the Chicago *Times*, Mar. 26, 1862.

hold a strategic position which probably saved the Union army from destruction.

William Tecumseh Sherman commanded the Fifth Division, and forty-two-year-old Brigadier General Benjamin M. Prentiss headed the Sixth. Prentiss was a native of Belleville, Virginia, who had been living in Illinois since 1841. He had served as a lieutenant of militia against the Mormons in Hancock County, Illinois, and during the Mexican War he was a captain in the First Illinois Volunteers, fighting at the battle of Buena Vista. Returning home after the Mexican War, he studied law and dabbled in politics, making an unsuccessful bid as a Republican candidate for Congress in 1860. Becoming a colonel of Illinois volunteers when the Civil War began, he had a misunderstanding with Grant at Cairo about who ranked whom. For a while Prentiss had refused to take orders from Grant, but that difficulty was now forgotten. Prentiss would find himself in the hottest of the fighting at Shiloh and in spite of the earlier pettiness, would prove to be one of the best soldiers in the Union army.

The most recently appointed of the division commanders, replacing the victim of the rowboat accident, General C. F. Smith, as leader of the Second Division, was forty-year-old Brigadier General William H. L. Wallace—no relation to Major General Lew Wallace. He was an Ohio-born, Illinois-educated lawyer who had served in the Mexican War as an adjutant. When the Civil War began, he entered the service as a colonel of Illinois Volunteers. He fought at Fort Donelson, handled himself well, and was promoted to brigadier general of volunteers following that battle. Popular and respected by his men, he was a natural choice when Grant had to find a new division commander to replace the ailing Smith.

On March 8, Wallace told his wife in a letter that he had been quite ill for several days and prayed for the "strength and wisdom to enable me to do my whole duty toward the country in this her hour of peril." In this and other letters he spoke often of his longing for the war to end and of how much he wanted to see his wife and all the family once more.[26] Ann

[26] Wallace, *Letters*, 174–76.

Dickey Wallace, twelve years younger than her husband, must have found his loneliness especially touching, for she decided to go south and visit him. Wallace had told her not to attempt the trip, and friends and relatives warned that she would not be allowed to pass, that all civilians were being turned back. Ann was not easily persuaded to change her course once she had made up her mind.

The daughter of Judge T. Lyle Dickey, one of the most successful lawyers in Illinois, she may have thought her father's name would help her get through. Most important in her decision, however, was her determination to see "Will" again. She had known her husband since she was a small girl when Will, as a young lawyer, had visited many times in her father's home. Often he had taken an interest in the bright child, sometimes suggesting books for her to read, sometimes watching her ride her pet pony or engage in some other sport, and on occasion just sitting and talking to her. Then, upon Will's return from the Mexican War, he made the pleasant discovery that little Ann had become a charming young lady of fifteen. When she was sixteen he pledged his love and asked her to become his wife. Soon after her eighteenth birthday they were married.[27]

Now, after all the years she had known him, it did not seem right to Ann for Will to be away, undergoing hardship and sickness, facing danger and possible death, while she remained passively at home. "Sometimes, Will, I can hardly restrain myself," she wrote on March 21. "I feel as if I must go to you, more so when I think of you sick. It seems wrong to enjoy every comfort of a good home and you sick in a tent. Is it indeed my duty to stay so far back and wait so anxiously?"[28] Three days later she dispatched another letter in the same vein. And in a few more days she was on her way south, leaving home in the midst of a high wind and raging rainstorm, which she later said only strengthened her resolve to make the journey. Her husband, of course, did not know she was coming.

[27] *Ibid.*, 62–64.
[28] *Ibid.*, 177.

When all divisions of the Union army, except the Third which remained at Crump's Landing, were in position at Pittsburg, they enjoyed high ground, which for camping, drilling, and exercising was admirable. The area occupied was a tableland extending some two and a half or three miles in both length and breadth. Near the landing and along the riverbank were a number of deep ravines cutting toward the Tennessee. Some of these had small creeks running through them carrying off the excess water from the recent deluge of rains. The tableland where the men camped was bounded on the north and south by two big creeks. To the south was Lick Creek, a large and swollen stream that poured into the Tennessee about two miles south of the landing. To the north was Snake Creek, joining the Tennessee about one-half mile north of the landing. As Snake Creek rushed toward the Tennessee from the west, it was joined by a major tributary coming into it from the southwest and known as Owl Creek. All three streams were broad, deep, and treacherous when swollen by the spring rains, sometimes as deep as 25 or 30 feet. With water protecting the rear and both flanks of the Union army, any enemy attack on Pittsburg Landing must of necessity come from the southwest in the approximately 3-mile interval between Lick and Owl creeks. And the frontage was certainly not excessive for the number of troops available to defend it.

Sherman and Prentiss, located southwest of Pittsburg Landing, held the most advanced ground and thus were encamped closest to the enemy at Corinth. All except one brigade of Sherman's division, as previously noted, were on the army's right near Shiloh Church, extending all the way to Owl Creek. The other brigade, under Stuart's command, occupied a position near the Tennessee River at the extreme left of the entire army. Stuart was a good mile and a quarter from the rest of Sherman's soldiers.

Prentiss' division was occupying an isolated and even more advanced position than that of Sherman. He was located east and south of Sherman's encampment at Shiloh Church. Thus Prentiss was several hundred yards away from Sherman's closest troops, both those at the church and those under

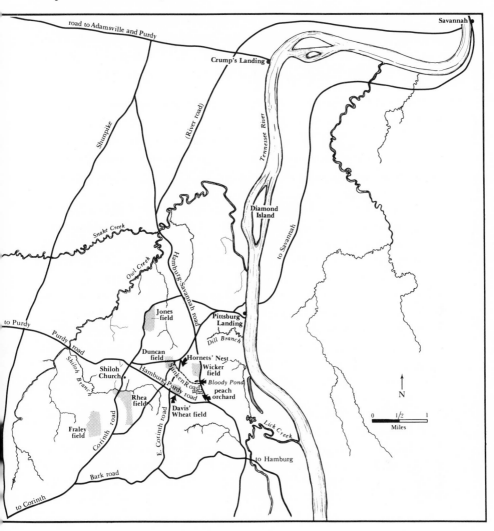

Map 2. The Battlefield of Shiloh.

Stuart by the river. McClernand's division was located a few hundred yards behind Sherman. Hurlbut and W. H. L. Wallace were back closer to the landing, Hurlbut's troops encamped only about a mile out from the river on the Hamburg road and Wallace's division being still nearer to the river.

Grant, looking upon Sherman as an informal field commander, instructed troops moving up from Savannah to report to Sherman. He also gave Sherman authority to organize the unassigned regiments and assign them to divisions as he deemed appropriate. Sherman gave orders that brigades should encamp facing west in order to be in the line of battle when called to arms. He further instructed that there should be no more than twenty-two paces between regimental encampments, and that convenience of fresh water, while it could be considered, must not be allowed to determine the placement of camps. These orders were widely disregarded, and Sherman did not correct the situation. One brigade immediately beside Sherman's headquarters had its three regiments each fronting in a different direction. Nor were regimental camps always kept close together. In one of the most flagrant violations, the Fifty-third Ohio, discovering a fresh spring, located its camp across a creek from and some 400 yards in advance of the rest of its brigade.[29]

Although Grant has been criticized for not keeping all of his army on the east side of the river until it was ready for offensive operations, this decision does not seem to be as censurable as the manner in which the army's divisions were encamped, scattered about without any tactical formation, with no semblance of a defensive line, and, above all, with no adequate provisions for outposting and patrolling.

No part of the army was entrenched. Grant seemed to be thinking only in terms of an offensive action. Halleck had instructed Grant not to let the enemy draw him into an engagement until he was "properly fortified" and received orders.[30] Such a phrase is subject to flexible interpretation, and there is no way of knowing exactly what Halleck meant by it.

[29] *OR*, x, part 2, 50.
[30] *Ibid.*, 50–51.

Grant did nothing whatsoever about fortifying, however. When he conferred with Smith, the old warrior who had been Grant's commandant at West Point, he was told that the men "have come here to fight and if we begin to spade it will make them think we fear the enemy." Besides, Smith boasted, "I ask nothing better than to have the Rebels come out and attack us. We can whip them to hell!" Grant also respected the opinion of Colonel James B. McPherson, thirty-three-year-old Ohioan on his staff. McPherson, who graduated first in his class at West Point and who would eventually lead the Army of the Tennessee until his death before Atlanta in 1864, was considered one of the brightest young minds in the regular army. McPherson did not think that breastworks were necessary, either.[31]

Sherman may have been a little worried at first about the army's position, judging by some remarks he allegedly made to newsmen. Nevertheless, he most surely remembered how he had lost his command in Kentucky several months earlier when certain newspapers indicated that he was insane because he seemed so nervous. Word spread that he feared that every little Rebel cavalry patrol heralded a major advance of the enemy, and he was said to have estimated that 200,000 men would be necessary to put down the rebellion in the Mississippi Valley alone. Doubtless Sherman did not intend to make such a mistake again.[32]

As time passed, Sherman seemingly became more confident that the Confederates were not likely to make an immediate attack in force. Yet there was more than ample evidence to put him on guard. How he could have so completely missed the signs is puzzling. He was perhaps overcompensating in an effort to avoid the kind of criticism he encountered in Kentucky. Attempting to justify himself later, Sherman referred to the many rumors, so often proved false, that had been circulating, saying that "for weeks . . . we had heard all sorts of reports . . . . For weeks old women had reported that

[31] Lewis, *Sherman*, 213.
[32] Foote, *Civil War*, 323.

Beauregard was coming, sometimes with 100,000, sometimes with 300,000 . . . ."[33] Beginning April 1, however, the warning signs were much more substantial than rumors spread by old women.

Sherman himself admitted that "From the first of April we were conscious that the Rebel cavalry in our front were getting bolder and more saucy."[34] This should have suggested to Sherman the possibility that the Rebel cavalry was being used to mask an advance by the entire army. Certainly after Friday afternoon, April 4, he should have been on guard. On that day an audacious reconnaissance in force was made by a portion of the Confederate cavalry in front of Sherman. Although not a wise move if the Confederates hoped to surprise the Union forces later, the Rebels carried off an officer and several men who were on picket duty out on the Corinth road.

Colonel Ralph P. Buckland of the Seventy-second Ohio, hearing the firing during this action, sent two companies forward to help the pickets. He also sent word of the fight to Sherman, his division commander. A few minutes later Buckland himself, apparently becoming apprehensive, gathered up men from three other companies and at a double-quick pace, sloshed through the heavy rain in the direction of the firing. About the time that Buckland arrived at the scene of battle, which was near a strip of fallen timber, the Rebels charged a portion of the Union troops but were driven back by a Federal countercharge. When the Union soldiers received additional support from about 150 troops dispatched by Sherman from the Fifth Ohio Cavalry Regiment, the Rebels retired. A number of men on both sides were killed and wounded.[35]

Primarily the Federals had been fighting Confederate cavalry, but they also reported that three or four pieces of artillery opened fire on them. Major Elbridge G. Ricker of the Fifth Ohio thought that at least two regiments of infantry were present.

Sherman, in the meantime, had called out an entire bri-

[33] Johnston, *Life*, 578.
[34] Sherman, *Memoirs*, I, 229.
[35] *OR*, x, part 1, 90–92, 248.

gade of infantry, which, according to Sherman, pursued the Rebels for about five miles without striking anything solid. The distance could not have been that great, however, because Hardee's infantry "corps," leading the advance of the Confederate army, was then less than five miles from Sherman's camps.[36]

When Major Ricker reported back to Sherman, he told the general that he had met and fought the advance of Beauregard's army, and that the Rebels were definitely advancing on the Union position. Sherman, according to Ricker, lightly dismissed the major's statement with the comment that such was impossible. Beauregard, he said, was not a fool to leave his own base of operations and attack the Federals in theirs—it was simply a reconnaissance in force.[37] Sherman was correct about the last part. The Confederate foray was only a reconnaissance in force, but it should have alerted and prompted him to take action in trying to learn what the Rebels might be planning, instead of merely assuming that the enemy would wait to be attacked at Corinth.

The skirmish caused considerable excitement in the Union ranks. The long roll was beaten in a number of encampments, and more than one division formed in line, readying for action. After that, a feeling of uneasiness, gradually spreading from soldiers to officers and from camp to camp, pervaded much of the front line of the Union army, especially Sherman's division. That night W. H. L. Wallace, James McPherson, and even Grant all rode out to Sherman's quarters, but everything was then quiet.[38]

On the following day, Saturday, April 5, Colonel Buckland visited the picket line several times and was convinced the woods were swarming with Rebel cavalry. The pickets claimed they had also discovered Rebel infantry and artillery close at hand. Buckland reported accordingly to Sherman, but the general took no action. Although the worried Buckland strengthened his pickets, there is no evidence that he pushed

---

[36] *Ibid.*, 93, 248.

[37] Johnston, *Life*, 579.

[38] Wallace, *Letters*, 181, H. V. Boynton, *Sherman's Historical Raid: The Memoirs in the Light of the Record* (Cincinnati, 1875), 30.

them out any farther toward Corinth to gain information about the Rebel intentions.[39]

During Saturday afternoon Colonel Jesse Appler of the Fifty-third Ohio Infantry, Sherman's most advanced regiment, sent him word that a large force of the enemy was approaching. It must have seemed a bit too much to Sherman. Whether his chronic asthmatic condition increased his irritability at the particular time or not, there is no doubt that he was genuinely upset with Colonel Appler. After listening to the communiqué in disgust, Sherman sent a message by an aide curtly telling Appler something to the effect that "there was no enemy closer than Corinth" and Appler could "take his damn regiment back to Ohio!" Of course Sherman knew from the various picket clashes that at least some Rebels were closer than Corinth, but his mind was closed; he obviously was convinced that the Gray army did not intend to do more along his front than to annoy the Blue host. It is certain that he took no adequate precautions against a surprise attack.[40]

As the Confederate forces moved toward Pittsburg Landing, they were amazed at the lack of Union pickets or outposts. The Rebels had their own pickets set out well in advance of their army as it ground forward and yet did not encounter any Federal outposts until they were almost on top of the Union camps. The deliberation with which the Confederates formed their lines for the attack was evident to the Federal soldiers examining the area after the battle.[41]

Sherman may have been unduly influenced by Grant's opinion that if the army faced any immediate threat—and Grant was careful to specify that he did not think the threat was real—it was Lew Wallace's Third Division at Crump's Landing that was in danger. On April 4, Grant wrote Sherman:

Information just received would indicate that the enemy are

[39] Johnston, *Life*, 579. Wallace, *Letters*, 191.

[40] *Battles and Leaders*, I, 537. Sherman, *Memoirs*, I, 229–230. Duke, *53rd Ohio*, 41.

[41] Alfred Roman, *The Military Operations of General Beauregard in the War between the States, 1861 to 1865*, 2 vols. (New York, 1884), I, 282. Johnston, *Life*, 530. *Battles and Leaders*, I, 604, 605.

sending in a force to Purdy, and it may be with a view to attack General Wallace at Crump's Landing. I have directed General W. H. L. Wallace, commanding Second Division temporarily, to reinforce General L. Wallace in case of an attack, with his entire division, although I look for nothing of the kind, but it is best to be prepared.

I would direct, therefore, that you advise your advance guards to keep a sharp lookout for any movement *in that direction*, and should such a thing be attempted, give all the support of your division and General Hurlbut's if necessary . . . (italics added).[42]

Confidence and offense were the orders of the day for the two key men of the Union army. Thus Sherman, on April 5, wrote Grant "I have no doubt that nothing will occur today more than some picket firing. . . . I do not apprehend anything like an attack on our position." Grant, having also concluded that the Confederates were simply making reconnaissances in force in recent days, and reassured by Sherman, wrote Halleck on the same evening: "I have scarcely the faintest idea of an attack (general one) being made upon us, but will be prepared should such a thing take place."[43]

Despite such a staunch avowal of preparedness, Grant had not made provisions—and never did—for adequate outposting and patrolling that would have unmasked an advance by the Confederate army. The position at Pittsburg Landing was potentially highly defensible, obviously an excellent site for training purposes, and, in spite of limited docking space, adequate for the beginning of an offensive movement on Corinth. Whether some other point or points of departure would have been more desirable for launching an offensive are moot questions. The failure of Grant lay not in the selection of Pittsburg Landing but rather in allowing his army to remain in badly aligned encampments for repelling an attack, with no entrenchments, on the same side of the river as the enemy camp which was only twenty miles away, and which he himself had estimated at 80,000 in number. And then he had

---

[42] *OR*, x, part 2, 91. Also see Manning F. Force, *Civil War Journal*, 133, Manning F. Force Papers, LC. John Y. Simon, ed., *The Papers of Ulysses S. Grant*, 5 vols. (Carbondale, Ill., 1973), v, 9, 10.

[43] *OR*, x, part 2, 93, 94; part 1, 89.

established his headquarters at Savannah, nine miles downstream and on the opposite side of the river from his army. These were not the lessons he had been taught at West Point.

Sherman must certainly be censured, too, but in the final analysis the responsibility was Grant's. The situation is graphically and accurately described in one sentence by Sir Basil Liddell-Hart, widely acknowledged as the foremost military analyst of this century: "Indeed the crowning irony of Shiloh is that Grant offered a perfect bait but omitted to set the trap."[44]

[44] Liddell-Hart, *Sherman*, 122. See also Otto Eisenschiml, "Shiloh—the Blunders and the Blame," *Civil War Times Illustrated* (Apr. 1963), 6ff.

3. *God and Beauregard*

THE REBEL ARMY was coming after the bait, although Albert Sidney Johnston was apparently directing the Confederates with a rather unsteady hand up to the very moment of attack. The avalanche of criticism of Johnston following the Confederate disasters in the West may have undermined his self-confidence during the period just before Shiloh. He certainly seemed to be unable to control the situation confronting him in the Rebel army at Corinth.

The army was lacking in transportation, supplies, organization, and discipline. Less than three weeks before the battle General Bragg had written Colonel Thomas Jordan about the "radical defects" of the army's organization which he said would prevent any movement against the enemy. The next day, in a letter to Beauregard, he seemed, if anything, even more discouraged. Drunkenness and plundering were problems, Major General George B. Crittenden finally being arrested for the former, relieved of his corps command and replaced by the recent Vice President of the United States, John C. Breckinridge. One of Crittenden's brigade commanders, Charles Carroll, was arrested on the same charge. Bragg, disturbed by his observations of widespread lack of respect in the army for property, even accused the bishop of the Episcopal Diocese of Louisiana, General Leonidas Polk, of "plundering." The army was also short on supplies, a condition that prevailed right up to the time of battle. For example, thousands of cartridges intended for the Enfield rifles of Hardee's "corps" were sent by mistake to Grenada, Mississippi. The problems may have seemed overwhelming to Johnston.[1]

[1] *OR*, x, part 2, 340, 341, 379. Connelly, *Army*, 145–47.

Indeed his actions suggest such an interpretation. On March 18, he mentioned to Jefferson Davis in a long letter from Decatur, Alabama, the possibility that the President himself, a West Point graduate, Mexican War veteran, and former secretary of war, might want to take command of Johnston's army. "Were you to assume command," he said, "it would afford me the most unfeigned pleasure, and every energy would be exerted to help you to victory, and the country to independence." Nothing came of the suggestion, but in August 1863, when Robert E. Lee considered resigning because of accusations concerning Gettysburg, Davis recalled that Albert Sidney Johnston, facing criticism just before Shiloh, had been "overwhelmed by a senseless clamor." When Johnston and Beauregard met at Corinth, a few days after Johnston had written Davis, Johnston this time offered to relinquish his command to the Creole.[2]

Beauregard refused the offer, but he nevertheless was the prime mover of the campaign that resulted in the battle of Shiloh. Beauregard was soon designated "Second in Command" of an army that he was basically responsible for assembling from throughout the Western Department. It was a force bearing the name "Army of the Mississippi," a title he had selected. It was an army organized into four "corps" as he had desired, and a command that marched to Shiloh according to an offensive program he devised. It also seems to have been Beauregard who played a major role in convincing Johnston that the time to attack had come.[3]

Pierre Gustave Toutant Beauregard was a small but muscular and strikingly handsome man, his olive skin accentuated by a neatly trimmed, jet-black moustache. Born in the parish of St. Bernard, just below New Orleans, he grew up speaking French and probably did not learn English until he was about twelve. He was raised in an environment that proudly man-

---

[2] Johnston, *Life*, 520. Thomas Connelly and Archer Jones, *The Politics of Command: Factions and Ideas in Confederate Strategy* (Baton Rouge, 1973), 52. Roman, *Beauregard*, I, 266.

[3] *OR*, x, part 2, 297. Roman, *Beauregard*, I, 266, 267, 269. Liddell-Hart, *Sherman*, 122, states "Johnston had not been as quick as Beauregard to appreciate the value of concentrating at Corinth. . . ."

The colorful P.G.T. Beauregard, popularly known as the "Napoleon in Gray," played a leading role in concentrating the Rebel army
at Corinth but thereafter suffered a decline in military fortunes.
Many Confederates blamed him for the "lost opportunity" at Shiloh.

ifested much of Gallic culture with its penchant for merry-making, luxurious living, and the maintenance of honor and good manners, but he was also influenced by the traits and customs of the plantation South. The ultimate product was one of the most volatile and colorful generals of the war. T. Harry Williams, in his biography of this "Napoleon in Gray," pictured Beauregard as having "more glamour and drama in his Gallic-American personality than any three of his Anglo-Saxon colleagues in gray rolled into one."[4]

In Beauregard's early teens his father sent him to a French school in New York, run by two brothers who had been officers under Napoleon Bonaparte. While there, studying the campaigns of the Corsican, Beauregard found a lifelong hero. In later years people would sometimes say that he looked like Napoleon in a gray uniform—a comment which doubtless gave him pleasure. He also found a profession, soon informing his father that he wished to enter the United States Military Academy at West Point. Described as rather quiet, studious, and somewhat reserved—at least in comparison with his demeanor of later years—the dark-haired young man graduated from the academy second in a class of forty-five. Although standing only five feet seven inches tall, he had excelled in sports as well as in his studies.

The passing years simply reinforced his martial bearing, as did his service in the Mexican War. But age brought a change in his personality, the quiet and reserve of his earlier nature giving way to more vocal, forceful, highly self-confident characteristics. Probably his heritage was asserting itself, although he was never a consistent personality.[5] If some thought him vain, pompous, and obnoxious—and they did, such as the newspaperman who spoke of "his godship" in reference to the Creole—many found him chivalrous, glamorous, inspiring in speech and bearing, and deeply devoted to the Confederate cause, "a host in himself" as Bruce Catton has written. If he was arrogant, his supporters would

[4] T. Harry Williams, *P. G. T. Beauregard: Napoleon in Gray* (Baton Rouge, 1954), 1.
[5] *Ibid.*, 1–8.

probably have said it was arrogance in the best Southern tradition.[6]

The reduction of Fort Sumter and the role he played in the first important battle of the war, the victory at Manassas, soon resulted in the idolization of Beauregard as a great popular hero of the Confederacy. Not even the reflections of his Napoleonic vanity in quarreling with President Davis in the Virginia newspapers soon after Manassas, or his fondness for dramatic phrases, such as the heading on one of his letters to a Richmond paper, "Centerville, Virginia—Within Hearing of the Enemy's Guns," could dampen the spirit of his admirers. In fact, a good case could probably be made for their contribution to his fame and popularity.

When he went west in early February 1862, the reception was sometimes astounding. A Memphis editor in a column headed *"THE HERO OF MANASSAS"* seemed to look upon Beauregard as a one-man gang. Upon hearing that Beauregard's health, which had been the subject of much anxiety in recent weeks, was improving, and that the Creole was assuming active command of the forces defending the Mississippi Valley, he wrote: "There is all confidence *now* that a vandal's foot will never tread the streets of Memphis." The New Orleans *Daily Picayune* made an appeal which sounded almost as though the war were being fought to save the forty-three-year-old Frenchman, rather than the Confederacy. Its issue of March 9, 1862, broadcast the cry "Creoles of Louisiana, arouse! Our Beauregard awaits you; he calls for men in this hour of peril. . . . Haste to his side ere the enemy surround him." And a Richmond correspondent of the New Orleans *Crescent*, after the fall of Fort Henry and Fort Donelson, declared simply that there is "no hope now in anybody but God and Beauregard."[7]

One senses that if there was one general in the Civil War who possessed the potential to be mobbed by his fans, it was Beauregard. He certainly was the favorite general of the

---

[6] Quoted in the Nashville *Daily Union*, Apr. 15, 1862. Catton, *Terrible Swift Sword* (Boston, 1963), 141.

[7] Memphis *Daily Avalanche*, Mar. 7, 1862. Quoted in the Cincinnati *Daily Enquirer*, Mar. 28, 1862.

ladies, who showered him with letters, flags, scarves, and flowers. One visitor to his office saw two vases of flowers on his table, one on each side of his maps and plans, and a bouquet of roses and geraniums being used as a paperweight. Some soldiers even claimed that he was accompanied on his marches by a train of wagons loaded with concubines and cases of champagne. Charges of immorality were to be expected, of course, inasmuch as infidelity was often alleged to be a Creole characteristic. Although most rumors about his immoral conduct were baseless, they did help add spice to his legend.[8]

From the time of his arrival from the East until Shiloh, it was Beauregard, saturated with Napoleonic concepts, who fervently proclaimed the absolute necessity of concentration of all available forces in the Western theater. General Johnston's son, William Preston Johnston, later contended that his father was responsible for the buildup at Corinth and the Shiloh campaign, but careful study of the Johnston and Beauregard correspondence in the weeks preceding Shiloh does not support this thesis. As early as February 14, Beauregard revealed his thinking in a letter to a friend in Richmond: "We must give up some minor points and concentrate our forces to save the most important ones, or we will lose all of them in succession."[9]

The fall of Fort Henry and Fort Donelson had separated the Confederate forces under Johnston in Middle Tennessee from those now placed under Beauregard in West Tennessee. If Beauregard then needed any nudge to assume the overall direction of affairs in the West, which seems doubtful, he received more than ample encouragement—and from Johnston himself. In a brief dispatch of February 16, Johnston told him, "You must do as your judgment dictates. No orders for your troops have been issued from here." Two days later Johnston repeated the advice! "You must now act as seems best to you. The separation of our armies is for the present complete." Another dispatch, on February 21, gave Beaure-

---

[8] Williams, *Beauregard*, 52.

[9] P. G. T. Beauregard to R. A. Pryor, P. G. T. Beauregard Papers, Duke Univ. Library, Durham, N. C.

gard still more support: "As you have had time sufficiently to study the field," said Johnston, "I hope you will advise General Polk of your judgment as to the proper disposition of his army, in accordance with the views expressed in your memorandum, unless you have deemed it necessary to change them."[10]

Although he was only a district commander and had no more than a "corps" under him—Polk's troops at Columbus, Kentucky—Beauregard was soon exercising full discretion in assembling an army. One of his first concerns was the disposition of Polk's troops, and Beauregard set out to inspect them but was forced off the train at Jackson, Tennessee, because of illness. Bothered by a bad throat, which had been getting worse for some time, he was unable to continue his journey; instead he summoned Polk to join him for a conference at Jackson. Polk was told that he must fall back to New Madrid, Missouri, for Columbus was dangerously exposed to Union attack. Beauregard was now planning a new defensive line. It would extend generally northwest from Corinth on the right through Jackson and Humboldt, Tennessee, to New Madrid on the left, thus protecting Memphis and its railroads until Beauregard could gather enough troops to take the offensive.

On February 21, "filled with profound anxiety," as he dramatically described himself, and convinced that the Rebels must boldly assume the offensive to prevent "an irrevocable defeat," he called upon the governors of Mississippi, Alabama, Louisiana, and Tennessee for 5,000 to 10,000 men each. The soldiers were to be armed and equipped. With these troops, augmented by whatever additional forces he could obtain, particularly from Earl Van Dorn in Arkansas, he proposed to take the field, capture Paducah, and close the mouths of the Tennessee and Cumberland rivers, thus cutting off the Union supply line. He also called upon Braxton Bragg for any troops he could spare from Pensacola and Mobile, and urged the general to come in person if possible. A similar request for troops was addressed to Mansfield Lovell at New Orleans, and Van Dorn was also urged to come at once to further swell the

[10] Roman, *Beauregard*, I, 232, 233. Johnston, *Life*, 526.

ranks of Beauregard's forces. Nor had Beauregard forgotten
to call upon God. "With the continued protection of the Almighty," he assured his troops on March 5, as he christened
them the Army of the Mississippi, "we must and shall
triumph."[11]

A dazzling vision of grandeur seemed to be unfolding, and
enlarging, as he wrote to Van Dorn. "We must . . . take the
offensive," he said, as he projected a campaign which would
not only overrun Cairo, Paducah, and the mouths of the
Tennessee and Cumberland rivers, but "most probably be
able to take St. Louis. . . ." Never one to be self-effacing, the
effervescent Creole triumphantly exclaimed, "What say you
to this brilliant programme?"[12] Beauregard could become
carried away, elaborating upon plans until they were unrealis-
tic and even ridiculous, but he was absolutely right in his
pronouncement of the necessity for concentrating and assuming the offensive. Fortunately for the Union, Van Dorn's
soldiers did not arrive in time for the great battle.

Next Beauregard turned his attention to Johnston's army.
As Johnston had retreated toward Murfreesboro, he still
seemed to be thinking of protecting particular places rather
than concentrating for a major blow at the enemy. And when
he continued his retreat along the Nashville and Chattanooga
Railroad toward Stevenson, Alabama, becoming farther and
farther separated from Beauregard's command in West Tennessee, the Creole urged upon him the wisdom of changing
direction in order to unite their forces in north Mississippi.
"Time is precious," he warned Johnston on February 26, as he
asked pointedly "can not you come here?" On March 2, he
said, "I think you ought to hurry up your troops to Corinth by
railroad as soon as practicable, for . . . thereabouts will soon
be fought the great battle of this controversy."[13]

Even if Johnston at this early date did have in mind the

[11] Roman, *Beauregard*, I, 240–42, 250.
[12] *Ibid.*, 242.
[13] Beauregard to Johnston, Feb. 26, 1862, Mar. 2, 1862, and Beauregard
to Mackall, Mar. 4, 1862, in Albert Sidney Johnston–P.G.T. Beauregard
Correspondence, mss Division, Howard-Tilton Memorial Library, Tulane
Univ., New Orleans. Hereafter cited as Johnston–Beauregard Correspondence.

eventual concentration of all available forces in the West for
the purpose of striking a counterblow at the Union army, it
was Beauregard who was spearheading the effort to bring
about such a junction at the earliest possible moment. (A full
month passed between Johnston's decision to move west—
announced to the Confederate secretary of war in a communiqué dated February 27—and the time he actually joined
Beauregard.) It was also Beauregard who was urging a concentration in an area where a successful counterblow would
hold the possibility of protecting the Mississippi Valley. The
direction in which Johnston had been moving would suggest
that he at first considered the valley of secondary importance.
Of course, Johnston's concern for the central South is readily
understandable. The wisdom of giving up the middle South
for the Mississippi Valley was a moot point. Not only were
Middle Tennessee's great corn, wheat, iron, and livestock
resources to be considered, but also East Tennessee and
northern Alabama were threatened by the Federal move up
the Tennessee River. If Union forces seized the Memphis and
Charleston Railroad, they would have a communication line
from the mouth of the Tennessee nearly all the way to the
great rail center at Chattanooga. But Johnston, in finally
electing to try to defend the Mississippi Valley rather than the
middle South, made the choice which most of the Rebel high
command favored.

When Johnston informed Beauregard, after the latter's
urging, that he was moving west to unite with him, the Creole
thenceforth bombarded Johnston with instructions couched
in language which would leave an unknowing reader with the
certain impression that it was Beauregard, rather than Johnston, who was in command. On March 8 Beauregard tele-
graphed Johnston: "Send me General Bushrod Johnson immediately. Also percussion caps to Ruggles at Corinth and to
Lovell at New Orleans." On March 10 he instructed Johnston
to collect no more cars and engines from the western part of
the road than were absolutely necessary, "lest they be cut off
at Tuscumbia." Two days later he cautioned Johnston again
about the same matter, and on March 15 he commanded
Johnston: "Great need of cavalry—spare me two regiments at

once." On another occasion he told Johnston to send him three infantry regiments, and specified the ones he wanted. Beauregard also advised Johnston to spread rumors that Hardee's men were going to Chattanooga instead of Corinth; that Johnston should send all available surplus ammunition to Corinth; and that it would be well for Johnston to telegraph the War Department for the generals he might require. He even asked for Johnston's own adjutant general, W. W. Mackall, and his chief engineer, Jeremy Gilmer, to be sent on ahead of Johnston's arrival, because Beauregard had need of them![14]

Johnston did not send the two staff officers, but he complied with most of Beauregard's other requests. When Beauregard and Johnston met at Corinth, the pattern had been set. Beauregard continued to be the driving force in managing the army's affairs.

Concerned about the need for more metal for guns and despairing of help from the War Department in Richmond, Beauregard took it upon himself to issue an appeal to the people of the Mississippi Valley. In dramatic terms, he asked them to sacrifice their plantation bells so that more cannon might be made for the defense of their homes, climaxing his appeal with the words, "Who will not cheerfully and promptly send me his bells under such circumstances? Be of good cheer; but time is precious."[15] Although some people responded, the number did not match Beauregard's expectations. General enthusiasm among the women was so great, however, that some of them were offering their brass candlesticks and andirons, and churches were giving up their church bells.

Beauregard was succeeding in bringing about a concentration of troops unprecedented in the expanse of geographical area from which they were drawn, a concentration which held a real promise of reversing the course of the war in the West. By the time of the battle of Shiloh all Confederate forces that

---

[14] Beauregard to Johnston, Mar. 2, 6, 8, 10, 12, 15, 17, 24, Apr. 2, 1862, all in Johnston–Beauregard Correspondence.

[15] Foote, *Civil War*, 307.

Beauregard had hoped to unite, except Von Dorn's Arkansas command, were gathered in one place. The Rebels were making the best strategic move available to them, and the most vigorous and assertive of the guiding hands were P. G. T. Beauregard's.

Nonetheless, the element of time was working against the Confederates. They needed more time to train their commands, secure additional weapons, and allow Van Dorn's troops to arrive; but time ran out on April 2. Benjamin F. Cheatham sent word from Bethel Station, some twenty miles north of Corinth, that Lew Wallace's force was advancing on him from Crump's Landing. Although Wallace's move was actually only a reconnaissance, the Confederates feared that he might be attempting to smash the Mobile and Ohio Railroad or that he might be moving on Memphis. There was no way of knowing what he intended.

Even more disturbing was information from scouts reporting that Buell, with 30,000 men, had finally left Columbia (his army had taken 12 days to cross the Duck River) and was moving to join Grant at Pittsburg Landing. Beauregard was convinced that the time for attack had come; it must be launched before the Federal forces came together. On Cheatham's report, which would be delivered to Johnston, Beauregard placed an endorsement, urging upon the army's commander the necessity of attacking at once. When Johnston received the message, he left his headquarters house in Corinth and crossed the street to arouse Bragg, who had already retired for the night. After a hurried consultation Bragg and Thomas Jordan, Beauregard's chief of staff then serving as adjutant general for the army, agreed with the Creole. The Rebels should attack at once. Johnston at first hesitated, arguing that he was not yet ready to advance, but finally consented. Although Jordan, who had been schooled by Beauregard, parried Johnston's arguments with some success, the necessity for action before Buell and Grant could join forces was probably the overriding factor in swaying Johnston to make war immediately.[16]

[16] *Battles and Leaders*, I, 594–95. Roman, *Beauregard*, I, 270. Connelly, *Army*, 152. Horn, *Army*, 121.

The Rebel plan of advance and attack appears to have been devised chiefly by Beauregard. As Thomas L. Connelly has written, it was not simple: "Dazzled by prospects for a grand offensive the Creole rose to the occasion with an impossible set of maneuvers ill suited to raw troops and unfamiliar terrain."[17] The Confederates would march from Corinth on two dirt roads that ran north and east and somewhat parallel until they converged at a house called Mickey's about eight miles from Pittsburg Landing. At that point the army would be deployed to attack. The easternmost route, the Monterey road, was the longest and crookedest, swinging out to the east of Corinth before turning north, while the more western and direct approach, the Ridge road, cut northeast from Corinth for several miles and then curved more sharply east toward Mickey's.

The Confederate army that marched to Shiloh was organized into four corps. The plan of march called for William J. Hardee's "Third Corps," numbering 4,545, to proceed toward Pittsburg Landing on the shorter Ridge road. Hardee would become known in Confederate legend as "Old Reliable," and was already famous as the author of *Rifle and Light Infantry Tactics*, commonly referred to simply as Hardee's *Tactics*, a manual of arms by which many of his soldiers drilled. He was a West Point graduate, class of 1838, who had distinguished himself in the Mexican War, continued in the old army, and held the rank of lieutenant colonel when the Civil War began. Because Hardee's corps, which would lead the attack, was relatively weak in numbers, A. H. Gladden's brigade from Bragg's corps was assigned to it also.

Hardee's command was to be followed on the Ridge road by the "First Corps," consisting of 9,024 men, commanded by Leonidas Polk. The fifty-six-year-old Polk was a graduate of West Point who resigned his army commission to study theology. He had been a missionary bishop to the southwest, the Episcopal bishop of Louisiana, and founder of the University of the South at Sewanee, Tennessee, before casting his lot with the Confederacy.

[17] Connelly, *Army*, 152.

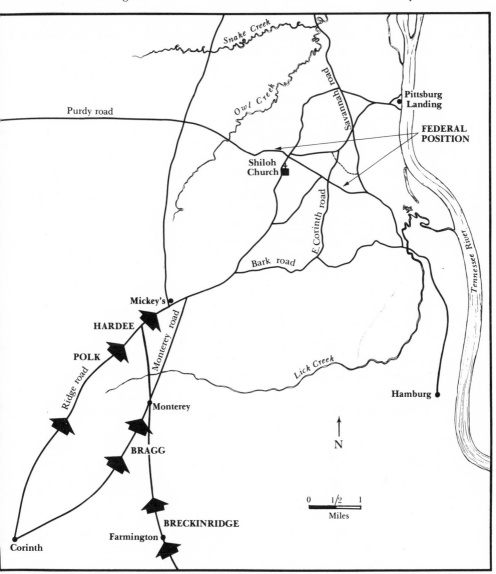

Map 3. Route of the Confederate Advance on Pittsburg Landing.

Braxton Bragg was to lead the "Second Corps," 14,868 strong, and the largest in the army, by way of the Monterey road—an odd arrangement that seems to defy logic, for it involved sending the largest number of troops by the longest road. Bragg was to be followed by John C. Breckinridge, commanding the "Fourth Corps," which actually consisted of only three brigades, and formed the army's reserve of 6,290 men.[18] Born in Kentucky in 1825, Breckinridge was a dark-eyed, swarthy fellow who had practiced law, had served in the Mexican War, had served in the United States Congress, was elected Vice President on the ticket with James Buchanan, and had been nominated for the Presidency by the Southern Democrats following the breakup of the Democratic Party in 1860. After the election of Lincoln he had worked for a compromise to avoid war, and did not join the Confederate army until the fall of 1861.

Hardee's corps was to reach Mickey's first and deploy in battle line in the fields beyond that place. Bragg was expected to form his corps in a second line behind Hardee. To accomplish this Bragg was to split up his troops at Monterey, a little town a few miles south of Mickey's. His first division was to continue on directly to Mickey's while his second division filed off to the west on a route intersecting the Ridge road where Hardee and Polk were marching. The plan called for Bragg's soldiers to swing in behind Hardee's troops and in front of Polk's, continuing by the Ridge road to Mickey's where they would join up once more with the rest of Bragg's command, deploying for attack on the left of his line.

After Bragg had formed his corps in line of battle behind Hardee, Polk would come up and form a third line behind Bragg. Then Breckinridge, having reached Monterey, was to choose whichever route seemed quickest, getting into position as a fourth line behind Polk, where he would act as a reserve.[19]

It was a curious plan. Not only was Bragg's corps, the largest, expected to take the longest route and perform the most complicated maneuver, calling for near perfect timing,

[18] The numbers for the corps are taken from *OR*, x, part 1, 398, and do not include the artillery and cavalry.
[19] *OR*, x, part 1, 392–95.

but the army was to attack in linear formation, with one corps behind another rather than side by side, obviously making communication, supply, and command on the battlefield more confusing and difficult. Finally, and almost unbelievably, the plan made no provision for a heavier attacking force on the Confederate right, where the Rebels supposedly intended to launch their strongest assault and cut off the Union army from the landing, the Federals' most likely source of reinforcements and supplies.

The Confederates may well have lost the opportunity to break the Union army at Shiloh when they adopted this program of battle. There was no doubt that the Blue army was vulnerable: resting in an undeveloped defensive position, overconfident, its highest ranking officers not expecting an attack, and lacking adequate pickets and patrols to give early warning in case the enemy should come. Grant's army was ripe to be smashed, but the Rebel battle plan practically guaranteed confusion in command and inefficient use of manpower. Predictably, chaos reigned in some areas of the battlefield soon after the fight began, and some commands simply stood around, lacking instructions on what to do and where to go.[20]

The origin of these basic tactical flaws has been a debatable point ever since the battle. Johnston's communication to President Davis on April 3 indicated that he fully intended, at least originally, to make the attack with his corps side by side—Polk on the left, Bragg in the center, and Hardee on the right wing, with Breckinridge in reserve. In his memorandum to corps commanders on April 3, Johnston specifically stated that in the approaching battle "every effort should be made to turn the left flank of the enemy so as to cut off his line of retreat to the Tennessee River, and throw him back on Owl Creek."[21]

How and why, then, were the plans so drastically changed? Johnston delegated to Beauregard, as second in command, the preparation of the orders for the advance and attack, and therein must lie the answer. Beauregard framed the orders

[20] *Battles and Leaders*, I, 599, 600.
[21] Johnston, *Life*, 557.

and afterward turned over his notes to Thomas Jordan for their final elaboration in finished form. In other words, it is reasonable to assume that Beauregard changed the plans. His was the kind of colossal ego that made him fully capable of scrapping a superior's instructions and writing his own. Perhaps he reasoned that with so many green troops in the field, it would be difficult to exercise command control regardless of the type of attack formation. Consequently, he would mass the corps in one line after another in the hope of presenting an overwhelming striking force while at the same time preventing gaps in the Confederate line. No force the enemy could amass could cut through three double lines of Confederates. By the combination of surprise and sheer weight of numbers he would simply power his way over the Union army. In an article written after the war, Beauregard claimed that the terrain to be traversed made any other kind of movement an "absolute impossibility."[22] It is doubtful that Beauregard, or any other Rebel officer, knew as much about the terrain as his statement implied. Otherwise the Confederates would not have expected to march from Corinth and deploy for attack at as rapid a pace as was projected. Furthermore, it is difficult to imagine how Johnston's side-by-side formation, whatever the terrain, could have resulted in any more confusion than did Beauregard's linear organization.

Obviously, at some point and for reasons unknown today, Johnston accepted Beauregard's changes in the attack formation and as supreme commander must bear the primary responsibility. Perhaps the most likely explanation is that Johnston's personality was not sufficiently forceful to control a strong-willed subordinate like Beauregard.

That the two men ever agreed on the arrangement to turn the Union left toward Owl Creek is doubtful. Johnston's actions on the day of the battle could be interpreted as indicating he still intended to carry out the original plan in this respect, although there is no indication that he ever tried to get a proper turning force on his right until after the battle was well begun. Beauregard's intentions are a little murky, but the

[22] *Battles and Leaders*, I, 581.

evidence available supports the thesis that he and Johnston were working at cross-purposes. Beauregard funneled a sizable number of reserves to the Rebel center and left, rather than to the right. Describing his actions in the morning and early afternoon, the Creole later wrote: "I had ordered General Hardee to gather all the forces he could and press the enemy on our own left. Stragglers that had been collected by Colonels [George W.] Brent and [A. R.] Chisholm and others of my staff, were also sent forward extemporized into battalions, and Colonel Marshall J. Smith with the New Orleans Crescent Regiment was added, with orders to 'Drive the enemy into the Tennessee.' "[23] Because he made no provision for placing a larger number of troops on the Rebel right, where Johnston said "every effort" would be made to turn the Union left, it seems likely that Beauregard was no more convinced of the wisdom of Johnston's flanking plans than he was of Johnston's attack formation.

[23] *Ibid.*, 590.

4. *We Attack at Daylight*

ABOUT MIDAFTERNOON of Thursday, April 3, some three hours later than planned, three Confederate corps finally began moving out of Corinth, heading northeast toward Pittsburg Landing and the Union army. Breckinridge's corps at Burnsville would not move until the next afternoon. The weather was clear as regiment after regiment fell into line. Hardee's corps was in the lead, followed by Bragg and Polk, but the movement was slow and the rear of Polk's column was still in Corinth as night came on.

Beauregard, attempting afterward to explain the army's late start, charged Polk with obstructing and delaying Hardee's march with his baggage trains. Polk denied it and claimed he himself was the one delayed because Hardee would not move. In detailing the plan of campaign Beauregard had told the corps commanders not to wait for written orders, but to move out at noon. Hardee, for some unexplained reason, was apparently not satisfied with oral instruction and waited for written orders which did not come until after 3 P.M.[1]

Because Hardee's corps was to lead the Confederate advance, the entire army was held up. Thus the pattern was set from the very first, for one delay would follow another as the Rebels plodded toward Pittsburg Landing. If the Confederate marching plan looked a little complicated on paper, the march itself turned out to be like a nightmare. The entire army was to cover the distance from Corinth to Pittsburg

---

[1] Roman, *Beauregard*, I, 275, 276. Joseph H. Parks, *General Leonidas Polk, C. S. A.: The Fighting Bishop* (Baton Rouge, 1962), 228. Johnston, *Life*, 563, 564. Roman, *Beauregard*, I, 275.

Landing and be deployed in battle line by late morning of April 4.[2] Well-trained troops marching over suitable terrain might have found it possible to attack on the morning of the fourth if they had started the march on time. However, the land over which the Gray army had to make its approach was heavily wooded and cut by creeks, ravines, swampy areas, and confusing dirt roads, and some of the troops, as Bragg said, had "never made a day's march."[3]

The plan called for Hardee's lead corps to reach Mickey's, about eight miles from Pittsburg Landing, by the night of the third, but it was the morning of the fourth when the head of the column at last came trudging in. Meanwhile, Bragg's big corps, marching on the Monterey road to the east of Hardee, was falling even further behind schedule. His first division marched all night on the narrow and muddy road to get to Mickey's on the morning of the fourth, where it was supposed to have been at sundown on the third. His second division did not even reach Monterey until the evening of the fourth. If Bragg now sent this division on over to Mickey's by the Purdy road as originally planned, where it was to pass in front of Polk's corps at the intersection of the Purdy and Ridge roads, he feared that the action would delay Polk's march; it seemed certain that Polk, having a shorter distance to cover and a smaller command, would be there first. Thus, hoping to avoid delaying Polk, Bragg took it upon himself to send his second division straight on to Mickey's by the Monterey and Savannah road, instead of the Purdy road. Unfortunately, however, Polk waited at the intersection of the Purdy and Ridge roads for three hours before Bragg's courier informing the general of what Bragg had done reached him.[4]

There were more delays. One of Polk's divisions, under Benjamin Cheatham, was on outpost duty to the north, near Bethel on the Mobile and Ohio Railroad. Coming in on the Purdy and Monterey road, Cheatham was not able to form a

[2] *OR*, x, part 1, 393. *Battles and Leaders*, I, 596.
[3] *Ibid.*, 463.
[4] Johnston, *Life*, 558, 564, 565. William Preston Johnston manuscript defending his *Life of Johnston* against criticism of General Daniel Ruggles, in the Johnston Papers.

junction with the rest of Polk's command until the afternoon of April 5. And Breckinridge's three brigades, moving from Burnsville through Farmington and toward Monterey, did not even leave Burnsville until midafternoon of the fourth. His artillery became stuck in the mud and stopped his entire train.[5]

Soon it had become obvious to everyone that no attack could be made on the morning of April 4. Johnston and Beauregard may have still hoped, for a while, to make the assault later in the day, but the afternoon brought rain, and still the army was not in position. It was decided, in a conference at Monterey, to put off the attack until the morning of April 5.

During the march, while the men would stand at arms, a short address from General Johnston was read at the head of each regiment. The Southern mind has always been peculiarly receptive to oratory. Johnston's words were well chosen to stir the emotions of the soldiers as he briefly but skillfully developed the theme of a people wronged, fighting, with God on their side, for land, country, home, Southern womanhood, and honor:

> Soldiers of the Army of the Mississippi: I have put you in motion to offer battle to the invaders of your country. With the resolution and discipline and valor becoming men fighting, as you are, for all worth living or dying for, you can but march to a decisive victory over the agrarian mercenaries sent to subjugate you and to despoil you of your liberties, your property, and your honor. Remember the precious stake involved; remember the dependence of your mothers, your wives, your sisters, and your children, on the result; remember the fair, broad, abounding land, and the happy homes that would be desolated by your defeat.
>
> The eyes and hopes of eight millions of people rest upon you; you are expected to show yourselves worthy of your lineage, worthy of the women of the South, whose noble devotion in this war has never been exceeded in any time. With such incentives to brave deeds, and with the trust that God is with us, your generals will lead you confidently to the combat—assured of success.[6]

[5] Johnston, *Life*, 558, 559.
[6] *OR*, x, part 1, 396, 397.

Johnston's address was received with evidences of deep feeling, and no doubt some of the soldiers were stirred to a greater resolve to conquer or die.

Throughout the night and early the next morning, the rain poured continuously, sometimes in torrents, until much of the ground was mud and water. With the coming of daylight Hardee was working to get his corps into formation to attack, but the soldiers were sometimes firing their weapons to learn if their powder was still dry, cracking away at rabbits scampering from the brush, shouting to each other upon sighting a deer, or becoming confused as they attempted to assume their proper positions. Once they were formed in line of battle, Beauregard, at Hardee's request, rode along in front of the soldiers, inspiring them for the coming struggle. Later he did the same thing for Bragg's corps. It was approaching mid-morning before Hardee's corps was finally deployed for attack.[7]

Bragg's situation was even worse. One of his divisions was lost. Bragg's right wing had deployed behind Hardee, but nothing was seen of the division which was to take position on his left. Finally Johnston sent word to Bragg inquiring why the troops on his left were not in place. Bragg replied that the head of their column had not yet appeared and that he had sent to the rear for information about it and would inform Johnston what had happened as soon as he himself learned.

As more time passed, Bragg's missing division still did not show, and Polk was becoming irritated and complaining that he could not move his troops into position behind Bragg until Bragg's men were first formed in line. Again Johnston sent a courier to Bragg for information. Bragg's reply was the same as before—he still did not know what had happened to the missing division. Johnston waited a while longer. The time was then past noon; still no troops appeared and no report came from Bragg. "This is perfectly puerile!" Johnston at last erupted, his patience gone. Gathering up some of his aides he rode to the rear in search of Bragg's men, and finally found the missing division standing still in an open field. Some of

[7] Johnston, *Life*, 561, 562. Roman, *Beauregard*, I, 276, 277.

General Polk's reserve troops were ahead of it, with their wagons and artillery blocking the road. Johnston ordered the road cleared and got the division moving forward once more, but by then the day was rapidly waning.[8]

The Rebel forces did not finally get into battle position until late afternoon—too late to begin the attack on that day with any hope of forcing a decisive engagement. It was then that the famous council of war, which will live forever in Confederate legend, took place. The council will never cease to be intriguing because the drama of a few moments, which involved the very highest stakes, has been obscured by the flaring of tempers, the uncertainty of some of the facts, and the even more disturbing uncertainty of the proper interpretation of the known facts.

Apparently the council was rather informal and occurred in the roadway hardly two miles south of Shiloh Church. Present were Johnston, Beauregard, the corps commanders except Hardee, and a few staff officers. Beauregard claimed Johnston called the council, but both Polk and Bragg later described the conference as developing from a somewhat casual, and in part, accidental meeting of the principal men involved. Polk said he was summoned by Beauregard, whom he found already talking with Bragg and expressing serious misgivings about making an attack after all the delay the army had experienced. Then Johnston, perhaps attracted by the gathering, came up and joined in the discussion.[9]

Polk said that his soldiers had already exhausted their rations and he had none in reserve. Bragg indicated that his men had enough food and that they could share it with Polk's troops.[10] It seems doubtful that Bragg enjoyed such a surplus, and it should be noted that he did not follow through with his offer. He could not, at best, have had much food to share, for his soldiers started out with the same amount that Polk's did—five days rations. There is evidence that some soldiers in other commands were also running short and the quartermaster wagons, containing a five-day supply of uncooked

[8] Johnston, *Life*, 563.
[9] *OR*, x, part 1, 407. Johnston, *Life*, 567, 568, 569.
[10] *Battles and Leaders*, I, 597.

reserve rations for the entire corps, were far in the rear, miles away and unable, because of the bad roads, to keep up with the army's advance.

There is truth in the old cliché that an army marches on its stomach, but food was not the chief topic of conversation at the council. Beauregard argued strongly against the offensive. His campaign was conceived on the basis that the Union troops were not entrenched and the belief that the success of the Rebel attack depended on a quick march that would take the Federals by surprise. The delays experienced in marching, and the accompanying noise made by the Rebels, had convinced Beauregard that the Union army must surely know its enemy was coming. All hope of surprise was gone. The Federals were probably well entrenched by now, and Buell would have speeded his march to join Grant. Thus Beauregard felt it would be unwise to attempt an attack against breastworks with such troops as composed most of the Confederate commands. Bragg apparently supported Beauregard's position, but Polk was irritated by Beauregard who implied, according to Polk's official report of the campaign, that Polk was responsible for the delays.[11]

It was then that Albert Sidney Johnston made the decision to proceed with the assault on the morning of April 6. He was, according to Polk, very displeased with the idea of calling off the offensive, and remarked, when Beauregard had presented his position, that "this would never do." Johnston stated, "We shall attack at daylight tomorrow," and concluded the council on a note of firm and complete commitment to battle. As he walked off he is said to have confided to a staff officer: "I would fight them if they were a million."[12]

The question of what actually happened, what really motivated the principal actors, in this historic drama of more than a century ago, is still debated today. Present-day biographers of both Beauregard and Johnston think that Beauregard had lost his nerve and that Johnston, in the moment of crisis,

[11] *Ibid.* William Preston Diary, Apr. 5, 1862, War Department Collection of Confederate Records, National Archives. *OR*, x, part 1, 407.
[12] *OR*, x, part 1, 407. Roland, *Johnston*, 324. Johnston, *Life*, 569.

emerged as the man of true courage and resolution.[13] Although such an interpretation of the events is possible, this judgment may be too harsh on Beauregard and too laudatory of Johnston. Beauregard's assessment was more realistic on the basis of the evidence available. Beauregard should have been right about the Union army being alerted and prepared. The Confederate march to Shiloh had been conducted almost as if the Rebels were trying to attract the enemy's attention. Beauregard later contended that he recommended as an alternative that the advance be turned into a reconnaissance in force to lure the Federal army away from its strong position at the river in order to attack it while in motion.[14] Such strategy might well have been a better idea than an assault with inexperienced troops against a prepared position. It was also Napoleonic; and Beauregard, of course, was steeped in Napoleonic concepts.

But the idea has usually been discounted as an afterthought by the Creole on the grounds that there is no evidence from anyone else at the conference that Beauregard made such a suggestion. This is not as strong an argument as it seems to be because two of the principal characters—Johnston and Polk—were never able to give their versions of the council. Johnston was killed the next day. Polk was to die before the war was over, killed during the Georgia campaign on June 14, 1864. Furthermore, Polk was an old friend of Johnston's. They had been roommates at West Point. Polk, in the time he did have left, might not have been willing to say anything that could have reflected badly on Johnston, particularly after Beauregard had angered him at the council. And Bragg may not have wished to tell all he knew after the war, particularly if it would have placed Beauregard in a better light. He and Beauregard were not then on very cordial terms. In fact Bragg came to blame Beauregard in scathing terms for the defeat at Shiloh.

Even if Beauregard did not make such a suggestion concerning strategy, the really essential point is that his argument for calling off the offensive could still have been a logical plea.

[13] Williams, *Beauregard*, 132. Roland, *Johnston*, 323, 324.
[14] Roman, *Beauregard*, I, 278.

A man with nerves of steel, given the situation as the Rebel commanders perceived it and not as students today know it, could have presented a soundly reasoned argument for not attacking. There was certainly ample reason to think an assault might be disastrous. "We do not wonder," wrote Sir Basil Liddell-Hart, "that on April 5 Beauregard advised its [the offensive] abandonment on the ground that surprise was no longer feasible. For only a surprise, crowned by a complete success, could rationally justify this plan of a direct assault on an enemy of almost equal numerical strength in a naturally strong position. Johnston, however, felt that it was 'better to make the venture'. . . . This habit of gambling contrary to reasonable calculations is a military vice which, as the pages of history reveal, has ruined more armies than any other cause."[15]

Johnston's motivations have been difficult to fathom. His sudden decisiveness, as several writers have noted, does seem somewhat out of character. Here was a man who had allowed Beauregard to assume much of the direction of the army's affairs; a man who, three nights before, when the chances for success seemed much brighter, had argued against attack, now calling with unflinching, unwavering, resolution for the battle to begin—and this in direct opposition to the strong arguments of Beauregard.

What was it that moved Johnston? One careful student of the Shiloh campaign has interpreted Johnston's determination to fight, whatever the odds, as possibly the decision of a desperate man attempting to regain his image as a successful commander. The biographer of Polk has suggested that Johnston may have finally gotten enough of Beauregard's tendency to dictate and determined to assert himself. It is interesting that neither of these writers interprets Johnston's decision to fight as a rational judgment based upon the interests of the cause and the merits of the situation.[16]

Possibly historians have tried too hard in their efforts to explain Johnston. Maybe the answer is relatively simple. Once

[15] Liddell-Hart, *Sherman*, 123.
[16] Connelly, *Army*, 157. Parks, *Polk*, 230.

the army was placed in motion, eager and primed for attack, Johnston simply had a "gut feeling" that to turn back was psychologically unacceptable. This would not rule out the possibility that, at the same time, Beauregard was irritating him, or that a victory was needed to save his reputation.

Although historians will probably never learn all they would like to know about that fateful war council meeting, one fact is certain: Albert Sidney Johnston had firmly committed the Confederate army to attack the Union forces at Pittsburg Landing.

The Rebels slept upon their arms that Saturday night knowing that Sunday morning could likely bring one of the biggest battles of the war, knowing that the fate of the Confederate cause in the West probably hung in the balance, and anticipating too that many of them would not see the sun rise but one more time. They slept within hearing of the Union camps. Beauregard, listening to a loud beating of drums near the hour of tattoo, immediately dispatched a staff officer with an order to suppress such thoughtless noise. The officer soon returned with the report that the noise came, not from the Confederates, but from the Union encampments.[17]

Despite strict orders to enforce quiet among the Rebel troops, here and there men shouted, drums were beaten, bugles were blown, fires were kindled, and even firearms were discharged before most of the army at last settled down for a few hours of sleep.[18] Yet, inconceivably, the Rebel army remained undetected by the Federals.

With the coming of dawn the woods were teeming with men quickly eating a bit of breakfast, readying their arms for conflict, and forming in line of battle. Beauregard, apparently, was again making a last-moment attempt to talk Johnston out of attacking when the firing of guns to the front signified that the struggle had begun. Swinging on his horse, Johnston exclaimed to his staff those historic, often quoted words: "Tonight we will water our horses in the Tennessee River!" A few moments later, to Colonel Randal I. Gibson, a close

[17] Roman, *Beauregard*, I, 282.
[18] *Ibid*.

friend of Johnston's son, he said: "We *must* win a victory."[19]

Most of the Confederate army seemed to be advancing with the same buoyancy and spirited impatience to close with the enemy as Johnston typified. Like their Union counterparts, many of the Rebels were anxious to "see the Elephant." The battle was going to be a great adventure, they thought, and some of them could hardly be restrained from rushing forward too quickly.[20]

The influence of Napoleon was ever present with the men in the ranks as well as with the officers in those Civil War conflicts. Most of the soldiers, of course, really knew little or nothing of Napoleon's campaigns, tactics, and strategy other than some clichés or disconnected references which they had picked up they knew not where. It was natural enough as the sun rose big and red through the trees on the morning of April 6 that more than one Confederate thought of Napoleon's most celebrated victory and exclaimed, in hope of triumph, it is the "sun of Austerlitz."[21] Actually, if there was any Napoleonic omen associated with the battle of Shiloh, it had probably already occurred when Colonel Jordan, Beauregard's chief of staff, wrote out the Creole's orders for the campaign. He used as a general model a set of Napoleon's orders—his orders at Waterloo.[22]

[19] Johnston, *Life*, 582, 583.
[20] *Ibid.*, 585.
[21] *Battles and Leaders*, I, 556.
[22] *Ibid.*, 595.

5. *Bad Luck All Around*

IT WAS SIX-THIRTY in the morning, Sunday, April 6; the "sun of Austerlitz" was creeping above the horizon across the river to the east of Pittsburg Landing, and many of the Union camps were stirring. Some of the men continued to sleep, however, or lay relaxed in their tents enjoying the pleasant feel of an early spring morning. Others, less fortunate for the moment, lay sick in their beds. Most of the Federal soldiers were looking forward to a typical Sunday morning in the army, perhaps even a more desirable day than normal: the weather seemed unusually promising. But some four miles out from the landing and only a few hundred yards to the southwest of the Union camps more than 40,000 Confederates, with rifled-muskets and bayonets held in readiness for rough work, were stalking toward the Union lines.

At that hour, unknown to most of the soldiers, a few companies of the Union army had already been fighting the Rebels for an hour or more. Despite the confidence of Grant and Sherman that the army was not about to be attacked at Pittsburg, some men in the Federal camps were very uneasy about the signs of Rebel activity just beyond their lines. One of the worriers was an officer of Prentiss' advanced division to the southeast of Sherman—Colonel Everett Peabody, commanding Prentiss' First Brigade, camped on the division's right. Peabody was a competent man, perhaps a little short-tempered and too outspoken for the liking of some of his superiors, but he did have the confidence of the men who served under him. After his graduation from Harvard as an engineer, he had acquired a reputation while constructing western railroads as "the best field engineer in the West." He made a formidable appearance, standing over six feet tall and weighing about 240 pounds. Peabody was convinced, on the basis of reports from subordinate officers, that the Rebels were gathered in force all along the Union army's front. On the night of April 5 he had suggested to Prentiss that the division be prepared to receive an attack, but the general, mocking the idea of a Confederate advance, refused to take Peabody's ideas seriously. Then Peabody acted on his own judgment. Long before daylight, about three o'clock that morning, Peabody sent Major James E. Powell out on a reconnaissance with three companies of the Twenty-fifth Missouri Infantry, a regiment which had left St. Louis only two weeks earlier.[1]

Powell's little band of less than three hundred men tramped southwest down the rough dirt road that passed beside their brigade camp and gradually bore off to the right between two open farm fields. The troops pushed on until the road finally intersected the main branch of the Corinth-Pittsburg road which passed Shiloh Church farther to the north. Groping their way in the darkness just before dawn, the troops in Blue had plodded across the Corinth-Pittsburg road and reached the edge of another field, belonging to a man named Fraley, when suddenly they stumbled onto a portion of Confederate skirmishers from Hardee's lead corps. By this time the Missourians were actually in front, and about a mile distant, from the camps of Sherman's division. The hour must have been about five o'clock.[2]

The Rebel picket post they encountered belonged to Major A. B. Hardcastle's Third Mississippi Battalion. Hardcastle was occupying high ground about a quarter of a mile in front of his brigade, which was just then beginning to form into a battle line. As Hardcastle later reported the incident, his cavalry vedettes sighted the Union troops about dawn, then

---

[1] *OR*, x, part 1, 282, 284. W. A. Neal, *An Illustrated History of the Missouri Engineer and the 25th Infantry Regiment* (Chicago, 1889), 124, 125. John Robertson, *Michigan in the War* (Lansing, Mich., 1882), 325.

[2] *Battles and Leaders*, I, 558, places the time at 5:14. *OR*, x, part 1, 591, 603; Wood's report says "as early as 5:00," while Hardcastle said it was about dawn. The sun rose at 5:38. Henry Stanley, who was in Hindman's brigade on Wood's right, said he first heard firing at 5:15, Henry Steele Commager, ed., *The Blue and the Gray* (New York, 1950), I, 353.

"fired three shots, wheeled, and galloped back" to rejoin his command. Although the Blue forces' Major Powell did not survive the day to make a report, perhaps he thought he had only flushed a Rebel scouting party, for he deployed his men for further reconnaissance and they scrambled forward toward a rise of high ground a few hundred yards to the south. As his men advanced, seven or eight Confederates who had been posted ahead of their battalion fired a volley at the oncoming Union line and then retired; a second small Rebel party, stationed behind the first, leveled another volley when Powell's men approached to within about a hundred yards and then also fell back. But at the top of the rise, Hardcastle, acting upon his brigade commander's orders to hold his position until the Confederates were ready to advance, now had his whole battalion ready to stop the Union infantry. At a distance of about 200 yards, the two lines began blazing away at each other, and the battle of Shiloh had begun.[3]

Major Hardcastle reported that this clash lasted for an hour or more until about six-thirty, without his command giving an inch. Then, seeing the full Rebel brigade formed in battle line to his rear and advancing to support him, he ordered his battalion to drop back and take its position near the right of the oncoming soldiers. In the face of this heavy Confederate battle line Major Powell's small Union command gave ground, retreating in the general direction from which it had come. Meanwhile, Powell had evidently sent word back to Peabody's brigade that he had encountered the enemy, because Colonel David Moore, commanding the Twenty-first Missouri Infantry, reported that at about six o'clock he was ordered forward by Colonel Peabody to reinforce the Union command that had been attacked. There is no report from Peabody, for he too, like Powell, was killed on the first day of the battle.[4]

Advancing with five companies of the Twenty-first for perhaps a half mile, Moore met Powell's force falling back with its killed and wounded. Taking command of all and ordering the wounded who were able to do so to stay and fight, Moore

---

[3] *OR*, x, part 1, 603.
[4] *Ibid.*, 282, 603.

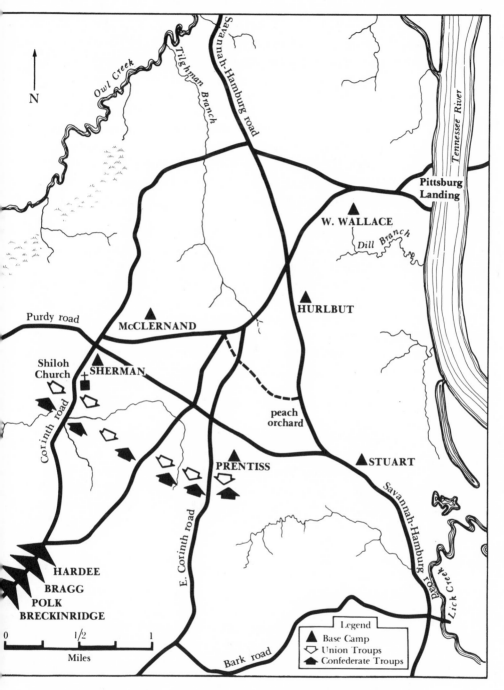

Map 4. Confederate Armies Advance on Federal Positions, 5–8 A.M., April 6, 1862.

dispatched a courier instructing the other half of his regiment to advance at once. About this time General Prentiss, probably notified by Peabody of the action, ordered Lieutenant Colonel Humphrey M. Woodyard to lead the remainder of Moore's regiment to reinforce their commander. Shortly thereafter, with all his regiment together, plus the remnants of Powell's command, Colonel Moore attempted to make a stand against the Rebels at the northwest corner of a cotton field, only to be cut down as one of his legs was shattered below the knee by an enemy shot. Colonel Woodyard took command and, being joined soon after by four companies from the Sixteenth Wisconsin, held a position on the brow of a slight hill on the cotton field. For a short time—half or three-quarters of an hour he later reported—he checked the enemy's march.[5]

It is clear from this action that General Prentiss, commanding the most advanced and isolated division of the Union army, had at least received some warning that the Confederates were coming. Few if any of his troops were surprised and bayoneted in their tents while still asleep, as some newspaper columnists reported. And the man responsible for preventing the division from being taken by surprise was Everett Peabody. He never received any commendation from Prentiss, however, who merely listed him as a brigade commander in his official report. On the contrary, Peabody was preparing to mount his horse after ordering the sounding of the call to arms as the firing of musketry came closer, when he confronted an angry Prentiss reining his horse and demanding to know if Peabody had provoked an attack. Peabody responded that he had sent out a reconnaissance patrol, to which Prentiss exploded that he would hold Peabody "personally" responsible for bringing on a battle. As the two infuriated men glared at each other, Peabody stated that he was personally responsible for all of his actions, and then he swung up on his horse and rode away.[6]

Sherman was also warned but at first took no action. The

---

[5] *OR*, x, part 1, 282, 283.
[6] *Ibid.*, 278. John G. Shea, *The American Nation* (New York, 1862), 356. Charles A. Morton, "A Boy at Shiloh," Military Order of the Loyal Legion of the U.S., N.Y. Commandery (New York, 1907).

alarm came not from Prentiss who seemingly did not think of sending word to Sherman, but from the Fifty-third Ohio, a regiment encamped in the front of his Fifth Division and resting about a quarter of a mile south and east of Shiloh Church, in a corner of a field belonging to a man named Rhea. Like most of Sherman's troops, the Fifty-third Ohio was a green regiment that had not even received muskets until it reached Paducah en route to Pittsburg Landing, had never been drilled except after arriving at the landing on March 20, was plagued with an unusually large number of sick in the camp—at one point two-thirds were reported unfit for duty —and, worst of all, was commanded by a nervous colonel, Jesse J. Appler, who possessed no knowledge of drill or army regulations and would flee from the front lines soon after the battle began.[7]

Unfortunately for the Union army, on a day when there was to be much misfortune in both armies, the soldiers who had some training and experience were generally located back toward the landing, while the rawest regiments were in Prentiss' and Sherman's advanced divisions. The Union front line did not contain one regiment that had previously been under fire.

On the night of April 5 the jittery Appler had sent a picket of sixteen men toward the southern end of the Rhea field on reconnaissance with orders to report any movement of troops in their front, not to fire unless attacked, and to return to camp at daybreak. Probably smarting from Sherman's recent rebuke that he could "take his damn regiment back to Ohio," he did not report this action to either brigade or division headquarters. Then, before dawn of April 6, Appler aroused his adjutant E. C. Dawes, telling him that he could not sleep, had been up all night, and could hear firing to the front. As the two men talked, the sixteen-man picket returned to camp, reporting they heard much firing to the south and were sure a large force of the enemy was in their front.

His excitement now mounting, Appler began giving orders—countermanding them in favor of other orders al-

[7] *OR*, x, part 1, 252, 278. Duke, *53rd Ohio*, 7, 8, 41, 42.

most as soon as he had uttered the first—when suddenly a soldier who had been shot in the arm came stumbling out of a thicket into the camp yelling, as Appler's adjutant remembered it, "Get in line! The Rebels are coming!" Colonel Appler ordered the long roll to be sounded, the regiment to be formed in line, and the sick to get to the rear, and he sent couriers dashing to inform his brigade commander, Jesse Hildebrand, and General Sherman that the enemy was advancing.[8]

Sherman was not impressed, realizing that the warning message came from the same Ohio regiment whose colonel had been so jumpy. He simply replied, with a touch of sarcasm, "You must be badly scared over there." Nevertheless, within a few minutes Sherman seemed to have second thoughts, called together his staff, and rode forward to learn for himself what was happening at the camp of the Fifty-third Ohio. He arrived in time to see the advancing line of Hardee's corps, with the "glistening bayonets of heavy masses of infantry," as his official report described the sight. Suddenly, finally, he realized what was happening; "My God, we are attacked!" he is reported to have exclaimed. Almost at the same instant his orderly beside him, Thomas Holiday, was struck and killed by Rebel fire.

Sherman told Appler to hold his position, for he protected the left flank of the entire division. Supporting units, Sherman promised, would be sent forward immediately. Next Sherman dispatched couriers galloping to inform McClernand, Hurlbut, and Prentiss of the attack (if he sent word to Grant he failed to mention the fact) and cautioned Captain A. C. Waterhouse's Battery E, First Illinois Light Artillery, to hold its fire until the Rebels had crossed the ravine in their front and started their ascent. Then Sherman rode off to see to the rest of his command.[9]

Nearly two miles back of Prentiss and Sherman, Lucius W. Barber of Company D, Fifteenth Illinois Infantry in Hurlbut's division, was in the midst of writing a letter home and only

[8] Duke, *53rd Ohio*, 42, 43.
[9] *Ibid.*, 43–45. *OR*, x, part 1, 249. Sherman, *Memoirs*, I, 230.

vaguely aware of a distant rattle of musketry (which he first thought was something else) when the warning of attack came to his regiment. As he heard the long roll beating, he tossed his unfinished letter to a sick companion telling him to finish it, grabbed his equipment, and hastened to take his place with his company. In less than five minutes from the time the bugle was sounded, as he remembered it, he was marching with his regiment toward the sounds of fighting. They marched "with drums beating and colors flying," he recalled, and as he looked over the column, he was surprised to see that his sick friend, even though weak from fever, was marching with them as they moved toward the front.[10]

About half a mile farther back, close to the landing, B. F. Thomas of the Fourteenth Iowa Infantry, in W. H. L. Wallace's division, was with a companion washing dishes when they first heard firing in the distance. The two, supposing it was only more picket action and not believing the army was really being attacked, joked about the Rebels' fierce intentions, wondering if the "secesh" would let them alone until the dishes were finished. They were still washing when they heard the long roll sounding over in the Second Iowa's camps, which lay close by, and in a short interval, the sound was being reechoed by their own regiment. A few minutes more and they were forming in line and advancing to the front. Some of the regiment's sick tried to follow, but when the command was given to move at a double-quick pace, they began to fall out.[11]

The Second Iowa had just turned out for Sunday morning company inspection when the warning began to sound, and over in the Eighty-first Ohio, also of Wallace's division, Corporal Charles Wright had finished breakfast and started toward the landing with a detail of men to help unload the boats when news of the attack came.[12]

In the camp of the Eleventh Iowa of McClernand's division, about a mile behind Shiloh Church, Colonel William Hall, commanding the regiment, had his wife visiting with him. She

[10] Barber, *15th Illinois*, 51, 52.

[11] Thomas, *14th Iowa*, ch. IV (pages are not numbered).

[12] John T. Bell, *Tramps and Triumphs of the Second Iowa Infantry* (Omaha, 1886), 15. Wright, *81st Ohio*, 32, 33.

later told a newspaper reporter that the first notice she and her husband had of the battle was when a cannon shot ripped through their tent early in the morning.[13]

On the army's left, where peach trees in full bloom skirted the streets of some of the company camps, the men of Stuart's brigade had just finished breakfast and were preparing for inspection; the same was true up ahead and to the right in the camp of the Sixty-first Illinois of Prentiss' division. Leander Stillwell of that regiment later recalled listening, in the calm early morning, to the staccato beat of a woodpecker attacking the limb of a nearby tree immediately before the regiment knew the Rebels were coming.[14]

Still farther to the right in the Seventieth Ohio of Sherman's division, resting beside Shiloh Church, sixteen-year-old John A. Cockerill, who had enlisted as a musician, had taken his place at the breakfast table when he began to hear firing to the front. Sensing that a battle was on, he rushed to the tent of his father who commanded the regiment and found him buckling on his sword. Not exactly sure of what to do, the boy gathered up his prized Enfield rifled-musket and a box of some twenty rounds of cartridges and ran across to the church where he was soon to behold what, through his innocent eyes, seemed at first glance to be "one of the most beautiful pageants . . . ever beheld in war."[15]

And on the army's extreme right, the Sixth Iowa of Sherman's command, with a mascot mongrel named "Jeff Davis," was soon to learn that their colonel was drunk. The regiment formed for action as soon as the alert was given, but when the commander attempted to put his troops through senseless and impossible maneuvers, he had to be removed and placed under arrest. Later in the day he sobered up somewhat, joined with another command, and gave a good account of himself, fighting in the ranks like an ordinary soldier.[16]

---

[13] Franc B. Wilkie, *Pen and Powder* (Boston, 1888), 160, 161.

[14] Leander Stillwell, *The Story of a Common Soldier of Army Life in the Civil War, 1861–1865* (n.p., 1920), 42.

[15] Cockerill, "Boy at Shiloh," 363, 364.

[16] Wright, *6th Iowa*, 77, 80. W. P. Kremer, *Sixth Iowa Infantry* (Rutherford, N. J., n.d.).

Ann Wallace was just arriving at Pittsburg Landing on a steamboat—her coming still unknown to her husband. As she was putting on her hat and gloves, readying to walk from the boat to her husband's headquarters, she could hear a great deal of firing in the distance. It was first explained to her that this probably involved nothing more than the men on picket duty exchanging a few shots with some Rebel patrol. A captain in the Eleventh Illinois who was on board suggested that perhaps it would be better for him to first find out how far it was to General Wallace's headquarters, for it would be better for Mrs. Wallace to ride if the distance were great.

As she waited for the captain to return, the sound of firing seemed to grow more pronounced. In less than thirty minutes, she thought, the captain was back with news that it looked like a major battle was shaping up. Ann's husband had already taken his command to the front, and now it was too late for her to see him. There seemed to be nothing she could do except settle down on the steamboat and wait—disappointed, frustrated, fearful for Will's safety as well as for her other relatives who were in the army. In addition to her husband, Ann's father, two brothers, two of her husband's brothers, and several more distant relatives were all fighting on the field of Shiloh.[17]

Nine miles down the river at Savannah, men in the camps of the Forty-first Ohio Infantry heard the sounds of firing, and at the William H. Cherry mansion, seated at the breakfast table, Ulysses S. Grant heard them also.[18]

Grant quit his breakfast while holding an untasted cup of coffee in his hand, according to some reports, and with his staff, headed down to the landing where he boarded his headquarters boat, *Tigress*, on which steam was continually kept up. Before casting off he sent notes to Buell, canceling their scheduled meeting at Savannah, and to Brigadier General William Nelson, whose division had arrived in Savannah the day before, ordering him to move his entire command to the riverbank opposite Pittsburg Landing. On the way up-

[17] Wallace, *Letters*, 186, 187.
[18] Robert L. Kimberly and Ephraim S. Holloway, *The Forty-first Ohio Veteran Volunteer Infantry* (Cleveland, 1897), 21.

stream at Crump's Landing, General Lew Wallace, having heard the sounds of fighting and supposing that Grant would soon be passing by, was waiting for instructions from the army's commander. He had already directed his three brigades to close up in preparation for action. The *Tigress* swung in close to the landing, and Grant, without stopping the boat, called out to Wallace to get his troops under arms and have them ready to move at a moment's notice. Wallace shouted back that he had already done so. The time seems to have been about eight o'clock, perhaps a little later.[19]

What happened in the next several hours to Lew Wallace at Shiloh has been one of the bewildering mysteries of the battle. Wallace, the brilliant author-to-be of *Ben Hur*, and a man who desired military fame, would spend the rest of his life trying to explain why he never got into the fight on the first day at Shiloh. Even after he had become world renowned as a writer, he could not forget this black mark on his career. For several years before his death he returned almost annually to Shiloh. Whatever the reason for his failure to get into battle on April 6, his marching and countermarching would deprive the Federal army of 7,000 men whose strength might well have turned the tide of the struggle on that day.

The Confederate army approached Shiloh with more men, probably in excess of 40,000, than they had ever thrown into a battle anywhere before—or would again in the Western theater until a year and a half later at Chickamauga. For one of the few times in a major battle in either the east or the west, the Confederates, on April 6, outnumbered the Union army. The Rebel bulge, using the figures of the recognized authority Thomas L. Livermore, was about 40,000 Grayclads to 35,000 Federals. Although, according to Livermore, the effective strength (able-bodied men) of the Union army was 42,682, Lew Wallace's division of 7,564 did not get into battle on Sunday, thus reducing the Federal strength to 35,118; and all the available evidence indicates at least 5,000 to 7,000 Union troops ran away, far more than deserted the Rebel army.[20]

[19] *OR*, x, part 2, 95; part 1, 170, 174, 175, 181, 185. Bruce Catton, *Grant Moves South* (Boston, 1960), 223–24.
[20] Livermore, *Numbers and Losses*, 79, 80. *OR*, x, part 1, 112, 398. See also

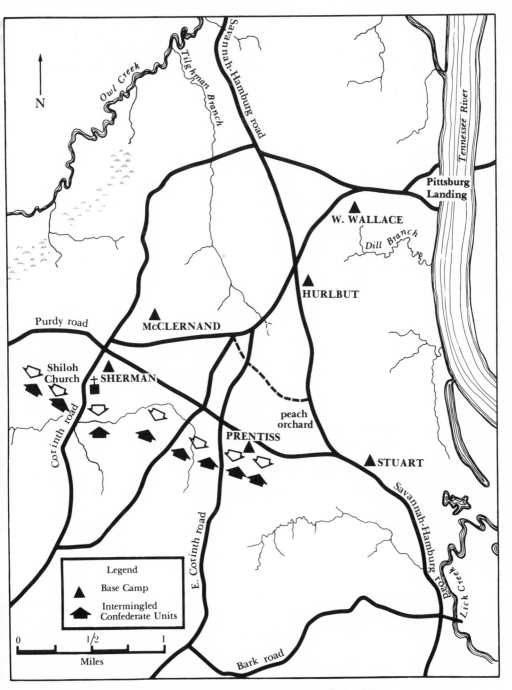

Map 5. The Front Line at Shiloh, 8–9 A.M., April 6, 1862.

The Confederates probably had more to gain by winning at Shiloh, plus a reasonably good chance for victory, than they would ever have again in the Western theater. A triumph at Shiloh held the bright promise of reversing the tide of war in the entire area, something which would have been much more difficult to accomplish a year later, even by a successful defense of Vicksburg, or by the Rebel win at Chickamauga. For by then the Union war machine, anaconda-like, was firmly wrapping itself in a death hold about the Western Confederacy; but in April 1862, having surprised the Confederates with its sudden strike through the rivers, it was still attempting to secure its grasp. Most of the Confederates sensed that the stakes were high, for both friend and foe testified to the fury and determination with which they fought.[21]

Albert Sidney Johnston dramatically captured the urgency of the day—perhaps better than any other man, perhaps more fully than even he himself realized—when, riding toward the front after sharp skirmishing had already begun, he met Colonel John S. Marmaduke, commanding the Third Arkansas Infantry Regiment. Marmaduke had been with Johnston in Utah, at Bowling Green, and in the retreat from Tennessee, and now he was close to the center of the Confederate front line as it advanced. Placing his hand on Marmaduke's shoulder, Johnston said, with an earnestness that the younger man long remembered: "My son, we must this day conquer or perish!"[22]

Johnston had informed Beauregard that he would go to the front, leaving the Creole in the rear. The precise nature of Beauregard's responsibilities was to become a subject of much controversy. Beauregard would claim Johnston had left to

---

David W. Reed, *The Battle of Shiloh and the Organizations Engaged* (Washington, D. C., 1903), 11, 12. Hereafter cited as Reed, *Shiloh*. Reed's work is particularly valuable. The major fought in the Hornets' Nest, was the Shiloh National Military Park's first historian, and was able to evaluate conflicting reports in the *OR* in light of personal interviews and correspondence with some of the participants, many of whom testified to the accuracy of his account. He placed the Confederate force present for duty on April 5 at 43,968.

[21] Johnston, *Life*, 585.

[22] *Ibid.*, 584.

him the general direction of the battle, while Johnston's sympathizers maintained Beauregard exaggerated his importance, that he was charged only with forwarding reinforcements and supplies to the front and had little to do with the actual command of the army.[23]

Whatever his instructions from Johnston may have been, the fact is that Beauregard was soon sending staff officers all over the field to gather information upon which he based decisions about dispatching reinforcements to the front, while Johnston was playing the role of a gallant combat leader rather than acting as supreme commander of an army. Beauregard's official report of the battle indicates that the influence he exercised was to mass reinforcements on the Rebel left and center. Beauregard and Johnston, as previously noted, probably never had a clear understanding about whether they were trying to turn the Union left and cut the Federals off from the river or drive them into the river. Unquestionably, the Creole's efforts were directed toward forcing the Blue army into the river. He stated in his report that it was expected that Grant "would be beaten back into his transports and the river, . . ." and when speaking of the situation Sunday afternoon, he said the Rebels were successfully "pushing the enemy back upon the Tennessee River."[24]

Hardee had four brigades of infantry in the Rebels' advance corps as he drove in and hit the Yankee line at and to the east and west of Shiloh Church. Bragg's corps was to his rear, ready to send support wherever needed, and his artillery was firing over Hardee's line, shelling the Union camps. On Hardee's left, thirty-four-year-old Patrick Cleburne was directing the brigade which was bearing in against Sherman's camps. A native of Ireland, Cleburne was an erect six-footer with gray-blue eyes and a heavy shock of dark-brown hair, who was to become one of the best division commanders in the Confederate army, only to fall late in the war in the ill-advised assault against John M. Schofield's forces at Franklin.

Cleburne took his men down a heavily timbered slope,

[23] *Battles and Leaders*, I, 586, 599. Roland, *Johnston*, 326–27.
[24] *OR*, x, part 1, 385, 387.

covered with thick underbrush, and hit the deep morass of Shiloh Branch, overgrown with shrubs, saplings, and vines, whose existence nobody had known about. This swampy area split the line into separate forces, two regiments going to the right and the rest to the left. Cleburne himself got bogged down in the entanglement and was thrown from his horse.[25]

When the Confederates finally staggered past the swamp, they started struggling up a rather steep hillside just south of Shiloh Church which lay open for 100 yards or more in front of Ralph P. Buckland's and Jesse Hildebrand's brigades of Sherman's division. As they moved into the open, they were swept by a galling musketry fire mixed with artillery. The artillery, posted on Sherman's left, enfiladed the Rebels with terrible effect. Cleburne described the devastating fire power as "an iron storm that threatened certain destruction to every living thing that would dare to cross. . . ." The Sixth Mississippi and the Twenty-third Tennessee penetrated the Union line briefly but were thrown back. That was enough for the Twenty-third, but the Sixth Mississippi charged again and still again, in what must have been one of the most courageous efforts of the war, until the unit at last collapsed and retreated in disorder over the dead and wounded.

One of the Rebels charging up the slope with the Sixth Mississippi was William C. Thompson, from Simpson County, Mississippi. He later described how the regiment picked up speed as it went forward until the men were practically running, and everyone seemed to be yelling and shouting. Up ahead he could see countless little clouds of smoke appearing, followed almost simultaneously by the cracking report of the Union rifles, and then by a storm of bullets tearing through the Rebel ranks. Thompson began noticing men on the ground, cut down by the firing. At first he could not see their faces and thought, perhaps, that he did not want to see them. The first wounded man he recognized was his cousin, shot in the face. He recognized another man whose eyes were glazed by death. Still another he knew was badly wounded. Then a sudden pain struck Thompson, his legs folded, and he too was on the ground. His cousin, who was blinded, had recognized Thompson yelling and was calling to him. Thompson tried to drag himself along the ground in that direction, but then everything went black. The Sixth Mississippi had gone into the attack with 425 officers and men; it came back leaving 300 dead and wounded on the field.[26]

Cleburne, assisted by Colonel Mat Martin, the former commander of the Twenty-third Tennessee, rallied and began reforming what was left of his right wing; then he galloped around the morass to his left where the rest of his command, badly outflanked by the Federal line, was fighting vainly in an attempt to overrun Buckland's position. Many Confederates seemed scornful of death. Major J. T. Harris, leading the Fifteenth Arkansas, which was skirmishing out in front of the brigade, boldly advanced within pistol range of the Blue line, firing on the enemy with his revolver and shouting to his men to come on. But the colonel went down, killed by withering fire from the Federal line. The Second Tennessee, which had been *en echelon*, came up on the brigade's left, charged the Union line, and was raked by a terrible cross fire from Federals on their left and front. The regiment suffered heavy losses (about 50 percent), including their colonel, who was severely wounded, and their major, who was killed.[27]

But there were some Rebels who were not so brave. Upon encountering the fierce defense of Sherman's troops, enjoying the advantage of high ground, some of Cleburne's men, as he noted in his official report, turned and fled to the rear. One of Cleburne's regimental commanders, Colonel Ben J. Hill of the Fifth Tennessee, was more specific, naming several of his men who left the fight without permission early in the day and were seen no more until the regiment returned to Corinth. Colonel Hill reported of one company captain who acted in a

[26] William R. Thompson, ed., "From Shiloh to Port Gibson," by William Candace Thompson, *Civil War Times Illustrated* (Oct. 1964), 20–21.
[27] *OR*, x, part 1, 568, 581, 585.

cowardly manner: "Several times I had to threaten to shoot him for hiding far back in the rear of his men."[28]

On Cleburne's right the weight of the Confederate front line—S. A. M. Wood's, R. G. Shaver's, and A. H. Gladden's brigades—pressed in against the left of Hildebrand's brigade and Prentiss' hurriedly formed division. Their line of advance bore off to the right, however, and a large gap developed between Wood and Cleburne. In such a heavily timbered area, any hope of communication between the two brigades was lost. Even so, the heavy Gray line routed the Fifty-third Ohio of Hildebrand's brigade and drove back the vanguard of Prentiss' command—the troops of Peabody's brigade who tried to make a stand but were unable to hold their ground.

Shortly thereafter a further Rebel problem developed. Someone among the Confederates, at the point where the brigades of Wood and Shaver came together, started retreating. An Arkansas major in Shaver's brigade reported angrily that one of Wood's Tennessee regiments was the cause because it broke and ran for the rear yelling "Retreat!" and the major's men began to follow; but Wood reported that it was a regiment in Shaver's command, the Seventh Arkansas, that first fell back and caused all the trouble.

Whatever the reason, some troops in both brigades had headed for the rear. Staff officers came galloping up, Wood himself saw the trouble and went to the spot, and after some anxious moments, most of the retreating soldiers were stopped, the ranks re-formed, the soldiers reassured, and the advance resumed.[29]

In spite of losses of communication, confusion, and attempts to retreat, the Rebel attack was now driven home with fury—and heavy casualties. General A. H. Gladden fell mortally wounded by a cannon shot; however, Daniel W. Adams took command of his brigade and pressed on. Chalmers came up with his brigade from Bragg's corps, strengthening the Confederate right as it bore in upon Prentiss. Albert Sidney Johnston was in the midst of the battle, directing a charge by

[28] *OR*, x, part 1, 582, 583, 589.
[29] *Ibid.*, 577, 591.

Gladden's brigade and also leading J. K. Jackson's brigade into line. Then he directed a charge by an Alabama regiment. The Confederates were loading and firing so rapidly that when General Thomas C. Hindman ordered one of his regiments to prepare to charge an enemy battery in their front, the regiment's major reported to the general that his ammunition was already nearly expended. Hindman responded laconically: "You have your bayonets!"[30]

The Gray line rose, yelling and shrieking, and swept forward for 300 or 400 yards over ground raked by musketry, and broke directly into the camps of Prentiss' division. Perhaps because Prentiss did not occupy as favorable ground as did Sherman, he received the full fury of the Rebel onslaught, and his line simply could not hold. He fell back to the rear of his encampment; yet the Rebels came on. Again his men fell back—and some of them did not stop retreating until they reached the landing.

Confusion, horror, and panic gripped many of the Union troops. Leander Stillwell said, "The main thing was to get out of there as quick as we could." As he ran down his company street, Stillwell saw something moving fast, with a jerky motion, that he described as sending a chill through him. "It was," he remembered, "a gaudy sort of thing, with red bars. It flashed over me in a second that that thing was a Rebel flag. . . ." Private Jeremiah Baldock ran into his tent to grasp a Bible with his name written in it, in order that his body might be identified if he were killed. Emerging from the tent with his Holy book and seeing three Confederates bearing down upon him, he fired his rifled-musket in their faces and then turned and fled as fast as he could in terror and shock at the sight of some Rebels bayoneting a wounded member of his company. A young fellow in the Eighteenth Missouri, with a hole blown in his abdomen from which a long section of intestine hung out, was pleading for help. A chaplain, horrified and sickened by the sight, quickly pressed the slippery intestine back inside, assisted the lad to a resting place beside a tree, and told him he must trust in Christ for salvation. Some of the tents in the

---

[30] *Ibid.*, 532, 548, 578. Connelly, *Army*, 164.

camp of the Twelfth Michigan Infantry were somehow set afire and the sick and wounded who could not be removed in the rapid retreat were burned to death, their charred bodies found the next day.[31]

Most of the Federal soldiers were contesting the enemy's onrush as best they could, firing from behind trees and logs, depressions in the ground, whatever offered a little protection. They tried to rally in still another position, but once more the pressure was too great. They continued to retreat until at last they found a slightly eroded wagon trace—the "Sunken Road" it was later called—which ran in a generally east to west direction. In a pinch it seemed to be the best natural defensive position at hand, and here, about a half mile behind his headquarters camp, Prentiss finally made a stand—a stand which probably saved the Union army at Shiloh. But thirty-one-year-old Colonel Everett Peabody, who had a premonition of his own death, was no longer with Prentiss. A little earlier, bleeding from four wounds, he had been riding among the tents of the Twenty-fifth Missouri's camps, trying to establish an effective line of resistance and shouting to his men to make a stand, when he was killed instantly by a shot through the head. His body was discovered after the battle, with the buttons and shoulder straps cut from his uniform, and his sword and pistols also missing.[32]

Many of the Rebels who had swept through Prentiss' camps were elated by their triumph. One Confederate soldier recalled that for an incredible instant he had an impression that "the battle was well-nigh over . . . ." Some of the Rebels, overcome with curiosity and hunger, were exploring the Yankee tents, foraging through the possessions of those they had just killed or driven off, and munching on the breakfasts they occasionally found half-eaten or maybe even still cooking. Sam Houston, Jr., who burned his arm snatching a joint of

[31] Leander Stillwell, "In the Ranks at Shiloh," *Journal of the Illinois Historical Society* (1922), 468. Jeremiah Baldock, *Soldiers and Citizens' Album of Biographical Records*, vol. 1—*Wisconsin* (Chicago, 1888), 746. Leslie Anders, *The 18th Missouri* (Indianapolis, 1968), 54. Franklin Bailey to parents, Apr. 8, 1862, Personal Accounts, SNMP.

[32] *OR*, x, part 1, 278. Shea, *American Nation*, 357.

meat from a cooking pot as he went by, remarked that if the Union army was not surprised it was blessed with the most devoted cooks on record. Not a few of these soldiers were lost to any future Confederate efforts for several hours, if not for the rest of the battle. But officers were soon re-forming the ranks and most of the Confederates plunged on.[33]

The center of Hardee's lead corps split off from Gladden's old brigade, now directed by Adams. Wood, with Shaver supporting, changed direction, advancing obliquely to the left against a Federal brigade from McClernand's division, while Adams moved on ahead and to the right, feeling for the enemy. The gap between Cleburne and Wood was being filled by brigades from Polk's command. By this time extensive intermingling of Rebel commands was taking place, but the sheer weight and determination of the Confederate attack at the left and center were carrying it forward. The Southerners were making it hotter than ever for Sherman and McClernand's men.

Meanwhile, James R. Chalmers' troops, who had driven on ahead of Jackson, were halted by order of General Johnston and commanded to resume their position on Jackson's right. Finally, more than a half hour later, Chalmers reported, a guide came to conduct the brigade around to the extreme right toward Lick Creek.[34]

Indeed, the time for someone to exploit the situation by attacking the Federals on the far right, turning their left flank, was long overdue. In this sector the Confederates were offered what was probably their best opportunity of the day. The Federal left was defended by Colonel David Stuart's lone brigade of three regiments, and when the Rebels finally did attack, Stuart's largest regiment, the Seventy-first Ohio, fled from the field with its colonel setting the example.

The Confederate plan of attack, as stated by General Johnston, had been to turn the Union left flank and cut the army off from the landing, driving it back into the swampy

[33] Stanley, *Autobiography*, 191. Foote, *Civil War*, I, 337. Roman, *Beauregard*, I, 288–89. *OR*, x, part 1, 391. Robert S. Henry, *The Story of the Confederacy* (Indianapolis, 1931), 117.

[34] *OR*, x, part 1, 532, 548.

morass of Owl and Snake creeks. In reality, however, the Rebels did not even find the Union left for a long time and, in fact, made virtually no effort to locate it. Neither Johnston, Beauregard, nor any other officer ordered a reconnaissance of the ground toward the river in time for the information gleaned to be of value. Apparently the only action taken was by Johnston when, on the night of April 5, he ordered Captain Samuel H. Lockett, Bragg's chief engineer, to sneak forward and survey the ground on the enemy's left flank near the river. Yet Lockett did not begin before 4 A.M., and the attack was planned for daybreak! He obviously did not have time to gather his information and return before the fight began.[35]

If Johnston knew the location of the Union left, which can be questioned, he apparently did not appreciate the difficulties involved in moving an attacking force over the extremely rough, heavily timbered ground. It was cut by deep ravines and also presented the formidable obstacle of entangling undergrowth. In defense of Johnston, it has been said that he hoped to surprise the Union army, and therefore did not reconnoiter the ground near the river earlier for fear of alerting his enemy, but this line of thought seems rather specious in view of the noise the Rebels made as they approached Shiloh. Furthermore, it does not explain why Johnston failed to provide for a force in the area adequate to cut the Federals off from the landing, as the battle plan envisioned. Only four out of fourteen brigades were on his right flank when the attack began.[36]

In view of these considerations, as well as some of the official reports by Rebel commanders, and especially noting the personal attention given by Johnston to the attack on Prentiss, it seems possible that Johnston thought that Prentiss' division represented the Union left.[37] In any case, the assault on the Union left, the attack on Stuart, did not get underway until more than four hours after the battle began.

What well may have been possible for the Confederates at

[35] *OR*, x, part 1, 397, 465. *Battles and Leaders*, 1, 604.
[36] Connelly, *Army*, 161.
[37] *OR*, x, part 1, 465, 532, 548, 554. *Battles and Leaders*, 1, 604. Roman, *Beauregard*, 1, 289.

dawn, when both the initiative and an overwhelming force were at their call against the meager Union left, was frittered away by a lack of reconnaissance and execution of the purported battle plan. Instead, the Rebels were attacking in a northeast direction and massing their reinforcements on their own left and center, as though the plan had been entirely different—one that would drive the Union army into, rather than away from, the landing at Pittsburg. The final, inevitable effect of the Confederate drive would be to compress the Union resistance into a more solid and shortened line—until it would be no more than a mile wide and resting behind the deep ravines of Dill and Tilghman branches which protected the landing.

6. *In Hell before Night*

As the morning progressed, the Rebel army continued to experience distressing and disheartening blunders which no one seemed able to stop.

One Confederate regiment, unable to withstand the withering Union fire, broke rank and, as it raced headlong for the rear, ran directly through the ranks of a regiment advancing behind it, even trampling that command's color-bearer in the mud. Worse yet, the men of the Orleans Guard Battalion, the elite organization with P. G. T. Beauregard's name still on the muster roll, were advancing into the battle wearing their dress uniforms—which, unfortunately, were colored blue. The Confederate regiment they were supporting saw the blue uniforms coming, concluded that a Union regiment was attacking them, and opened fire on the Orleans Guard. The Louisianans, led by their Creole Major Leon Querouze, immediately began returning the fire. When a distraught staff officer came riding up frantically screaming "Cease fire!" and explaining that they were shooting fellow Confederates, the major replied: "I know it! But dammit, sir, we fire on anybody who fires on us!"[1]

While Wood's brigade was trying to storm a Union battery, the Rebels suddenly found themselves under fire from the rear by two Confederate regiments. The two units had just topped a hill behind Wood's men and, in their eagerness to close with the enemy, apparently mistook the Rebels in front of them for Federals. Several of Wood's command were killed, and his men threw themselves down behind some logs, exposed to the fire of the Union, preferring to be killed, if

[1] Foote, *Civil War*, I, 337.

they must, by the enemy rather than their own men. Wood and part of his staff rode toward the crest of the hill yelling for the Confederates to stop firing. Another volley crashed through them, wounding the general's horse, which, in its pain, became unmanageable, throwing Wood to the ground and dragging him for some distance before he finally struggled free.[2]

A young Rebel officer, mounted on a fine horse and handsomely dressed in a uniform resembling that of the Union army, galloped toward the Fourth Louisiana from the front, holding a Federal banner in his hand. Almost instantly both the horse and rider went down as some men of the Fourth opened fire on what appeared to be the enemy. Too late it was discovered that a fellow Confederate, returning in triumph with a captured Union flag, had been killed.[3]

In spite of all the problems and tragic mistakes, however, the left and center of the Confederate line were being carried forward. The pressure on Sherman's and McClernand's men, who stood in the way, continued to mount.

The pressure was already too great for the commander of the Fifty-third Ohio on Sherman's left front. His regiment had slowed down the initial Confederate assault, but the Rebels rallied and kept coming. Again they were beaten back, but once more they re-formed and came on. It was too much for Colonel Jesse Appler, who yelled to his men: "Retreat, and save yourselves." Many of his regiment followed at once, although some men did not hear the order and continued firing until they saw the others falling back. Part of the regiment re-formed some distance to the rear where the colonel found refuge behind a tree and lay down. When the regiment's adjutant, E. C. Dawes, found him and suggested that they go to the support of another Ohio regiment that was being driven back, the colonel still could not face the action. He got to his feet and headed for the rear, with many of his men following behind.[4]

---

[2] *OR*, x, part 1, 592.
[3] Richardson, "Shiloh." For another similar incident, see *OR*, x, part 1, 605, 606.
[4] Duke, *53rd Ohio*, 45–47.

Adjutant Dawes set out to find someone to take command of the remainder of the regiment. He finally came upon a company captain, W. S. Jones, who consented to lead these troops, and a Captain J. R. Percy, who offered to help. In fact, Percy seemed almost as rash as Appler had been fearful. Waving his sword in the air he yelled out, as Dawes recalled: "Tell Captain Jones I am with him. Let us charge!" Adjutant Dawes convinced Percy that it would be best to wait on charging until they could get more troops together.[5]

Union reinforcements were coming toward the front as rapidly as possible, making their way along roads cluttered with hundreds of disorganized soldiers stumbling back toward the landing. The refugees included retreating batteries of artillery, squads of cavalry, litter bearers with sick and wounded, and panic-stricken infantry who had fled from the conflict. To the reinforcements meeting these retreating troops, some of them obviously terrified, the scene was both despicable and unsettling. Some of the men in the Fifteenth Illinois Infantry, marching to support the area where Sherman's and McClernand's lines overlapped, heaped bitter curses upon the stragglers.[6]

The Fourteenth Iowa, advancing on the run to reinforce Prentiss' division, which was in the center of the Union line, to the left of McClernand and Sherman, encountered stragglers and wounded shouting to them that all was lost, that a large Rebel army was carrying everything before it and the Union army would be driven into the river. The Second Iowa, moving at a double-quick pace to the front, was meeting equally frightened soldiers. It was the "Bull Run" story all over again, the stragglers said. Their regiments had been "cut to pieces." One man was standing by the roadside, waving his arms and yelling, "For God's sake don't go out there; you will all be killed. Come back, Come back!"[7]

There was so much confusion that some reinforcements were having trouble finding the front. One blundering guide led two regiments in the wrong direction, crossing a deep

[5] Duke, *53rd Ohio*.
[6] *OR*, x, part 1, 286, 288. Barber, *15th Illinois*, 52.
[7] Thomas, *14th Iowa*, ch. IV. Bell, *2nd Iowa*, 15. Belknap, *15th Iowa*, 107.

Behind the Union lines, wounded soldiers and stragglers fall back to
the river landing as ammunition wagons advance to the front.

ravine and struggling through thick underbrush for some
distance before the mistake was discovered. Finally, with a
new guide, the column was turned around and groped its way
to the conflict. One of these particular regiments, having just
arrived at the landing, had been exposed to a rumor as they
came up the river that a great battle had already been fought.
Some of the men were clearly disappointed, complaining that
they had been deprived of their "share of glory." In a little
more than two hours after they joined the battle, the regiment
had lost over two hundred men and their colonel had been
shot through the neck.[8]

As reinforcements reached the front lines, the sound of
artillery and musketry became almost deafening. Cannon
shots tearing through the branches of the trees made a terrifying noise, and the air was becoming filled with the smoke from
burned gunpowder, stifling and smarting to the eyes. Some of
the tents were burning, horses lay killed or writhing in agony,
and all about were the dead and dying soldiers, some of them
horribly mangled.

Men react in varied ways to the experience of such carnage.
When the Fifteenth Illinois reached the area of conflict and
halted to await orders before going in, the gory battle site
plainly visible before them, Lucius Barber remembered that a
few of the men were making jokes and laughing. Barber and
most of the others, however, did not find anything about the
scene to amuse them.[9]

Over in the ranks of the Eleventh Iowa of John McClernand's division, Thomas Hains of Company E felt a minié ball
pass through the creased crown of his hat. Upon discovering
the four holes made by the missile, he placed the hat upon his
ramrod and hoisted it in the air, shouting to the rest of his
company to see what a close call he had survived. Almost at the
same instant a shell burst immediately above his head and
killed him.[10]

In the partial shelter of a ravine a short distance to the rear
of McClernand and Sherman, a regimental surgeon was at-

[8] *OR*, x, part 1, 288. Belknap, *15th Iowa*, 17, 105.
[9] Barber, *15th Illinois*, 52.
[10] Downing, *Downing's War Diary*, 41.

BATTLES AND LEADERS OF THE CIVIL WAR

The first field tent hospital in history, permitting treatment of the wounded on the battlefield itself, was set up at Shiloh on April 7, 1862.

tempting to minister to the wounded, cutting out bullets and dispensing morphine to the most severely injured. Suddenly, what he described as "a cyclone of musketry, shot and shells" swept the ravine, tearing the intestines out of a man who was already suffering from a gunshot wound in the leg. Blood and flesh spattered everywhere. An injured soldier, whose wound the surgeon had just dressed, was still partially elevated, resting on one arm, and witnessed the ghastly scene. "This is a hell of a place for a hospital," he muttered.[11]

Across the way in the Rebel lines Colonel Robert Trabue's brigade was moving at double-quick pace to reinforce a portion of Hardee's corps when a Union shell tore through the ranks, killed two men, and carried away both hands of another soldier. The man clasped the bleeding stumps in anger and despair, exclaiming: "My Lord, that stops my fighting!"[12]

Somewhere in the midst of the gory scene on the Union right was Sherman. He impressed those who saw him in battle. Edward Bouton remembered that soon after the fight began, Sherman rode up on the left of his battery and, while watching the effect of the artillery shots and praising the gun crews' accuracy and rapidity of firing, was wounded by a minié ball that passed entirely through the palm of his right hand. As Bouton watched, Sherman drew a handkerchief from his pocket and wrapped it about the injured hand, which he then thrust inside the breast of his coat. He scarcely took his eyes away from the scene of conflict. Later in the day Sherman was slightly wounded again, and three horses were killed from under him, but the man who had sometimes seemed highly nervous was cool and proficient as he directed his division in the heat of battle. Observers said he seemed to be where he was needed, to have a grasp of what was taking place all along the line, and sometimes to anticipate what would occur before it happened. Soon after the battle he wrote a letter to his wife that reveals something of the impression Shiloh was making

[11] Belknap, *15th Iowa*, 109.
[12] A. D. Kirwan, ed., *Johnny Green of the Orphan Brigade: The Journal of a Confederate Soldier* (Lexington, 1956), 26.

Although the Union troops commanded by General William T. Sherman were surprised at Pittsburg Landing—evoking his exclamation, "My God, we are attacked!"—Sherman went on to become one of the nation's finest military commanders.

on him: "The scenes on this field," he said, "would have cured anybody of war."[13] This was the bloodiest battle that Sherman ever saw. It was to him, no doubt, a confirmation of his simple, classic description: "War is hell."

Sherman has sometimes been criticized for holding his ground when the attack began rather than dropping back to join up with McClernand's division. Sherman would have been unwise to move, for the front of his three right brigades was protected by Shiloh Branch, a tributary of Owl Creek, and also enjoyed the defensive advantage of high ground. If he had initially fallen back, it would probably have only shaken the confidence of his men to resist the Rebel onslaught and added to the general confusion that already plagued much of the Union army.

McClernand, on Sherman's left and rear, had sent a brigade early in the fight to support Sherman's flank and soon, with most of his division up, was trying to plug the gap between Sherman and Prentiss, who was farther to the left. James Veatch's brigade from Hurlbut's division also came to shore up Sherman's left. But the Confederate attack was increasing in intensity.[14]

The weakest link in the line continued to be Sherman's left brigade, from which most of the Fifty-third Ohio had fled early in the battle. Portions of another regiment began streaming to the rear; then virtually the whole brigade (Jesse Hildebrand's) disintegrated, although its commander stayed in the thick of the struggle as an aide to McClernand. Waterhouse's Battery E, First Illinois Artillery, which had been fighting with the brigade and doing an effective job against the Rebels, was nevertheless compelled to fall back a hundred yards or more. Three Illinois regiments, plus small portions of the regiments that had fled, tried to support the battery in its new position, but the Confederates, driving with grim determination, could not be stopped.

The Fifteenth Illinois now found itself in the thick of battle.

[13] Edward Bouton, *Events of the Civil War* (n.d.), 61. *OR*, x, part 1, 110. Lewis, *Sherman*, 222, 223. Simon, *Papers of Grant*, v, 141. Howe, *Home Letters of Sherman*, 222, 223.

[14] *OR*, x, part 1, 203, 220, 228, 250. Catton, *Grant Moves South*, 228.

A Rebel battery was cutting through the regiment with canister, and a column of infantry, bayonets glistening in the sun, was bearing down upon it. The Fifteenth was loading and firing furiously. Lucius Barber watched as a Rebel sergeant triumphantly planted the "Star and Bars" on top of a piece of Union artillery just overrun by the Gray line, and then saw him fall, riddled with bullets.[15]

The Confederates continued to press their advantage. Sherman and the entire right wing of the Union line fell back, and three of Waterhouse's guns were captured. E. C. Dawes remembered that the Rebels "swarmed around them like bees." He said "they jumped upon the guns, and on the haybales in the battery camp, and yelled like crazy men." A dead Union officer lay near the guns, and keeping guard over his body was a pointer dog that refused to allow the Confederates to approach the body. The fighting seemed to be swirling now in all directions in that sector. One of the soldiers who was wounded was told to go to the rear. He started back, only to encounter gunfire in every direction he turned. He came back to his company commander and said: "Captain, give me a gun—the blamed fight ain't got any rear."[16]

Sherman's left was crumbling. The Rebels were driving all along his front and on his flank. Among them was Patton Anderson, who had brought his brigade up from Bragg's corps to support Cleburne. Anderson took his men down the same heavily timbered slope in front of Sherman's line where Cleburne had gone earlier and found the densely interwoven undergrowth so thick, he reported, that he sometimes had to cut through it with a knife. Emerging at last from the entangling morass, he charged up the open ground in front of the Federal troops of Buckland's brigade, was driven back, charged again, and finally, supported by three regiments of Preston Pond's brigade which had come up on his left, held on under the brow of the hill where the Union fire was not as effective.[17]

Cleburne had re-formed ranks after the disaster of his

---

[15] *OR*, x, part 1, 249. Barber, *15th Illinois*, 53.
[16] Duke, *53rd Ohio*, 48, 49. Reed, *Shiloh*, 14.
[17] *OR*, x, part 1, 496. Roman, *Beauregard*, I, 290.

initial attack when his line had been split into two parts and
badly mauled, and was coming to help. The Fifth Company,
Washington Artillery, was now shelling Sherman's artillery
with good effect. The Rebel brigades of Bushrod Johnson and
R. M. Russell had come up from Polk's corps, but Russell's
men found the undergrowth so thick that only seven companies of two regiments struggled through in time to join in
the first charge made by their units. Johnson's and Russell's
men plowed into the Union line just to the right of Cleburne
and Anderson, and when Bushrod Johnson's line wavered
under the heavy Federal fire (and Johnson himself was severely wounded), order was restored in one regiment by its
colonel who, standing in the rear with drawn pistol,
threatened to shoot any stragglers.

The portion of the Rebel line that was advancing upon
Sherman's and McClernand's divisions was now strung out
from Shiloh Branch on the Confederates' left for a distance of
approximately a mile and a quarter to their right. On the far
left was Pond's brigade, and to his right along the line were, in
this order, the brigades of Anderson, Cleburne, Johnson,
Russell, Alexander P. Stewart, Wood, and R. G. Shaver. Alexander Stewart's brigade had just come in between the commands of Russell and Wood, applying more pressure to the
most vulnerable point of the Federal line in that sector—
Sherman's left. And on Wood's right, R. G. Shaver's brigade
was now getting on McClernand's left flank.[18]

The intense fire and frantic action was described by a Confederate of Shaver's brigade, whose small group of a dozen or
so soldiers was firing from behind a fallen tree, the trunk of
which was still resting a short distance above the ground. Not
only was a hail of bullets passing above the crouching soldiers,
he said, but many missiles were smacking into the opposite
side of the log and some were coming underneath. He noticed
that a man beside him expanded his chest as if to yawn, but the
fact was that a bullet had just gored the man's face and penetrated his chest. Another soldier was hit and then rolled over
on his back and died, face to the sky. He heard still another

[18] *OR*, x, part 1, 416, 444, 445. Roman, *Beauregard*, I, 290.

Private Robert Patterson (*above*) was a member of the Twelfth Tennessee Infantry, C.S.A., commanded by Colonel Robert M. Russell, which saw heavy action at Shiloh.

soldier yell "It is getting too warm, boys!" and follow the yell with curses on those commanders who kept their troops hugging the ground. As the soldier raised his head, perhaps getting ready to move out, a bullet hit the center of his forehead and he collapsed forward on his face. Then there was the sound of an officer commanding "Forward, Forward!" and the ensuing scramble as the men got to their feet and charged. Someone was screaming "Give them hell!" Another was urging "Come on, boys!" Everyone, to this particular observer-participant, seemed to be yelling or screeching as the Rebels moved agonizingly ahead.[19]

The Confederates had at last mustered sufficient manpower. Up and over the top of the ridge and into the camps of Sherman the Gray line swept, leaving, as Lew Wallace later described the scene, a pavement of their dead; and finally, Sherman's whole line retreated, followed by McClernand who otherwise would have been outflanked. It was about ten o'clock.[20]

Sherman and McClernand tried to establish a new line along the Hamburg-Purdy road a quarter of a mile or more to the north of Shiloh Church, but everything seemed to go wrong. John A. McDowell's brigade on Sherman's right, part of which had been virtually unengaged with the enemy thus far, spread confusion as it fell back over a broken and wooded terrain, with its heavily loaded wagons moving to the rear and blocking the road. And when Sherman ordered Frederick Behr's Sixth Indiana Battery to unlimber for action, Behr had scarcely given the order when he was shot from his horse; the men serving his guns panicked and fled, carrying off the caissons. The Rebels, taking advantage of the turmoil, poured in and captured five cannon.[21]

The Union soldiers simply could not regain their balance; again they retreated to find a new line of defense. And S. A. M. Wood's Rebel brigade overwhelmed Jerome Burrows' Fourteenth Ohio Battery as McClernand retreated, capturing all six guns. Sherman and McClernand finally stabi-

[19] Stanley, *Autobiography*, 193, 194.
[20] *OR*, x, part 1, 249, 250.
[21] *Ibid.*

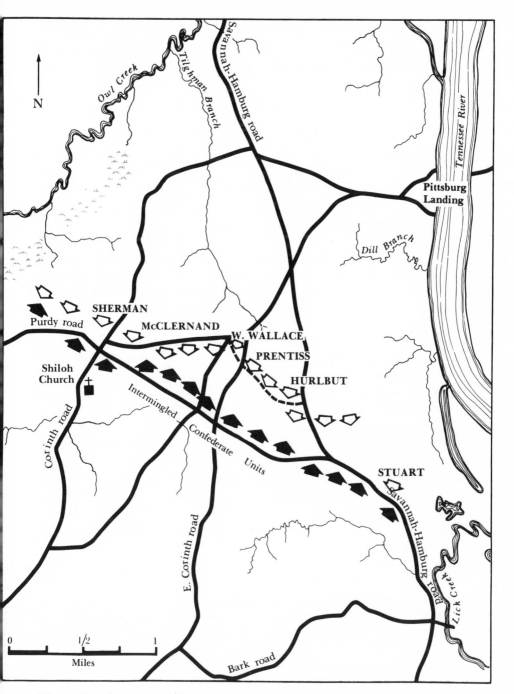

Map 6. Development of the Hornets' Nest, 9–12 A.M., April 6, 1862.

lized their commands nearly a half mile farther back toward
the landing sometime around ten-thirty, and here they held
on for the next four hours.

Their portion of the Union line then extended from the
edge of the Duncan field, on their left, for a distance of
three-quarters of a mile to the right. Anchoring the left of the
line was Abraham Hare's First Brigade of McClernand's division, and to his right, in order, were the brigades of James
Veatch from Hurlbut's division, C. Carroll Marsh and Julius
Raith of McClernand's command, and finally what remained
of Sherman's division. Sherman's left brigade, under Colonel
Hildebrand, had, of course, disintegrated sometime earlier.
Consequently, Buckland's brigade now composed Sherman's
left, joining with the right of McClernand's division, while
McDowell's brigade was on Sherman's right—at least it was
there until about twelve-thirty when McDowell was severely
injured by a fall from his horse. This, plus increasing Rebel
pressure on his exposed right flank, caused McDowell and his
three regiments to retire to the landing. McClernand's men
and Sherman's lone brigade then continued to hold the Federal line in that sector.[22]

Midmorning was approaching when the commander of the
Union army rode his horse off the *Tigress* at Pittsburg Landing after the nine-mile trip upstream from his headquarters at
Savannah. The scene before Grant must have been disheartening. Already hundreds of men, perhaps thousands, who
had fled from the battle were cowering under the bluff on the
west bank of the river. Some were trying to cross the river to
the safety of the east bank. Grant first acted to provide for a
reserve and to stop the people who were running away. At the
top of the bluff he found the Fifteenth Iowa, which had just
debarked, and the Sixteenth Iowa, which Prentiss had sent
back to the landing to get ammunition which, unaccountably,
had been left behind when the regiment moved forward to
Prentiss' camp. Grant sent a staff officer to form these regi-

[22] *Ibid*. Also Wood's report, p. 592. Reed, *Shiloh*, 16, 17, 54, 56, 57. Reed's
account is also contained in *Shiloh: Campaign and Battle*, as a part of John
Obreiter, *History of the 77th Pennsylvania Volunteers* (Harrisburg, 1905), 269.
Hereafter cited as Reed, *Battle of Shiloh*.

Scenes of panic-stricken Union troops fleeing the battle site greeted Grant as he disembarked at Pittsburg Landing at mid-morning, April 6.

ments into a line where they could both act as a reserve and shoot the stragglers if they did not stop. An additional deterrent to those running away, in the form of a battery, was placed in position to command the main road leading from the battlefield. Then the stragglers were to be re-formed to add to the reserve.[23]

Grant now started to the front. About half a mile up the Corinth road he met one of his division commanders, W. H. L. Wallace, who briefed him on the progress of the battle. Up to this time Grant had probably feared that the Rebels might also be planning to attack Lew Wallace's division at Crump's Landing. For several days before the battle he had seemed to think that if the Confederates made an attack anywhere, it would be against Lew Wallace because that division was isolated from the rest of the army. But now, from what he had learned from W. H. L. Wallace, and what he himself had witnessed at Pittsburg, Grant firmly concluded that the Rebels were launching an all-out attack from Corinth; hence, there was no longer any reason to fear an attack at Crump's Landing. He ordered James Rawlins back to the river to send an officer instructing Lew Wallace to bring his division forward at once. Grant sent another message to Nelson's division in Savannah instructing that general to "hurry up your command as fast as possible. The boats will be in readiness to transport all troops of your command across the river. All looks well, but it is necessary for you to push forward as fast as possible." Then he continued toward the front.[24]

Grant found Sherman about ten o'clock when, according to Sherman, "the battle raged fiercest." Sherman was covered with dust, and his face and red beard were darkened with powder. He told Grant the situation was not too bad, but that he was worried about running out of ammunition—an understandable concern in view of the varied sizes of ammunition needed. Because weapons in the Union army had not yet been standardized, more than a hundred kinds were being used altogether, and in Sherman's division alone, there were

[23] *OR*, x, part 1, 109, 286, 288, 559 ff. Kenneth P. Williams, *Lincoln Finds a General*, 5 vols. (New York, 1952), III, 361, 362.

[24] *OR*, x, part 2, 95, 96.

weapons of six different calibers. Grant assured him that he had already made provision for more ammunition, encouraged him to continue resisting the Rebel advance as stubbornly as possible, and rode off to another part of the line. Grant had more confidence in Sherman than in any other commander on the field and later wrote that he never considered it necessary to stay long with him.[25]

Moving on to visit McClernand, Grant sent word back to the landing for the Fifteenth and Sixteenth Iowa to come forward to McClernand's support. Although these regiments constituted the heart of the "reserve" he had tried to form, Grant evidently felt that McClernand's need was greater—and, furthermore, he was expecting Lew Wallace's 7,000 men to arrive soon.[26]

Grant also visited Prentiss, whose command had by then settled down into the area of the "Sunken Road." Actually not very sunken at all, the road provided a rather shallow trench in the midst of a wooded area about half a mile to the rear of Prentiss' former headquarters. His troops had already repelled at least one Confederate charge against this position, and probably more, before Grant came up. On Prentiss' right, and angling back toward the north, stretched W. H. L. Wallace's division, also occupying the line of the Sunken Road; a large open field stretched out ahead of Wallace's position. To Prentiss' left and advanced slightly ahead of him, was Hurlbut's division, part of it occupying a peach orchard.[27]

Evidently satisfied that Prentiss had been offered no choice but to fall back from his original position, Grant commended him for the present disposition of his forces and then ordered him to hold that position "at all hazards"—an order from which Prentiss never flinched.[28] Grant may have gone on to confer with Hurlbut and Stuart on the extreme left, but the only evidence of such visits is the statement in his memoirs that he "was with each division commander in person."[29]

---

[25] *OR*, x, part 1, 109, 559 ff. Grant, *Memoirs*, I, 343.
[26] Williams, *Lincoln*, III, 367.
[27] *OR*, x, part 1, 278. Commager, *The Blue and the Gray*, 1, 363.
[28] *OR*, x, part 1, 279.
[29] Grant, *Memoirs*, I, 348.

Stuart's brigade, close to the river and in the midst of what was probably the roughest terrain on the battlefield, could have used help from someone. It was about ten-thirty that the Confederates finally got the attack in this sector underway. The colonel of Stuart's largest regiment, the Seventy-first Ohio, seeing the Rebels pouring out of the woods, reined his horse around and galloped toward the rear. The second in command tried to rally the regiment but was killed, after which most of the regiment then followed their colonel's example and headed for the landing. The Fifty-fifth Illinois and the Fifty-fourth Ohio fell back to their left some 300 or 400 yards where Stuart rallied the units, and they made a stand on a heavily timbered ridge with their flanks protected by thick underbrush and their front facing an open field. Here they fought valiantly for some time, well over two hours, but according to their brigade commander's report, not more than 800 effectives were available for the attempt to hold the line.[30]

The wounded presented a ghastly spectacle. A Union private, not yet seventeen years old, was hit seven times before he died. One Federal soldier who looked at the boy's body said he was "as red as if he had been dipped in a barrel of blood." "Only the excitement of battle," another Yankee wrote, "could sustain a man in the midst of such carnage. As man after man was shot down or mutilated, a feeling of perfect horror came over me at times, and I berated the powers which placed us in such a position and left us alone to our fate." Although the Rebels had greater numbers, they could not drive Stuart's men from the ridge.[31]

About noon Grant returned to his headquarters near the landing. The situation for the Union was desperate. Fugitives from the battle were still making their way to the rear in spite of the straggler line and the work of the officers trying to rally

[30] *OR*, x, part 1, 258, 259.

[31] Lucien B. Crooker and Committee, *The Story of the 55th Regiment Illinois Infantry in the Civil War, 1861–1865* (Clinton, Mass., 1887), 124. Elijah C. Lawrence, "Stuart's Brigade at Shiloh," read before the Commandery of the State of Massachusetts, Military Order of the Loyal Legion of the United States (Boston, 1900), 494. B. F. Wilkinson, Letter, Apr. 16, 1862, Department of Archives and MSS, Louisiana State Univ., Baton Rouge.

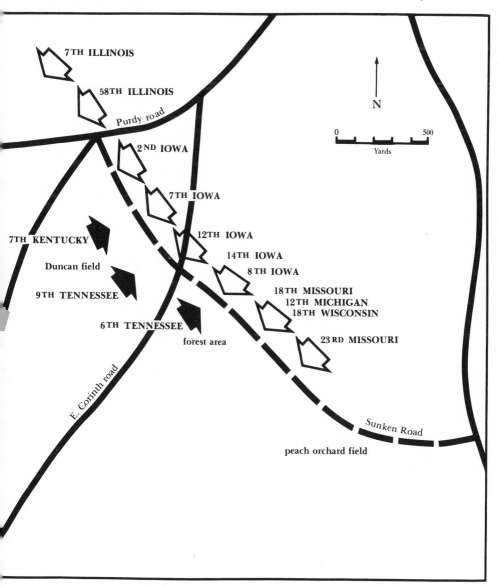

Map 7. Assault on the Hornets' Nest, Led by William H. Stephens, About 10:30 A.M., April 6, 1862.

them. Several thousand men were beneath the bluff, totally useless for the fight. Sherman and McClernand had been driven back twice from their original lines, and if either command should break into a rout, the battle would be over, since the Rebels would have a straight shoot to the landing. And should a breakthrough develop at any point of the Union line, no reserve was available to plug the gap.

By now, Lew Wallace should have arrived. The man who delivered Grant's order telling Wallace, at Crump's Landing, to come forward at once had been back for an hour and a half. Where was Wallace? James McPherson, who was with Grant at the time, wrote: "About 12m., General Wallace not having arrived, General Grant became very anxious, as the tide of battle was setting against us, and shortly after dispatched Captain Rowley, one of his aides, to hasten up General Wallace."[32]

Nor had anything been heard from Nelson across the river. Grant sought to hurry him with a message that probably reveals his anxiety more clearly than any other evidence:

> The attack on my forces has been very spirited from early this morning. The appearance of fresh troops on the field now would have a powerful effect both by inspiring our men and disheartening the enemy. If you will get upon the field, leaving all your baggage on the east bank of the river, it will be a move to our advantage, and possibly save the day to us. The Rebel force is estimated at over 100,000 men. My headquarters will be in a log building on top of the hill, where you will be furnished a staff officer to guide you to your place on the field.[33]

Grant's gross overestimate of the Confederate force may be a further indication of his marked concern, for he had spoken earlier, before the battle, of the Rebels having 80,000 at Corinth. Now, he seems to doubt that even the arrival of Nelson's division will be sufficient to "save the day." The ferocity of the Rebel attack and the panic which gripped segments of the Union army could be expected to color the commander's thinking to some degree.

The Confederates were pressing in with confidence now;

[32] *OR*, x, part 1, 181.
[33] *OR*, x, part 2, 95.

they believed they could destroy the Union army. Sam Watkins of the First Tennessee Infantry later recorded his impressions of the Rebels as the Union line had fallen back: "We were crowding them. . . . Then their lines waver and break. They retreat in wild confusion. We were jubilant; we were triumphant. . . . The Federal dead and wounded covered the ground." A Confederate cavalryman remembered the exhilarating effect upon him as, riding up beside some of Breckinridge's Kentuckians who were going into action about noon, the regiment nearest to him struck up the favorite song of the Kentuckians, "Cheer, Boys, Cheer." The effect, he said, was "animating beyond all description."[34]

And no doubt some of the Rebels, perhaps many of them, were certain that God was with them. A chaplain with the Seventeenth Alabama Infantry wrote the governor of Alabama after the battle:

> We were under a cross fire from the left wing from three directions. Under it the boys wavered. I had been wearied and was sitting down, but seeing them waver, I sprang to my feet—took off my hat—waved it over my head—walked up and down the line, and, they say, "preached them a sermon." I reminded them that it was Sunday: that, at that hour (11:30 o'clock) all their home folks were praying for them. . . . I called upon them to stand there, and die . . . for their country. The effect was evident. Every man stood to his post . . . with desperate resolve to conquer or die.[35]

Although the chaplain may have overestimated the effect of his words upon the soldiers, his example was convincing. Newspaper reports credited the chaplain himself with killing a colonel, a major, and four privates in the Union army.[36]

At high noon the Confederate line of advance still lay generally northeastward, pressing up against an irregular, crooked semblance of a Union line that stretched from Sherman's right flank near Owl Creek almost to the Lick Creek

---

[34] Watkins, "*Co. Aytch*," 66. Stanley F. Horn, ed., *Tennessee's War, 1861–1865, Described by Participants* (Nashville, 1965), 88, 89.

[35] Charles F. Pitts, *Chaplains in Gray: The Confederate Chaplain's Story* (Nashville, 1957), 96, 97.

[36] *Ibid.*

General Hurlbut's division charges and turns back the rebels at the Peach Orchard in this scene from Leslie's *The Soldier in Our Civil War*. Below, in today's tranquil Peach Orchard, four cannon and a cabin similar to the one that stood there more than a century ago are reminders that the site was once a bloody battleground.

area on the left—a distance of three miles. The struggle had settled down into what most of those participants who survived the war would describe as the fiercest they ever saw. There were charges and countercharges. One regiment remembered fighting back and forth over the same ground a half-dozen times.

Both armies had by then thrown in all their reserves. The Confederate commands were split up and intermingled all over the field, and the same was true of some Federal units.[37] The terrain was so concealing that no continuous view of any large body of troops was possible. The fight was now a mass of keyed-up men, dirty, sweaty, and darkened with gunpowder, crowded up more or less into battle formation. Under the hot sun and in the dense undergrowth they grappled frantically amidst their dead and dying and wounded that lay sprawled about, their bodies resting across each other in all the unseemly deformity of violent destruction. Broken guns, abandoned caissons, dead horses, and the other debris of war littered the ground. A pall of gunsmoke hung over the entire scene. Survivors reported also the added horror of the furious sounds, frightening and at times deafening in their intensity. The din of thousands of rifled-muskets firing was joined by the roar of cannon and explosion of shells and, most unsettling of all, the sounds of men yelling, shrieking, moaning, and crying. Shelby Foote has suggested that it must have "resembled Armageddon."[38]

It was somewhere behind the Union line, shortly after noon, that the Forty-first Illinois of Hurlbut's First Brigade, which had been badly shot up, was moving toward the rear. It passed another regiment advancing to the front. Colonel Isaac C. Pugh of the Forty-first, a white-haired man who had seen service in Mexico, called out to the new troops: "Fill your canteens boys! Some of you will be in hell before night and you'll need water!"[39]

---

[37] *OR*, x, part 1, 165, 166, 278.
[38] Foote, *Civil War*, I, 338.
[39] F. Y. Hedley, *Marching through Georgia* (Chicago, 1890), 46.

7. *Thar' Ain't No Good Way*

SHILOH CHURCH HAD BECOME the headquarters of P. G. T. Beauregard by early Sunday afternoon. A Confederate soldier recalled seeing him near the church "standing on a stump. . . . He cheered the boys as we passed telling us we had them whipped and to fall in on them—keep cool and shoot low." All morning Beauregard had been supervising the rear area and forwarding reinforcements to the front lines. Staff officers were continually bringing him reports of the progress of the battle, and he probably knew more about the overall situation than any Confederate officer on the field.[1]

Albert Sidney Johnston was where he had been all day—up front, riding from place to place; conferring with his corps, division, and brigade commanders; observing the terrain and the enemy positions; and occasionally even leading units into attack position. Beauregard's chief of staff, Thomas Jordan, was also up front. Together with his friend Colonel Jacob Thompson he had ridden to the front early in the day, and there he had found, according to his report, that critical problems of command control were plaguing the Rebels. Asserting that corps commanders were located ahead of or separated from substantial portions of their troops, Jordan said he repeatedly encountered soldiers halted for want of orders, whereupon the chief of staff, "assuming the authority of my position," simply took it upon himself to give orders in the name of General Johnston. For a time Jordan actually had the chiefs of staff of Hardee, Bragg, and Polk all consulting with

[1] Nathan Parker, Diary, Apr. 6, 1862, Univ. of Kentucky, Lexington. Roman, *Beauregard*, I, 524–34.

him! He was employing them in pressing the Confederate troops toward the heaviest firing.[2]

Because of the extensive intermingling of Confederate units, the front was eventually divided into four sectors, with a corps commander over each, in an effort to restore some degree of command control and communication. The arrangement apparently was worked out by the corps commanders themselves independent of Johnston's help. Hardee and Polk took the left, and Bragg and Breckinridge the right.

Most of Johnston's time during the morning had been devoted to the Rebel center, but he had also ridden to the left to observe Cleburne's attack, and had been on the right when Brigadier General Jones M. Withers with Chalmers' and Jackson's brigades began the advance against Stuart's brigade. He never seemed to leave the center for long, however, and shortly before noon was back on the right-center where the command of Breckinridge was fighting. In fact, by early afternoon not only Johnston, but the weight of the Confederate army, was gradually becoming marshaled at the center.

The focal point, pulling the Rebels to it almost like a magnet, was the "Hornets' Nest," the name given by the Confederates to the Union position where a part of Prentiss' command, supported by Hurlbut on his left and W. H. L. Wallace on his right, held on in the Sunken Road. The site was actually an old wagon road that formed only a slight depression in the terrain along most of its route, and at the time of the battle apparently was not considered to be a significant topographical feature. Both Union and Confederate officers in their reports were impressed by the strength of the Federal position here but seemed to attribute the strength to the thick underbrush and rising ground on the Union center and left and to an open field of fire on the right. Although the road gained considerable prominence as "sunken"—in retrospect and in the memories of veterans—only one participating officer, B. Franklin Cheatham, mentioned it in his report,

---

[2] *Battles and Leaders*, I, 599, 600. The chief of staffs were known in 1862 as assistant adjutant generals.

referring to it simply as "an abandoned road."[3] Regardless of name, however, here would occur some of the bloodiest fighting at Shiloh.

The portion of the road occupied by the Federals was well over half a mile long. From its intersection with the Corinth road near the western extremity of the Union line, the abandoned road ran in a southeasterly direction to about midpoint of the line and then bore due east to its junction with the Hamburg-Savannah road, at this point passing just north of a peach orchard in full bloom. The Union troops were aligned along the north side of the road, except on the east where some of Hurlbut's units were advanced a short distance to the south. Undoubtedly the Federals occupied a more favorable position than did the attacking Rebels. Sheltered by woods and commanding generally higher ground in the center of the line, the Yankees looked southwest across the road to large expanses of open area. To the southwest, they faced a farm field alluded to as the Duncan field, and on the eastern extremity of the line they looked south across a cotton field, its openness unbroken except for a log cabin and the peach orchard in one corner. Only near the center of the road—the place known as the Hornets' Nest—were both forces protected by wooded areas. Even here, however, at this highest point in the gently rolling land, the Federals looked down upon the Confederates, and the wooded slope between them was covered with dense, entangling underbrush.

This particular section of the Union line was manned with infantry along its entire length. In addition, artillery strategically placed at intervals could sweep a large circuit and rake a charging column from the flank as well as head-on. When fully formed, the Federal troops were aligned, from right to left, in the following order: the Seventh and Fifty-eighth

---

[3] *OR*, x, part 1, 438. William Kay, "The Sunken Road," unpublished paper in SNMP. As late as the 1880s most writers were ignoring the existence of the road and still emphasizing the underbrush and the hill. But gradually the road seemed to become more significant in retrospect among subordinate commanders and soldiers. The importance of the road as cover became magnified in the minds of the veterans, both from romantic and from faulty memories, as well as from attempts to justify the choice of the position.

Gibson's Confederate brigade charges Hurlbut's troops in the "Hornets' Nest," the scene of prolonged and bloody fighting during the battle of Shiloh. Shown below are the Sunken Road and thicket of the Hornets' Nest as they appear today, looking from west to east. At right is Duncan Field, across which Rebel soldiers made many charges in an attempt to dislodge the enemy.

Illinois (Thomas W. Sweeney's brigade), the Second, Seventh, Twelfth, and Fourteenth Iowa regiments (James M. Tuttle's brigade), and the Eighth Iowa of Sweeney's brigade, all of Wallace's division; then came portions of the Twelfth Michigan, the Eighteenth Missouri, the Eighteenth Wisconsin, and all of the Twenty-third Missouri (Prentiss' division), and finally came the Third Brigade of Hurlbut's division, a major portion of which was stretched on out into the peach orchard.

A section of artillery rested between the Twelfth and Fourteenth Iowa and another between the Fourteenth and Eighth Iowa; a full battery was located between the Eighth Iowa and Prentiss' men and still another to Hurlbut's left rear. In addition, from about noon until 2 P.M., a section of Mann's Missouri Artillery was pushed forward on the Union left to a site west of the peach orchard where it could enfilade the Rebels as they charged through the woods in front of the Federal line.

Here the center of the surging Confederate line was brought to a halt. Time and again the Rebels attempted to storm this Union strong point; they came across the open fields, and they came through the timber. Major D. W. Reed, who fought in the Hornets' Nest and was a careful student of the history of the battle, said as many as twelve separate charges were made against the Federal line. Ten can definitely be established by the official reports of officers who participated in the battle. When the Confederates continually recoiled from the slaughter dealt out by the Yankees, somebody said that the spot was like a Hornets' Nest, and the name stuck.

Major General Bragg, by late morning, was commanding the majority of the Confederates who were making the assaults. Bragg was a brave man. At the battle of Buena Vista he had held his ground with his artillery even when his infantry support left him. And Bragg believed that the Hornets' Nest could be carried by bayonet charge. Taught the value of the bayonet at West Point, Bragg had confirmed its effectiveness in his own mind by his Mexican War experience. No doubt he was also aware of the importance Napoleon had attached to the weapon, Bonaparte once writing that "the bayonet has

Confederate General Braxton Bragg, a puzzling mixture of compe-
tence and ineptness at Shiloh, has been referred to as "a man who
could snatch defeat from the jaws of victory."

always been the weapon of the brave and the chief tool of victory."[4]

But the Union troops in the Hornets' Nest had something that neither Napoleon's foes nor the Mexicans had possessed: rifled muzzleloaders. A trained soldier could load and fire the weapon three times a minute; it was deadly accurate for 200 yards; and it could kill at a distance of 1,000 yards, still possessing at that point sufficient power to penetrate a one-inch board of soft pine. The rifled-musket was so superior in range and accuracy to the old smoothbore musket that it often made bayonet charges virtually suicidal.

Making the situation more deadly for the Rebels was Bragg's failure to demonstrate much imagination as he persisted in reliance on frontal assaults; worse yet, he sent his troops against the Yankee line in piecemeal fashion in a series of uncoordinated charges rather than as a single mass of soldiers.

For a while, at least, the charging Rebels were literally slaughtered. The Twelfth and Fourteenth Iowa were holding the Union line across the road from where the central wooded area adjoined Duncan field. The Twelfth fronted on the field, and the Fourteenth faced the timbered area. Describing the repulse of one of the Rebel charges, the colonel of the Fourteenth said he ordered his men to lie down and hold their fire until the Confederates were within thirty paces; and then,

> When the order to fire was given, and the 12th and 14th opened directly in their faces, the enemy's first line was completely destroyed. Our fire was only returned by a few, nearly all who were not killed or wounded by it fleeing in every direction.[5]

On the left of the Fourteenth, the Eighth Iowa, after about eleven o'clock, was protecting a battery that was being fired for a time, and effectively, under the immediate supervision of General Prentiss. Between one o'clock and two-thirty it bore the brunt of some of the heaviest assaults the Confederates launched against the Hornets' Nest. The colonel of the

[4] Quoted in Grady McWhiney, *Braxton Bragg and Confederate Defeat*, 2 vols. (New York, 1969), I, 231.

[5] *OR*, x, part 1, 153.

Eighth Iowa who had two horses shot from under him in the battle, said that the Rebels, attempting to silence the Union battery, "hurled column after column on my position, charging most gallantly to the very muzzles of the guns." A soldier of the Fourteenth Iowa confirms the colonel's account, testifying that the Confederates, charging like "maddened demons," got "so close they almost laid their hands upon our cannon. . . ."[6]

Just to the left of Prentiss was the Thirty-first Indiana of Hurlbut's division. The regiment was in a portion of the most depressed area of the wagon road and was in the thick of the action from about midmorning to two-thirty in the afternoon. Colonel Charles Cruft, commanding the regiment, recalled that the initial assault upon his position carried to within some 10 yards of his line before it was thrown back with a terrible slaughter. He reported that a second charge was made with still more fury and that this time his men were almost out of ammunition when the Rebels finally fell back. By then the dead and wounded were lying all through the woods to his front.

The regiment barely had time to replenish its supply of ammunition before the men could again see the gleam of bayonets flashing between the trees in front of them. The Confederates were attacking a third time. Again the Rebels were driven back, but again they came on, and at some point of this murderous Sunday which Lloyd Lewis, biographer of Sherman, has described as possibly "the bloodiest one-day strife in proportion to the number of men engaged" in the entire war, the woods in front of the regiment caught fire. A choking wood smoke now mingled with rifle smoke, and soon the stench of burning bodies began to fill the air. Wounded men, facing what may have seemed an even more terrifying death than that from cannon and rifled-musket, were strug-

---

[6] *Ibid.*, 166. Thomas, *14th Iowa*, ch. IV. F. F. Kiner, *14th Iowa Infantry: Embracing the Battles of Fort Donelson and Shiloh* (Lancaster, 1863), 55, 56. The commander of the 14th Iowa as well as the colonel of the 8th Iowa bore witness to the fury of the attack borne by the 8th Iowa. *OR*, x, part 1, 154, 166. Thomas, *14th Iowa*, said it "seemed like the heaviest battle fought that day."

gling to drag themselves along the ground away from the flames.[7]

All along the line a spectrum of bizarre and often tragic events was occurring in the midst of the continuing violence. One soldier in the Second Iowa Infantry remembered how a shell burst directly in his front, and though he was unharmed, he saw the man lying next to him, who was close enough to touch, look down to see his arm nearly torn off by a jagged piece of iron from the exploding missile. The arm appeared to be hanging by only a slender bit of flesh and muscle. Crazed with shock, the wounded man leaped to his feet, shouted something that seemed to make absolutely no sense, and then fell to the ground unconscious.[8]

Another man forgot to remove the ramrod from his gun before firing it and realized his mistake only when he saw it quivering like an arrow in the body of a Rebel soldier who had been charging the Federal line.[9]

One Union soldier, who had fled in terror from the fight into the shallow wooded ravine behind the Federal line, regained a little of his nerve and came creeping back and took up a position behind a big tree near the firing line. Another man came up and got behind him; then came another and still another, until soldiers were huddling one behind the other in a line stretching back from the tree. Then, making up one of the most weird scenes imaginable, a company officer, obviously beside himself, was observed simply pacing back and forth from one end of this line to the other.[10]

The Third Iowa Regiment, helping to anchor the right of Hurlbut's Third Brigade, was on the east end of the Hornets' Nest, holding an advanced position in front of the road. Soon after the regiment went into action, a battery of artillery, the Thirteenth Ohio came galloping up from the rear and unlimbered. Charges were being rammed down the barrels and the

[7] J. T. Smith, *The Thirty-First Indiana* (Cincinnati, 1900), 28, 29. Lewis, *Sherman*, 232. Stillwell, *A Common Soldier*, 64. *OR*, x, part 1, 233, 235. John H. Rerick, *The Forty-Fourth Indiana Volunteer Infantry* (La Grange, Ind., 1880), 52, 53. Richardson, "Shiloh." New Orleans *Daily Picayune*, Apr. 8, 1862.
[8] Bell, *Tramps and Triumphs*, 15–17.
[9] Lewis, *Sherman*, 224.
[10] Catton, *Grant*, 233.

Their wooded position in flames, soldiers of the Forty-fourth Indiana endure choking smoke and the stench of burning bodies, as well as cannon and rifle fire, in the holocaust at the Peach Orchard. Below, Company H of the same regiment poses for a picture in calmer days.

guns pointed toward the ranks of the Rebels when, from directly in front, shot and shell from Confederate cannon tore through the trees and virtually destroyed the Union battery. It had not fired a single shot. What were left of its personnel disappeared in the direction from which they had come.[11]

An Iowa private, told that his brother had just been killed, asked where he was. When the body, which lay not far away, was pointed out to him, the Iowan walked over, bent down, saw that the man was truly dead, and then took his position beside his brother's body, loading and firing at the Rebels. He stayed there as long as his regiment remained in that area.[12]

Sometime in the late morning Captain Andrew Hickenlooper, sitting astride a white horse spattered with blood, was busy supervising the placement of two guns from his Fifth Ohio battery when he was startled by the sight of his sixty-five-year-old father. Hickenlooper had thought his father was safe back home in Ohio; actually he had enlisted in a cavalry regiment hoping to be near his son. Arriving at Pittsburg Landing the elder Hickenlooper had been assigned to General Grant's escort. There was little more than an instant for father and son to be together before each had to resume his work.[13]

William Shaw, colonel of the Fourteenth Iowa, recalled that in a lull after the repulse of one of the Confederate assaults, he and one of his captains walked out to where a Rebel officer, leading his regiment, had fallen within 50 feet of the Union line. Shaw's captain reached the body first and said the Confederate spoke once or twice just before he died. Before the two Union officers returned to the line, the captain turned the Rebel on his back, placed a pocket handkerchief over his face, and crossed the dead soldier's hands over his breast.[14]

---

[11] Warren Olney, "The Battle of Shiloh, with some Personal Reminiscences," Johnston Papers.

[12] Catton, *Grant*, 233.

[13] Andrew Hickenlooper, "The Battle of Shiloh," *Sketches of War History, 1861–1865*. Military Order of the Loyal Legion of the United States, Ohio Commandery, vol. 5 (1903), 432.

[14] Shaw to W. R. Reed, Apr. 6, 1896, SNMP. Shaw always thought the dead man was Lt. Col. John M. Dean, commanding the 7th Arkansas Regiment, who was killed while assaulting the Hornets' Nest.

A Confederate soldier who was in battle for the first time recalled the gruesome sight of a fine horse "galloping between the lines, snorting with terror, while his entrails, soiled with dust, trailed behind him." Another soldier was amazed to watch a rabbit, trembling with fear in the midst of such intense noise, come rushing out of the brush and snuggle up close to him, apparently seeking refuge.[15]

All along the line, again and again the Rebels charged and then recoiled, retreating back across corpses, some cleanly cut down by small-arms fire but others horribly mangled by the artillery barrage. One Federal officer was appalled to see not only that the ground was covered with dead and wounded, but that the bodies lay in piles, some in grotesque poses, others headless, some disemboweled, others cut in half.[16] Always present, too, was the pitiable sight of hundreds of wounded men, still living but often writhing in agony and unable to escape the scene. Some of the Union soldiers noted how the charging Confederate lines seemed to undulate when a volley cut through them, like tall grain waving in a wind. Others likened the effect to a loose rope shaken at one end.

The Confederates flung a total of 18,000 attackers at the Hornets' Nest, which at no time was manned by more than about 4,300 Union troops. Yet, contrary to what has often been assumed, the Federals were never outnumbered by their adversaries at any one time, for the Rebels never made an attack with more than about 3,700 men in any single assault.[17]

The Confederates missed one of their best opportunities for success when they failed to break this Federal line before it was fully formed. Earlier, at about nine in the morning when John S. Marmaduke led some 500 men of the Third Confederate Infantry in the initial attack on the position, both of Prentiss' flanks were exposed. On Prentiss' left, the Twenty-third Missouri did not come up to support him until about nine-thirty, and the Eighth Iowa did not fill the gap on his

[15] Stanley, *Autobiography*, 198. Bell, *Tramps and Triumphs*, 17.
[16] *OR*, x, part 1, 233, 235.
[17] Donald F. Dosch, "The Hornets' Nest," unpublished paper, SNMP, 38, 39. Dosch did an excellent job in compiling and analyzing the numbers of troops involved in the attacks on and the defense of the Hornets' Nest.

right until approximately eleven o'clock. From a historical
vantage point, it can be seen that Marmaduke probably would
have broken the Union line before it was completely formed if
he had massed his attack on either flank. Instead, the attackers
simply rushed in pell-mell, engaging the troops they had been
pursuing and withdrawing after one assault.[18]

After the repulse of Marmaduke's initial charge, the Confederates marshaled some 3,300 troops made up of Gladden's
brigade (then led by Adams) and Shaver's brigade, and
launched a more formidable attempt to storm the Yankee line
to the northwest of where Marmaduke had failed. Adams
advanced through the woods, bearing in upon the Union's
Fourteenth, and Twelfth Iowa regiments, and Shaver, to his
left, moved toward the Duncan field. But Adams was driven
back by a withering fire as soon as he neared the Federal line,
whereas Shaver's brigade advanced hardly more than halfway
across the field before it too recoiled from the devastating
storm of lead. At this time there was still a gap in the Union
line between the Fourteenth Iowa and Prentiss' command,
but it continued to remain unexploited by the Rebels because,
apparently, no one was aware of its existence.[19]

Next came William H. Stephens' brigade of about 1,800
men, directed by General Cheatham, charging across the very
same ground where Adams and Shaver had just failed. The
time was probably about ten or ten-thirty in the morning. By
now the Federal position in the western sector was even more
formidable, for the Seventh and Fifty-eighth Illinois regiments had set up in a line along the Corinth road, firing
directly into the left flank of the advancing Rebels. The Confederates, out in the open field, found themselves raked by
fire from every direction except the rear. Shocked by the
rapidity with which they were caught and sustaining heavy
losses in the murderous cross fire, the Rebels once again
reached only halfway across the field before the assault
bogged down, at which point the tide of survivors went rolling

---

[18] *OR*, x, part 1, 280, 281, 574, 575. Reed, *Battle of Shiloh*, 265–271, 304, 320.

[19] Reed, *Battle of Shiloh*, 269, 320, 321. Bell, *Tramps and Triumphs*, 8–9. *OR*, x, part 1, 153. Dosch, "Hornets' Nest," 12–16.

back.[20] Stephens' brigade may have re-formed and made a second charge farther to the right—the evidence is not clear—but if the charge was made, its fate was the same.[21]

About this time, eleven to eleven-thirty, General Hindman brought up his command to attack the Yankee line. A cannonball blasted into his horse and the dying animal smashed the general to the ground under its weight, disabling him for any further action. Brigadier General Alexander P. Stewart took charge of Hindman's troops, and with portions of Wood's brigade and his own command, he launched another attack on the Federal line. Cleburne came on with his patched-up command and attached himself to the left wing of the Confederate advance. Cleburne's help had the effect of outflanking the Seventh and Fifty-eighth Illinois, which were forced to drop back to their right and rear, abandoning some log cabins in the Duncan field which they had just occupied. But except for this western flank the Union line along the Sunken Road held firm.[22]

The Confederate attack, consisting of about 3,600 soldiers, was stretched too thin, extending all the way from the front of the Eighth Iowa (which had taken its position about eleven o'clock completing the Union line) to beyond the Corinth road. Braxton Bragg was watching as the Union artillery fire and blazing musketry swept through the faltering Gray lines of Stewart's brigade—an attack that was ultimately no more successful than the previous ones. Nevertheless, Bragg, who by this time surely knew something about the failure of former assaults, as well as being eyewitness to Stewart's abortive charge, ordered Colonel Randall I. Gibson to bring his brigade of four regiments forward and storm the Union position. By Bragg's orders Gibson charged the Union stronghold *four* times between about noon and two in the afternoon.

Gibson described the carnage from the attacker's viewpoint:

[20] *OR*, x, part 1, 164–66, 438. Henry George, *History of the 3rd, 7th, 8th, and 12th Kentucky, C. S. A.* (Louisville, 1911), 29–30. Dosch, "Hornets' Nest," 17–20. Reed, *Battle of Shiloh*, 269, 343.

[21] Reed, *Battle of Shiloh*, 343.

[22] *OR*, x, part 1, 466, 574, 597. Reed, *Battle of Shiloh*, 270, 338, 339. Dosch, "Hornets' Nest," 21, 22.

I was commanded by Major General Bragg to attack the enemy in a position to the front and right. The brigade moved forward in fine style, marching through an open field under a heavy fire and half way up an elevation covered with an almost impenetrable thicket upon which the enemy was posted. On the left a battery opened that raked our flank, while a steady fire of musketry extended along the entire front. . . . Our line was broken and the troops fell back; but they were soon rallied and advanced to the contest. Four times the position was charged and four times the assault proved unavailing. The strong and almost inaccessible position of the enemy—his infantry well covered in ambush and his artillery skillfully posted and efficiently served—was found to be impregnable to infantry alone.[23]

It was sometime in the early afternoon that General Hardee apparently discussed the possibility of ordering a portion of John Hunt Morgan's cavalry to charge some Union batteries that were located on a rise just west of the Hornets' Nest. Lieutenant Basil Duke of Morgan's command turned for advice to a young soldier in his unit who formerly was with a Confederate battery, now disabled. Thinking he could get some information from one experienced with cannon, Duke asked what was the best way to charge a battery. "Good Lord, Lieutenant!" the man exclaimed, "I wouldn't do it, if I was you. Why your blamed little cavalry won't be deuce high agin' them guns!" Duke reminded the soldier that he wasn't interested in an opinion of the wisdom or lack of wisdom of the charge and repeated his question, "What's the best way to charge a battery?" Duke said the man looked him straight in the eye and replied in his Southern drawl: "Lieutenant, to tell you the God's truth, thar' ain't no *good* way to charge a battery!"[24]

His statement might well have been applied on a much broader scale. Indeed there was no good way to make a frontal assault on the Hornets' Nest. Some of the Confederate officers, particularly those leading the charges, tried to tell Bragg that some other tactics were necessary. When Gibson's first assault was thrown back, he sent his aide-de-camp to

---

[23] *OR*, x, part 1, 480.
[24] Basil W. Duke, *Morgan's Cavalry* (New York, 1906), 84, 85.

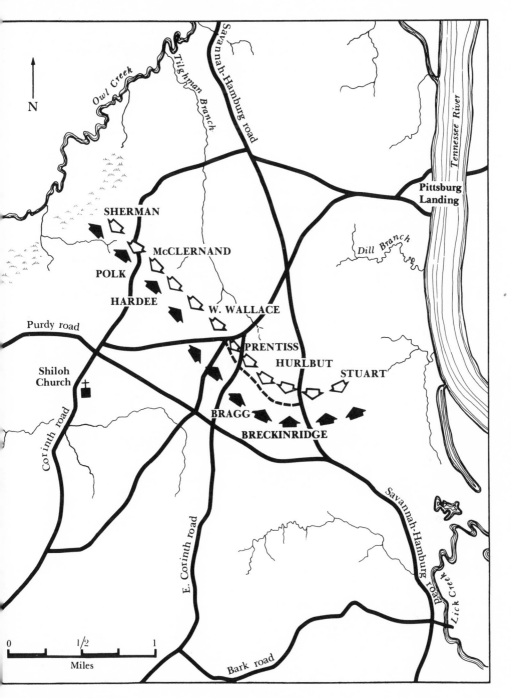

Map 8. The Federals Give Ground on Both Flanks, 12–2 P.M., April 6, 1862.

Bragg for artillery support. The only answer he received was an order to advance again on the enemy. The colonel of the Nineteenth Louisiana of Gibson's brigade, when ordered by a staff officer from Bragg to charge the Hornets' Nest a second time, did so; but he also told the staff officer to advise the general that it was impossible, in his opinion, to force the Union line by frontal assault and that a battery firing on one flank with infantry charging the other flank might be more successful.[25]

Bragg was still not satisfied after the second repulse of Gibson's command. Calling regimental commanders of the brigade together, he emphasized the importance of the position and the necessity of its immediate capture. Disregarding the protests of all four of the regimental commanders that it was a needless sacrifice, and refusing to act on Gibson's request for supporting artillery, he ordered a third and even a fourth advance, only to see his men repulsed and routed from the field.

As Gibson's brigade recoiled from its second advance, Bragg sent Captain Lockett, his chief engineer, galloping forward to the Fourth Louisiana, the central regiment in the brigade, telling Lockett to take the Fourth's colors and carry them forward. He climaxed his order with the admonition: "The flag must not go back again." Both the national and regimental colors carried in battle were regarded as almost sacred, and it was considered a signal honor to carry them. It was also a dangerous responsibility, because the opposing troops were equally determined to cut down the enemy's colors. Lockett dashed up to the color-sergeant and secured the flag, but he had not finished talking to the color-bearer when the man was shot down. A moment more and Lockett found himself confronted by the regiment's colonel, Henry W. Allen, a startling figure with a bullet hole in each cheek and blood streaming from his mouth. The wounded officer demanded to have the colors back, reported Lockett. "If any man but my color-bearer carries these colors, I am the man," the colonel said. "Tell General Bragg I will see that these

[25] *OR*, x, part 1, 483, 493.

colors are in the right place. But he must attack this position in flank; we can never carry it alone from the front."[26]

Surely by then, after the second unsuccessful attack by Gibson, Bragg should have realized the futility of further frontal assaults in this fashion. The general, however, not only ordered a continuation of the same tactic, but when Gibson finally retired with a fragment of his command left, Bragg ordered still another brigade to storm the Hornets' Nest. This time it was Shaver's command, which had already attempted the feat earlier in the day, afterward retiring to replenish its ammunition. Now, probably about two-thirty or so, Shaver's troops charged through the thick woods directly in front of the Hornets' Nest, at the Union position's strongest point. Advancing directly into the mouth of cannon as well as massed rifle fire, Shaver reported that

> on the enemy's right was a battery of the presence of which (so completely was it concealed) I was not aware until it opened. . . . I pressed forward, the enemy remaining close and quiet until my left was within about 50 and my right within about 60 yards from their lines (a dense undergrowth intervening), when a terrific and murderous fire was poured in upon me from their lines and battery. It was impossible to charge through the dense under-growth, and I soon discovered my fire was having no effect upon the enemy, so I had nothing left me but to retire or have my men all shot down. . . .

Shaver informed General Bragg that he could not carry the position and that his command was badly cut up, whereupon the general directed him to fall back, re-form his brigade, and await orders.[27]

One of the last Rebel assaults upon the Hornets' Nest was led by Patton Anderson, whose brigade of a little less than 1,500 men attempted to cross Duncan's field around three-fifteen or three-thirty. Anderson reported that the Union canister fire was particularly well directed, the musketry fire was galling, and the right of his line, attempting to crash through a portion of the woods, still found the underbrush so

[26] *Battles and Leaders*, I, 605.
[27] *OR*, x, part 1, 574, 575.

thick, in spite of all the firing through that area, that it was impossible to see a company officer at platoon distance.[28]

The reasons that the Rebel assaults did not succeed become obvious when they are thus individually examined. The Confederates failed to find and exploit the gaps and exposed flanks of the Union line in the morning hours when the Federal position was not fully formed. More important, the Rebels never attacked with enough men to assault the Union line as a whole, making it possible for the Union troops to pour oblique fire into the enemy's flanks from an overlapping position. Nor did the Confederates, with the two possible exceptions of the Adams and Stewart charges, mass a large enough force at any one point along the line to possess even a bare numerical advantage over the Union defenders at that position. To have cracked the Federal line in a massed assault upon a given point would probably have required at least a two to one advantage in the number of attacking men plus a column poised to immediately follow up on the initial break. The Rebels, however, were lined up in such a way that they faced on the same front an equal or greater number of men in Blue. And finally, when it had become obvious to many subordinate commanders that something other than these piecemeal frontal assaults was imperative, the high command, in the person of Bragg, remained wedded to the tactic which had been proved a failure.

[28] *OR*, x, part 1, 498.

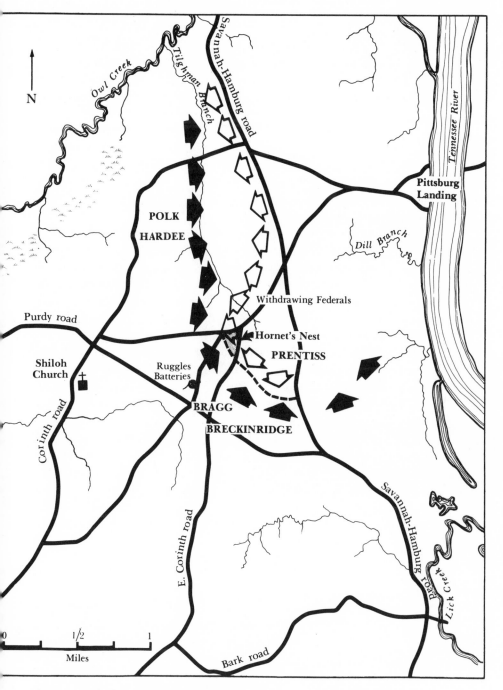

Map 9. Isolation of the Hornets' Nest, 2–5 P.M., April 6, 1862.

8. *Bayonets and Blunders*

BRAXTON BRAGG was not the only member of the Confederate high command who believed in the bayonet and frontal attack. Albert Sidney Johnston was applying the same tactics farther to the Rebel right. Earlier in the day he had exclaimed to an Arkansas regiment: "They say you boast of your prowess with the bowie knife. Today you wield a nobler weapon—the bayonet. Employ it well." A little later he remarked to Governor Isham G. Harris of Tennessee, concerning a portion of the Union line, "Those fellows are making a stubborn stand. I'll have to put the bayonet to them." About two o'clock, General Breckinridge, who had been assailing Hurlbut's line in and east of the peach orchard, told Johnston that he could not persuade one of his regiments (the Forty-fifth Tennessee) to advance again. The general sent one of his staff, Governor Harris, to address the regiment to urge it on for another charge. But following the speech by Harris, Breckinridge still was not satisfied that the troops were convinced, and so Johnston himself then rode along the front of the regiment, touching their bayonets and saying, "These will do the work. . . . We must use the bayonet." At the center of the line the general is reported to have wheeled his horse and yelled: "I will lead you!" The freshly inspired soldiers charged and this time drove the enemy back from its line among the peach trees.[1]

One of the most careful students of Johnston's career is uncertain whether Johnston actually led the assault all the way. It is clear, however, that he was under heavy fire and that he came back with rips and tears in his clothing and with one

[1] Johnston, *Life*, 583, 584, 613–15. Edward W. Munford, "Albert Sidney Johnston," Johnston Papers.

boot sole cut nearly in half by a minié ball. He must have been extremely keyed up, for he shouted something to the effect that "They didn't trip me up that time!" Then he dispatched Governor Harris with instructions to Colonel W.S. Statham's brigade to silence a battery that had opened fire from the woods off to the left.[2]

When Harris came galloping back a little later, he found Johnston alone—having dispatched all his staff with messages—and reeling in the saddle. Harris supported the general, to keep him astride his horse, while guiding the bay into a nearby ravine for shelter. The army's commander, now pale from loss of blood, was lowered to the ground, and Harris began loosening his clothes in a search for the wound. He finally found it. Just above the hollow of the knee a bullet had torn into the leg and severed the artery. Although it may have been too late at this point to save Johnston's life, Harris could not provide help. He lacked the knowledge and training to administer emergency aid himself, and the staff physician had recently been dispatched by Johnston. In a few moments Johnston's chief of staff came up but, like Harris, did not know what to do. He knelt beside the general's prostrate form and asked, over and over, "Johnston, do you know me? Johnston, do you know me?"[3]

It has been said that if Johnston had lived, the outcome of the battle on April 6 would have been different, that a lull occurred in the fighting following his death, precious time was lost, and the weak Union left which he was then in the process of exploiting in a drive to the landing was ignored. Among the propagators of this thesis were Bragg and Hardee. At the moment of the "irreparable disaster" of Johnston's death, Bragg reported, "the plan of battle was being rapidly and successfully executed under [Johnston's] immediate eye and lead on the right." But, Bragg contended, a "great delay" occurred when he was stricken down, and this loss of time was the loss of success. Hardee was even more emphatic than Bragg. In a rather fanciful account Hardee spoke of how Johnston, just before his death, was leading the Rebels as they

[2] Roland, *Johnston*, 336.
[3] *Battles and Leaders*, I, 564, 565. Roland, *Johnston*, 338.

"swept down the river" toward the landing, "cheering and animating the men and driving the enemy in wild disorder to the shelter of their gunboats." Then, with Johnston's death, Hardee claimed, came a lull in the attack on the right and "precious hours" were wasted.[4]

The historical accuracy of Hardee's dramatic and colorful account is, of course, highly questionable. Hardee, commanding on the left of the Rebel line, could not have seen what was happening on the right. Furthermore, he did not write his report until nearly a year later, dated February 7, 1863. It is obvious that "hours" could not have been wasted due to Johnston's death, inasmuch as he died about two-thirty, and no later than three-thirty the Rebels were assembling a row of cannon to try and break the center of the line, the Hornets' Nest. The content of Bragg's report, while of a lower key than Hardee's, was also embellished. Actually there is no reliable evidence to support Bragg's statement; his words ignored the fact that at two-thirty in the afternoon the Rebels attacking the Hornets' Nest were in approximately the same position they had occupied as early as ten in the morning, and failed to note that he was still employing the same tactics against the Hornets' Nest that had been costing them so heavily while gaining no ground. If the Rebel chance for victory by marching for the landing on the Union left was as obvious at Johnston's death as Bragg alleged, it is curious that Bragg himself did not exploit the opportunity. Furthermore, Johnston's actions up to the time of his death furnish no evidence that had Johnston lived, he would have struck for the landing at two-thirty rather than flanking the Hornets' Nest as the brigades of Bowen, Chalmers, Jackson, and Statham did.

Nor was there any "great delay" in the Rebel attack following Johnston's death, as Bragg asserted. Bragg, upon being informed that Johnston had fallen, rode farther to his right and assumed command in that area where Johnston had been exercising it. Beauregard, told of Johnston's death, continued the battle virtually without interruption. Also, General Breckinridge was soon striving to move the attack forward on the Rebel right. Breckinridge discovered that the brigades of

[4] *OR*, x, part 1, 469, 569.

Bowen, Chalmers, Jackson, and Statham were already wheeling in an arc to the northwest as they moved toward the sound of the heaviest firing in the vicinity of the Hornets' Nest. Colonel Joseph Wheeler of Jackson's brigade placed the time about 3 P.M. If there was indeed a temporary lull in the fighting, it may be attributed more accurately to the disorganization resulting from the long and hard struggle, which is borne out on page after page of the official reports.[5]

Precious time was lost by the Confederates, but the loss was before, not after, Johnston's death, and both Bragg and Johnston were apparently responsible. Their preoccupation with piecemeal frontal assaults on the Hornets' Nest in the center of the line had stymied a full Rebel advance for approximately five hours.

Only when the Confederate flanks to the right and left of the Hornets' Nest began to press forward with some success did that Union position become precarious. In fact, by 3 P.M. when Beauregard had learned that Johnston was dead, the Union army was crucially dependent upon the stability of the Hornets' Nest. On both flanks, the Federal regiments were falling back toward the landing. Only W. H. L. Wallace, Prentiss, and a portion of Hurlbut's command—all in the Hornets' Nest—were holding fast.

Grant was at the landing, struggling to form Sherman's and McClernand's troops, which had just been forced to retreat from their position on the right of the Hornets' Nest, into a last line of defense. He was also putting into the line stragglers from the rest of the army who could be rallied to fight. On the left flank of the Hornets' Nest John A. McArthur's brigade, separated from the rest of W. H. L. Wallace's division, had been plugging the gap between Hurlbut's and Stuart's troops since about eleven in the morning. The Fiftieth Illinois Regiment from Sweeney's brigade was also with McArthur's men. But McArthur's command broke up and retreated about one-thirty in the afternoon. McArthur himself was wounded, and his Ninth Illinois Regiment of 617 men suffered 59 percent casualties, the highest loss of any Federal unit in the

[5] *Ibid.*, 213, 215, 553, 554, 558, 622. Joseph Wheeler, "The Battle of Shiloh," *Southern Historical Society Papers* 24, (1895), 122.

battle.[6] Hurlbut's left flank was thus open and had to be recessed in an angle back toward the north. Nearly a half mile then separated Hurlbut from Stuart, on the far left flank of the army; and Stuart, like McArthur, could no longer hold his ground.

The Confederates had too many men and too much fire power. About two in the afternoon Stuart's brigade fell back again, and the troops of the Fifty-fifth Illinois Regiment were caught by the oncoming Confederates as they tried to flee up a narrow ravine. The Rebels lined both sides of the ravine, shooting as fast as they could load and fire while the Federals scrambled to get away. One of the Confederates who witnessed the slaughter later said that it was like shooting into a flock of sheep: "I never saw such cruel work during the war." The Fifty-fifth took more than 50 percent casualties. Lucien B. Crooker, wounded shortly before the retreat began, was one of the men stumbling down the ravine. He collapsed at the foot of a tree, and a comrade, Parker Bagley, himself wounded in the left arm, tried to help Crooker. As the two staggered along with Crooker leaning on Bagley, another Rebel bullet found its mark, first passing through Crooker's shoulder and then striking and killing Bagley. Stuart tried to rally remnants of the brigade some distance to the left rear of the Hornets' Nest. He could not stabilize his men, however, and finally led them along the Hamburg-Savannah road to the landing where they too became a part of Grant's last line.[7]

And still Lew Wallace had not arrived, nor was there any word from him. When Captain W. R. Rowley, whom Grant had dispatched at noon to hurry up Wallace, had not returned by two-thirty, the commander had then sent out a search party to look for Wallace.

The mystery of why Lew Wallace and his 7,000 men never saw battle on that fateful Sunday remains unsolved even today. According to Wallace's account, the first instructions he received from Grant, after seeing Grant at Crump's Landing

---

[6] George Mason, "Shiloh," *Military Essays and Recollections*. Military Order of the Loyal Legion of the United States, Illinois Commandery, vol. 1, (1891), 99. Reed, *Shiloh*, 91. *OR*, x, part 1, 158.

[7] *OR*, x, part 1, 259. Crooker, *The 55th Illinois*, 110, 123.

as the commander was passing up the river toward Pittsburg, came at eleven-thirty in the morning. He was ordered, he said, to leave a detachment to guard the public property at Crump's Landing, then march his division to form a junction with the right of the army, Sherman's division, and be governed by circumstances. Unfortunately for the sake of historical accuracy, the written order was subsequently lost. Wallace recounted later that his adjutant put it under his sword belt, forgot it, and somewhere along the line it disappeared.[8] The adjutant himself, Captain Frederick Knefler, in a letter written years later, acknowledged that the order had been placed in his hands and afterward lost, but he did not shed light on the contents.[9]

The order almost did not get written in the first place, for Grant when he arrived at the front earlier that morning had simply told James Rawlins the order he wanted conveyed to Wallace. But Captain A. S. Baxter, the army's quartermaster whom Rawlins asked to deliver the message, insisted that it be in writing. Rawlins therefore dictated the message, which Baxter scribbled out on some paper. It was the only copy and, according to Rawlins, contained a message quite different from what Wallace claimed he received. Rawlins' version was that Grant ordered Wallace to move to Pittsburg Landing by the road nearest to and parallel to the river, form in the rear of W. H. L. Wallace's Second Division, and await further instructions.[10]

Except that three other men who were present when the order was delivered gave essentially the same account of the message that Lew Wallace did, logic would dictate the acceptance of Rawlins' version as the more accurate.[11] Grant needed a ready reserve as quickly as possible—which a direct march of about five miles by the river road would provide—and not more troops on his right. The forces on his right already overlapped the Confederates early in the morning,

[8] Lew Wallace, *An Autobiography*, 2 vols. (New York, 1906), I, 463, 464.
[9] *Battles and Leaders*, I, 607.
[10] *OR*, X, part 1, 185. *Battles and Leaders*, I, 607. The weight of evidence available indicates that Wallace probably received the order earlier than 11:30. See also *OR*, X, part 1, 174, 175, 179, 181.
[11] *Battles and Leaders*, I, 607.

when the order presumably was dispatched. Furthermore, the route to his right flank called for a difficult march of some twelve miles over a road that traversed, for part of its route, an otherwise impassable swamp and led to a bridge over Owl Creek that was defended by two Confederate infantry regiments and a battery of artillery.

Did Wallace ignore Grant's order in favor of the dazzling thought that he might deliver a staggering blow to the Rebels by coming in on the flank? He claimed in his autobiography that he had actually placed himself in the rear of the entire Confederate army when ordered to turn around; and Grant later seemed to credit Wallace with a scheme of this nature.[12] Yet there is no evidence from Wallace's conduct before or after that time to indicate he would deliberately ignore his superior's orders. Another possible explanation is that he became confused about which road to take from Crump's Landing to Pittsburg and, after realizing his mistake, tried to justify his actions. He apparently did not know the roads well when, about the turn of the century, he revisited the battlefield in the company of Major D. W. Reed, then historian of the Shiloh National Military Park Commission. That his knowledge of the roads would be vague after being away from the area for years is only natural, however. It is also possible that the blame rested with Rawlins, that he garbled Grant's order in transmitting it through Captain Baxter to Wallace and attempted to cover up his error by making Wallace the scapegoat. Grant later acknowledged that he could not be certain what order Wallace had received.[13]

Regardless of the contradictory testimony on the content of the order, Wallace's actions after Baxter handed him the order were consistent with his description of it. Wallace did set out on the longer route, presumably to join the army's right flank. He left Crump's Landing by a road leading due west to Purdy; then at a place called Stony Lonesome he bore off to the southwest on a route known as the Shunpike that would have eventually brought him to an intersection with the

---

[12] Wallace, *Autobiography*, I, 467. Irving McKee, *"Ben-Hur" Wallace: The Life of General Lew Wallace* (Berkeley, 1947), 55.
[13] McKee, *Wallace*, 55; Grant, *Memoirs*, I, 183.

Hamburg-Purdy road, at a point more than three miles west of Shiloh Church. He had marched about seven miles from Crump's when the first of Grant's follow-up messengers, Captain Rowley, overtook the rear of his column. Rowley said he found the division halted, some of the men sitting by the roadside, some with their arms stacked—the entire scene conveying an impression that there was no haste—and Wallace, whom he found at the head of the column, when told he was on the wrong road, replied that this was the only road he knew anything about.[14]

The division was then told to turn around and head back, but Wallace gave the order to countermarch rather than reversing the column to march the rear in front, which would have saved time. Rowley stayed to act as guide, according to his account, although Wallace said he left. After retracing its route for about two miles the column bore off to the right, taking a shortcut toward the River road. It was at this point that Grant's second follow-up messengers, the search party consisting of Rawlins, McPherson, and two aides, finally galloped up to the lost column and accompanied it to Pittsburg Landing. In search of Wallace they had ridden nearly to Crump's Landing and then turned westward by the road they learned Wallace had taken. According to their report, they found the column, with Rowley still present, at about three-thirty.

Rowley, Rawlins, and McPherson all testified to what they thought was an unnecessarily slow march, but their efforts to speed it up were largely to no avail. Wallace himself said Rawlins wanted to arrest him, but McPherson talked him out of it. It was nearly dark, and the fighting had ceased when Wallace and his 7,000 men finally came across the bridge at Snake Creek and took position behind Tilghman Branch, ironically on Sherman's right flank, which by that time was about two and one-half miles back of the position it had occupied when the battle started.[15]

There is no compelling evidence to accept the verdict of

[14] *OR*, x, part 1, 179, 180.
[15] *Ibid.*, 180, 187. Rawlins testified that Rowley was with Wallace when he and McPherson came up about 3:30. Wallace, *Autobiography*, I, 470.

Grant's aides that Wallace was lost. Wallace's remark, in reply to Rowley's assertion that he was on the wrong road, saying that he knew nothing about any other route was only natural if Wallace was acting on an order to take position on the right of Sherman's original line. Indeed no other road led to that point. Wallace later wrote that in the last week of March he had ridden with Major Charles S. Mayes of the cavalry over the entire route to Shiloh Church by the Shunpike and the Hamburg-Purdy road.[16] There is no reason to suspect he was not telling the truth. It is inconceivable that a commander of Wallace's intelligence would reside for a month with his three brigades spread out at Crump's, Stony Lonesome, and Adamsville without acquainting himself with the only two roads by which his troops could be united with the rest of the army, roads which he could not avoid intersecting when he traveled between his brigades at Crump's Landing and Stony Lonesome.

The charge by Grant's aides that Wallace was slow arose because he countermarched the division rather than merely reversing it. However, since Wallace had begun his march in battle formation, with a proper displacement of cavalry, infantry, and artillery, he may have been thinking about the probable confusion in organization which would result upon entering the battle if he marched the rear in front. The charges that Wallace, at the head of the column, stopped more than once to rest may also be misleading. Wallace could have been trying to ensure that his division kept its ranks closed up in order that the command would not straggle into the battle, thus negating some of its strength and probably increasing its losses.[17]

It is interesting to compare the speed of Wallace's march, from the time that he began his countermarch, with that of Nelson's leading brigade from Savannah to Pittsburg Landing, approximately the same distance. Nelson received no criticism for being slow, and yet there was little difference in the speed of their marches.[18] And it should be remembered

[16] Wallace, *Autobiography*, I, 453.

[17] Harold Lew Wallace, "Lew Wallace's March to Shiloh Revisited," *Indiana Magazine of History* 59 (Mar. 1963), 29.

[18] *Battles and Leaders*, I, 609.

that Grant's aides were with Wallace for only part of his total march of about fifteen or sixteen miles and six and one-half hours.

Probably Wallace should be faulted for being overly concerned with proper procedure in a crisis situation, but the charges that he failed to follow orders, became lost, or was slow to the point of unconcern and indifference appear to be unwarranted and excessive. The most likely explanation of all Wallace's troubles is that Grant's intended order became garbled between its inception and its transmission to Wallace.

While Wallace was finding his way to the battlefield, Grant was also still wondering what had become of General Nelson and his lead division of Buell's Army of the Ohio. Unbelievable as it may seem, Nelson, by his own admission in his official report, never left Savannah until one-thirty in the afternoon, this in spite of Grant's instructions of the early morning, which were repeated later in the morning, with the admonition to hurry up his command "as fast as possible."[19]

Apparently Nelson did not move until General Buell ordered him to do so by "reiterating" Grant's orders. And ironically, Buell said in his report that he *knew* of Grant's order for Nelson to march to the river opposite Pittsburg Landing. Buell said he examined the road up to the river, found it impracticable for artillery, and ordered Nelson to leave his guns to be carried forward by steamers. He did not explain, however, why that prevented Nelson's troops from marching until one-thirty. In an article written years later he offered the rather feeble explanation that "Nelson only waited for the services of a guide . . . ."[20]

Perhaps Buell, Nelson, and some other officers at Savannah believed that nothing more than a hard skirmish between outposts of the armies was taking place. Buell said this impression existed at Savannah. Both Colonel Jacob Ammen, commanding the Tenth Brigade of Nelson's division, in his diary, and Buell, in the later article, record how they visited with C. F. Smith, and the old warrior made light of the idea that a real battle was in progress. Thomas J. Wood, commanding the

[19] *OR*, x, part 1, 323; part 2, 95.
[20] *Ibid.*, part 1, 323, 292, 293. *Battles and Leaders*, I, 492.

Sixth Division, adds further testimony to this effect in his report. Another possibility is that Buell was a bit jealous of Grant and resented the latter's orders to one of his division commanders.[21]

After waiting around at Savannah for a while, Buell, in his own words, "determined to go" up to Pittsburg and find out what was happening. Also by his own account, he did not arrive there until about one o'clock. When Nelson's men finally started, they marched eagerly enough, many of them anxious to get into the action. But it was about five o'clock before they reached the river opposite Pittsburg, and then they had to be ferried across the Tennessee.[22]

Wallace's men marched the long route. Buell's men were slow to get started. Another immense number of soldiers still cowered under the bluff at Pittsburg Landing. Grant and his staff worked to form a last line of defense covering the landing while the Union command in the Hornets' Nest fought to stave off disaster.

When Beauregard took command of the Confederate army shortly after three o'clock, he moved immediately to reduce the Hornets' Nest. Brigadier General Daniel Ruggles was to push the attack on the left and center and Bragg on the right. Ruggles was convinced that infantry alone could not take the Union stronghold. He sent out an order for all the cannon on the army's left to be marshaled at the western side of the Duncan field.[23] From about three-thirty to four-thirty, teams of horses and scores of men were kept busy as a line of 6-pounder smoothbores, 12-pounder rifles, 12-pounder howitzers, and 3-inch rifles was stretched longer and longer until it probably extended for a fifth of a mile—62 cannon, hub to hub, unleashing a fierce cannonade, striking across 500 yards of open field into the ranks of the Blue line. Firing approximately three to four times a minute (about 180 shots per minute) and continuing in full force for well over an hour, the bombardment of Ruggles' batteries literally darkened the sky with smoke.

[21] *OR*, x, part 1, 292, 331, 377. *Battles and Leaders*, I, 492.
[22] *OR*, x, part 1, 292, 332, 333. *Battles and Leaders*, I, 492.
[23] *OR*, x, part 1, 472.

Commanding the Army of the Ohio, General Don Carlos Buell
believed he had arrived just in time to save Grant's army from
disaster at Pittsburg Landing.

Besides Ruggles' guns, several batteries may have been playing upon the Hornets' Nest from the Rebel right. The overall effect was a murderous barrage that virtually pinned the Union troops to the ground. Some men found that if they tried to go back, they were in even worse danger than if they stayed put.

The hail of iron was at last too great. The Union batteries in the Hornets' Nest were forced to pull back, and Hurlbut's command began streaming toward the landing. Prentiss and Wallace, however, conferred and agreed to hold the position "at all hazards," hoping they could save the army from destruction. But Wallace himself was next struck down, severely wounded by a shot that struck him in the head, and many of the soldiers thought he was dead. More of the troops began falling back as the Rebel line of infantry closed in around the Union flanks. As if things were not bad enough, the shells from the Union gunboats *Tyler* and *Lexington*, which had come up the river and were attempting to help by shelling the Confederates with their big guns from the river, were severing limbs from the trees all around Prentiss, with the result that heavy pieces of timber were crashing down on his men.[24]

Prentiss recessed his lines to fight on all sides. Finally about five-thirty, seeing that further resistance could result in the slaughter of virtually every man then in his command, he surrendered. When he raised the white flag, he was turning over about 2,200 men, primarily of the Eighth, Twelfth, and Fourteenth Iowa regiments and the Fifty-eighth Illinois—all four of them from Wallace's division.[25]

Wallace himself now lay unattended within the Rebel lines. His brother-in-law, Cyrus Dickey, was riding by his side when Wallace was wounded, and Dickey and an orderly carried the stricken commander about a quarter of a mile toward the rear. But as they saw the Gray line closing in upon them, and thinking the general was dead, they abandoned their burden in order to save themselves.[26]

Confusion reigned as Prentiss surrendered. Some Rebels,

[24] *OR*, x, part 1, 166, 279.
[25] *Ibid.*
[26] Wallace, *Letters*, 196, 198.

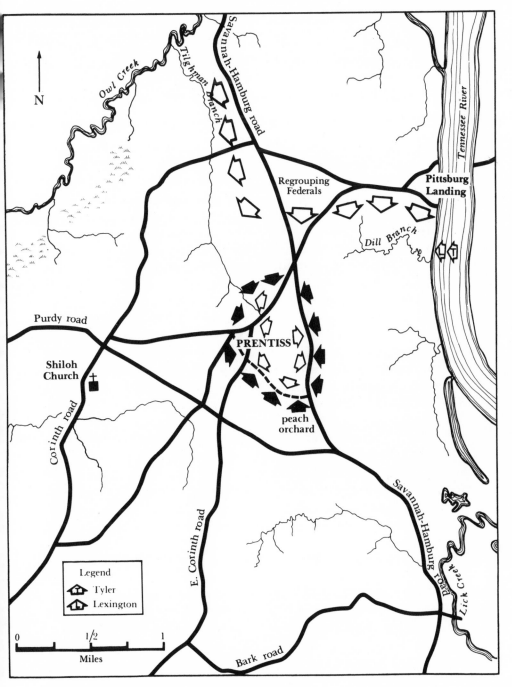

Map 10. Collapse of the Hornets' Nest, 5–6 P.M., April 6, 1862.

not realizing that the battle had been decided in that area, kept firing, inflicting casualties on both Union soldiers and Confederates. Colonel Madison Miller, leading a part of Prentiss' Sixth Division, came rushing into the area only to realize too late that Prentiss had just surrendered. The colonel and his men had no alternative but to also lay down their arms. Here and there wild and foolish acts occurred. A Confederate private rushed forward, grabbed the bridle of a horse ridden by a Union officer, and yelled at the Yankee to surrender. The officer put his pistol in the Rebel's face and fired. At the instant he pulled the trigger, however, the officer's aim was deflected by a shot from an unknown source that struck him in the side. The Confederate's life was spared as the Union officer fell fatally wounded from his horse, and the frightened mount then galloped away dragging his body through the Rebel lines. Some of the Union prisoners, refusing to surrender their arms, began smashing their rifled-muskets against the trees. When the Southerners saw what was happening, they opened fire again, killing some of the men who were still trying to destroy their weapons. After the shooting finally ceased, the Rebels, though surprised that the Yankee force they had captured was not larger, were jubilant, particularly so as word spread that they had captured a commanding general of one of the Federal divisions. A couple of Confederate cavalrymen galloped up and grabbed the silk flag and banner belonging to the Twelfth Iowa and then rode back and forth through a puddle of water and mud, dragging the colors behind them. Another, seizing the flag of the Fourteenth Iowa, was joined by other Rebels in tearing it to pieces and trampling it in the mud.[27]

As galling as these sights were to the Union troops, there was no way the Confederates, for all their fury, could undo what the Federal soldiers had here accomplished. Manning Force, who fought at Shiloh, wrote: "Prentiss, having never swerved from the position he was ordered to hold, having lost

[27] Madison Miller, Diary, 1862, Missouri Historical Society, St. Louis. Watkins, "Co. Aytch," 67. Mildred Throne, ed., "Letters from Shiloh," *Iowa Journal of History* 52 (1954), 276. Thomas, *14th Iowa*, ch. v.

everything but honor, surrendered the little band."[28] A noble tribute; but in another sense the Union troops in the Hornets' Nest had gained everything. They had delayed the Confederate advance most of the day, taking a terrible toll of Rebel manpower, and for well over an hour when time to form a defensive line at the landing was so important in the late afternoon, they had occupied the attention of virtually the entire Confederate army. Force might well have added that the stand made by these soldiers and their dead comrades had saved the Union army from destruction on the first day at Shiloh.

When Braxton Bragg wrote his official report of the battle of Shiloh, he described the failure of Gibson's four assaults upon the Hornets' Nest as "due entirely to want of proper handling."[29] He had reference to what he considered improper handling by the regimental officers of the brigade. Bragg would have been more accurate if that judgment had included the entire Rebel effort against the Hornets' Nest, particularly his own direction of it.

[28] Williams, *Lincoln*, III, 373.
[29] *OR*, x, part 1, 466.

9. *Lick 'em Tomorrow, Though*

LONG AFTER BEAUREGARD lay in his tomb in Metairie Cemetery in his beloved New Orleans some Confederates who fought at Shiloh continued to talk and write of the "Lost Opportunity" on April 6—for which they blamed the Creole. The Rebels did lose a chance to wreck the Union army at Shiloh, but it had probably passed before the time of the particular "lost opportunity" for which some writers attempted to hold Beauregard responsible.

If a large striking force had been on the Confederate right when the battle opened, when the Rebels had the element of surprise and momentum, when nothing but Stuart's undermanned brigade defended the Union left, the chances are good that they could have smashed through and driven to the landing, just as the proposed battle plan called for them to do. Although the ground next to the river was too rugged for the passage of artillery, there was nothing in the area that a sufficiently large, fresh, and determined bunch of infantry could not have surmounted.

Another "lost opportunity," already discussed, occurred when the Confederates expended too much time and manpower on frontal assaults on the Hornets' Nest, but the critics of Beauregard had in mind neither the Union left at the start of the fight nor the Hornets' Nest. They referred to the situation following the surrender of Prentiss, during the last moments of the struggle on April 6. The then shortened Confederate line, so it was alleged, could have made one more assault and destroyed Grant's army. The Rebels were on the threshold of victory, but Beauregard called off the attack.

A prime propagator of this thesis was Braxton Bragg. His memory of what happened seemed to improve and change in almost direct ratio to the distance he was removed in time from the battle. In a letter to his wife written immediately after the struggle on April 8, Bragg described the Confederates on Sunday evening as "disorganized, demoralized, and exhausted." Stating that the army came under a heavy fire from the Union gunboats as it approached the landing, he added an intriguing comment that "universal suffrage, furloughs, and whiskey have ruined us."[1]

By April 30, the date of his official report, Bragg had decided that the shells from the gunboats "though terrific in sound" did no damage, "as they all passed over" his troops, and that he was starting a final attack "with every prospect of success" when an order was received from the commanding general to withdraw the army beyond the enemy's fire. In almost the same breath, however, Bragg also noted the condition of the soldiers. They were "greatly exhausted by twelve hours incessant fighting, without food . . ." and the "heavy battery in our front and the gunboats on our right . . . seemed determined to dispute every inch of ground." When compared with these latter statements, Bragg's optimistic assertion that an attack would have had "every prospect of success" is rather surprising, especially when one recalls the lack of success of his assaults on the Hornets' Nest earlier in the day.[2]

About ten years after the war—when Bragg and Beauregard were no longer on cordial terms—Bragg gave General Johnston's son, Preston, some statements which the latter used in a biography of his father to support his contention that Johnston had led the army to the very brink of a great victory but Beauregard let it slip from his grasp. Preston's biography did much to popularize the "lost opportunity" thesis.

Also after the war was over, Bragg's chief engineer at Shiloh, S. H. Lockett, gave an account of how Bragg, when informed by a staff officer from Beauregard that the army was to be withdrawn and that the victory was "sufficiently complete," erupted with: "My God, was a victory ever 'sufficiently

[1] Braxton Bragg to wife, Apr. 8, 1862, Braxton Bragg Papers, William K. Bixby Collection, Missouri Historical Society, St. Louis. Lewis, *Sherman*, 229.
[2] *OR*, x, part 1, 466, 467.

complete?' " Lockett recounted how Bragg was allegedly on the verge of disobeying the withdrawal order in an attempt to save the "victory" until the general saw the troops on his left had already received the order and were falling back. Then, becoming even more impassioned, he exclaimed in anguished resignation: "My God, My God, it is too late!" Lockett concluded—"and *the victory was lost*."[3] In such manner the legend of the "lost opportunity" was born, nourished, and finally cherished in the memory of some Confederates.

In addition to the letter to his wife, further evidence indicates that Bragg was not nearly so upset by the withdrawal order as was later alleged. Captain Clifton Smith, the staff officer who carried the order from Beauregard to Bragg, said that Bragg received the news without comment. This statement was confirmed by the account of Dr. J. C. Nott, Bragg's medical director, who likewise remembered that Bragg made no protest after he received the order. When Bragg rode to Beauregard's headquarters a little later in the evening, Colonel Jacob Thompson, who heard their conversation, stated that the two talked of troop exhaustion, stragglers, and other problems. If Bragg was upset by the withdrawal order, he apparently did not express his concern to Beauregard.[4]

The actual situation at the landing late in the afternoon is not particularly difficult to reconstruct. Grant had stopped trying to rally the soldiers who had fled to safety below the bluff. Earlier, about four-thirty, he had made a final effort, riding to the landing and begging the stragglers to go back to the fight and redeem themselves. Promising that reinforcements would soon be on the field, and saying that he did not want to see his men disgraced, he threatened to send the cavalry down to drive them out if they did not immediately return to their commands. In about fifteen minutes a squadron of cavalry did come up. As the squadron separated into two forces, one at each end of the landing, and rode toward each other with drawn swords, the skulkers fled for security, many of them scrambling up the bank where some hung on by the roots of trees exposed on the eroded slope. When the

---

[3] *Battles and Leaders*, I, 605.
[4] Connelly, *Army*, 170.

cavalry left, however, the majority were soon in their same old place under the bluff. Here, by all accounts, were several thousand men, but Grant never was able to command their help on April 6.[5]

Nevertheless, the Union position was becoming more formidable all the time. Grant's line of defense at the landing was being strengthened as regiment after regiment fell back from around Prentiss in the Hornets' Nest, joining up with Sherman and McClernand who had been forced back by midafternoon. Sherman held the right with McClernand on his left. The Union army was now holding high ground with a relatively short line—which, of course, strengthened it—beginning at the mouth of Dill Branch, on the left, and sweeping westward in a shallow semicircle protecting the road leading up from the landing. At the Hamburg-Savannah road, on the right, the line bent back sharply to the north and covered that road for a short distance to keep it open for the expected arrival of Lew Wallace's division. Here it was covered by Tilghman Branch.

Grant's chief of artillery, Colonel J. D. Webster, meanwhile had been busy placing cannon on the left side of the line. When the Rebels came up after Prentiss surrendered, they faced about fifty Federal guns in strategic location. Some of the guns extended around to the mouth of Dill Branch where they could enfilade the attackers, but the majority were positioned to protect the landing. Infantry was massed all along the line except on the left, where the terrain made large-scale support for the batteries unnecessary. Parts of four regiments were stationed here behind the guns, and other troops could have been brought over quickly if needed.[6]

The Rebels attacking the Union left had to first cross Dill Branch, which flowed through a deep ravine in front of the Federal line. The ravine was almost impassable at the mouth;

[5] Cockerill, "Boy at Shiloh," 369.
[6] *OR*, x, part 1, 274. Wright, *6th Iowa*, 88. *Battles and Leaders*, I, 474, 590. Reed, *Battle of Shiloh*, 273. The 50 guns are established primarily on the basis of the works of Joseph W. Rich, *The Battle of Shiloh* (Iowa City, 1911), p. 73, and Manning Force, cited in Williams, *Lincoln*, III, 374. For the infantry support see Manning Force, *From Fort Henry to Corinth.* (New York, 1862), 156. Also see Simon, *Papers of Grant*, v, 33.

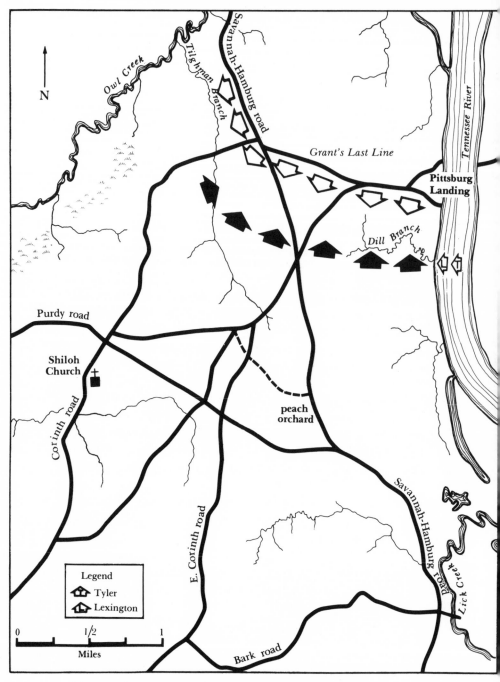

Map 11. Grant's Last Line, 6–7 P.M., April 6, 1862.

its sides were extremely steep and heavily timbered, and it was filled with water clogged with undergrowth. Even a quarter of a mile and more upstream, where the water was not as deep, the ravine was still a formidable obstacle. Another deterrent to the Rebels was the Union gunboats, *Tyler* and *Lexington*, which were anchored in the Tennessee at the mouth of the branch and were firing over the bluff and up the ravine.

The effect of the gunboat fire in influencing the Rebels to retire has been one of the many controversial aspects of the conflict. The commanders of *Lexington* and *Tyler* claimed much credit for helping to turn back the Confederate drive on the Union left in the late afternoon. Lieutenant William Gwin stated that "at 5:35, the Rebels having succeeded in gaining a position on the left of our line, . . . both vessels opened a heavy and well directed fire on them, and in a short time, in conjunction with our artillery on shore, succeeded in silencing their artillery, driving them back in confusion." Lieutenant James W. Shirk reported that the gunboat fire "silenced the enemy, and as I hear from many army officers on the field, totally demoralized his forces, driving them from their position in a perfect rout in the space of ten minutes." Grant himself said that in the repulse of this final Rebel assault on Sunday evening "much is due to the presence of the gunboats *Tyler* and *Lexington*. . . ."[7]

These accounts initially seem impressive, but a more careful examination produces a different conclusion. From the reports of the Confederate commanders who were in the area being shelled, the Rebels were not suffering heavy casualties from the gunboats. The worst damage that was done was psychological—Confederate troops and most of their commanders throughout the war had an inordinate dread of the gunboats. A number of Confederates refer to the terrible noise of the screaming shells and the heavy and fierce firing of the gunboats. Some soldiers may have been terrified and panicked thereby, supposing the danger to be far worse than it actually was. The majority, however, must have realized in

[7] *Official Records of the Union and Confederate Navies in the War of the Rebellion*, serial I, 22 vols. (Washington, D. C., 1908), XXII, 762–66. *OR*, X, part 1, 109.

The U.S.S. *Lexington* was one of two Union gunboats that supported the Federal line late on April 6 and helped thwart the Rebel attempt to seize Pittsburg Landing.

time that the shelling was not really hurting them. One Rebel reported that the gunboat fire sounded terrible, looked ugly, but hurt only a few. His men, he said, soon began to discover this fact. Another reported that the fire proved more noisy than destructive.[8]

Because of the angle of elevation which boat gunners had to use to clear the bluff, the majority of the missiles probably overshot the Rebels attacking on the Union left. Although the guns firing up the ravine at Dill Branch may have been effective at its mouth, the crooked ravine made a turn to the north a short distance from the river, making it very difficult to achieve accurate trajectories. It seems more reasonable that, rather then being decisive in turning back the Confederate attack on the Union left, the gunboats were simply another element in the Federal armor.

At the point, a short distance from the mouth of Dill Branch, where the ravine bore off first to the north and then west, it formed what resembled a crude "Y", with one arm extending toward the massive line of Union batteries that had been assembled by Colonel Webster. When the Confederates succeeded in struggling across this natural barrier, they came up to an open area looking directly into the face of Webster's cannon.[9]

The official records of the Union and Confederate armies leave no doubt about what happened; the Rebels never had much of a chance to break the Union line late in the evening. On the Union right the Confederates sporadically assaulted Sherman's and McClernand's men without ever seriously threatening the Blue line. Stragglers and the casualties of battle had depleted their ranks, and those still fighting were near exhaustion. The situation was no better for the Confederates attacking the Union left where the Gray army supposedly missed its opportunity. Bragg had the remnants of two brigades—Chalmers' and Jackson's—trying to carry the

---

[8] *OR*, x, part 1, 386–87, 410, 434, 440, 455, 466–67, 555, 559, 612, 616, 622.

[9] Anyone who thinks the Rebel attack in this area could have succeeded should spend some time tramping around in this ravine.

Infantry of the Ninth Mississippi, one of the regiments commanded at Shiloh by General Chalmers, pose here in a camp setting.

fight across the ravine with orders from him to "drive the enemy into the river."[10]

Chalmers' report speaks for itself: "In attempting to mount the last ridge we were met by a fire from a whole line of batteries protected by infantry and assisted by shells from the gunboats. Our men struggled vainly to ascend the hill, which was very steep, making charge after charge without success. . . . During this engagement Gage's [Tennessee] battery was brought up to our assistance, but suffered so severely that it was soon compelled to retire. This was the sixth fight in which we had been engaged during the day, and my men were too much exhausted to storm the batteries on the hill."[11]

Jackson's brigade was in worse shape than Chalmers'. One of his regiments had been detailed to escort prisoners to Corinth. The other three—the Seventeenth and Nineteenth Alabama and the Second Texas—possessed no more ammunition, advancing with bayonets as their only weapons. Jackson said their approach to the landing was under "a heavy fire from light batteries, siege pieces, and gunboats." After struggling through the ravine, he reported, they came up "near the crest of the opposite hill upon which the enemy's batteries were, but could not be urged farther without support. Sheltering themselves against the precipitous sides of the ravine, they remained under this fire for some time."[12]

From the Union viewpoint Stephen Hurlbut described the action: "The enemy appeared on the crest of the ridge, . . . but were cut to pieces by the steady and murderous fire of our artillery."[13]

Those who have criticized Beauregard for ordering the army to fall back about six o'clock have shown little understanding of the condition of the Rebel army or the terrain they had to cross. He has been criticized for not consulting the other commanders before withdrawing the army,[14] but his decision was the right one and was probably based, at least in part, on intelligence of the total situation of his tired and

[10] *OR*, x, part 1, 550.
[11] *Ibid.*, 550–51.
[12] *Ibid.*, 555.
[13] *Ibid.*, 205, 208.
[14] McWhiney, *Bragg*, I, 245, 246.

exhausted troops as supplied by his staff officers. Though
Beauregard would not have known it, Union reinforcements
were then at the landing; even had it been possible for the
Rebels to have stormed the Union line earlier, which appears
very doubtful, the opportunity was now gone.

The first of Buell's troops were finally arriving at the landing about 5 P.M., led off the steamer which ferried them
across the Tennessee by their division commander William
"Bull" Nelson. A blustery, profane, swaggering type, standing
well over six feet tall and weighing about 300 pounds, Nelson
put spurs to his horse and jumped him over the ship's gun-
wale. At the same instant he drew his sword and rode straight
into the crowd of stragglers (which he estimated at 7,000 to
10,000 in number) and shouted, according to a witness,
"Damn your souls, if you won't fight get out of the way, and let
men come here who will!"[15]

Jacob Ammen, who led the Tenth Brigade of Nelson's
division, was following his commander ashore. Crowding
through the mass of humanity that clogged the landing, he
heard a chaplain exhorting the stragglers with words monot-
onously repeated: "Rally, men, rally and we may yet be saved!
O Rally, for God and your country's sake, rally . . . ." It
seemed that no one was paying the least attention to his words
except for Ammen. The usually mild-mannered Ammen was
so irritated and upset by the total situation (he estimated
10,000 to 15,000 demoralized men were cowering under the
riverbank) that he shouted at the chaplain: "Shut up, you
Goddamned old fool, or I'll break your head! Get out of the
way!"[16]

Nelson, approaching the top of the bluff at the head of
three regiments, turned in his saddle and ordered his men to
"Shout 'Buell.' " Then he beat time with his saber as the soldiers came rushing up from the landing while their bands
played "Hail Columbia" and "Dixie." Their shouts were heard
above the roar of the battle by the men already in combat, and

---

[15] Wright, *6th Iowa*, 89. Cockerill, "Boy at Shiloh," 369. Nelson said in his
official report that he tried sarcasm and finally asked permission to fire on
the "Knaves" at the landing. *OR*, x, part 1, 324.

[16] *OR*, x, part 1, 333. Catton, *Grant*, 239.

all along Grant's line, the soldiers began to cheer. They cheered, as one man remembered it, "till the whole woods on either bank fairly shook." There was one man who later wrote that he was mighty glad to see the reinforcements arriving but that he did not cheer because he was not going to give Buell's troops that satisfaction.[17]

His comment points up the fact that Nelson's arrival, for all its pageantry, probably did not affect the outcome of the fight on April 6. Grant already had a line established that the Rebels in their weakened and disorganized condition could not have taken. Nelson's official report left a different impression, almost as though he were the savior of Grant's army, and it twisted the truth. He said he found a semicircle of artillery at the landing, "totally unsupported by infantry" and that "the left of the artillery was completely turned by the enemy and the gunners fled from their pieces."[18]

These statements are evidently not true, for none of the other reports confirms them. To the contrary, several reports from other sources tell of infantry supporting artillery on the left. As for gunners fleeing from their pieces, no one else from Buell's command who was there, not Ammen, nor the commanders of the Thirty-sixth Indiana and the Sixth Ohio which were stationed on the extreme left to support Captain George H. Stone's Battery K, First Missouri Light Artillery, nor Buell himself, had anything to say in their official reports about any cannon deserted by its gunners. Buell did seem to "recall" it later, but this was an assertion he took up in an article published after the war.[19] By that time he was caught up in a swirl of controversy about his contribution to the battle, which may well have destroyed his objectivity.

It might have been natural, nonetheless, for Nelson to have imagined that the Union army was then in a critical situation. He had Grant's exaggerated report from earlier in the day that the Rebel force was estimated at 100,000 men. He came

[17] Horace Cecil Fisher, "A Staff Officer's Story," 13, SNMP. Catton, *Grant*, 239. George H. Daggett, "Thrilling Moments," *Glimpses of the Nation's Struggle, A Series of Papers Read before the Minnesota Commandery, Military Order of the Loyal Legion of the U. S.* (St. Paul and Minneapolis, 1889–1909), 450.

[18] *OR*, x, part 1, 323.

[19] *Ibid.*, 292, 328, 333, 334, 337, 339. *Battles and Leaders*, I, 506.

across the river to face a swarm of stragglers, some of them trying to swim across the river or even paddle across on logs, and he had to struggle through the mob and up the bank amidst such panic-stricken cries as "We are whipped, cut to pieces." He could also see the wounded all about him. Then upon reaching the top of the bluff, one of the men riding with his staff was decapitated by a cannonball; another shot dismounted a second member of his staff, breaking the back of his horse, and then the ball plunged on through the infantry line causing several casualties. Nelson had suddenly found himself in the midst of awesome smoke, sound, and destruction such as he had never encountered before. In the near approaching twilight Confederate batteries were shelling the Union line, Webster's fifty-two guns were blazing, scores of muskets were crashing up and down the line, and this also was apparently the time—between five and six o'clock—when the gunboats opened their heaviest fire, creating a low-throated rumble that seemed to make the ground quiver as they slammed their 8-inch and 32-pounder projectiles into the Rebels from the river.[20]

At least one man who had been in the battle all day long thought the sound at this time was the worst it had ever been. Another described it as loud enough to deafen a person. Men of the Eighty-first Ohio, positioned slightly in front of some of Webster's guns, claimed that the thunderous discharges knocked their hats off. One soldier believed that the concussion had almost broken his neck. Some discovered blood coming from their noses and ears because of the violent concussion, and not a few experienced permanent damage to their hearing.[21]

Such were the scenes that Nelson and his command were marching into. It is not surprising that some of them thought they had arrived "in the nick of time" to save Grant's army, despite the fact, probably unknown to them, that the Union position was by then much more favorable than that of the Confederates. The shortened line along easily traversable

[20] *Battles and Leaders*, I, 324. Cockerill, "Boy at Shiloh," 369, 370. Fisher, "Story," 13, 14.

[21] Cockerill, "Boy at Shiloh," 369. Catton, *Grant*, 240. Wright, *6th Iowa*, 88.

ground gave the Union army the ability to quickly send reinforcements to any threatened point, certainly before the Rebels, admittedly disorganized and facing rugged terrain, could assemble enough troops to solidify a temporary advantage.

Although it seems highly likely that Grant's army could have held its line if Buell's troops had not started arriving on April 6, the most important point is that several thousand of Buell's men were there by nightfall, whether needed or not. Even if the Rebel "lost opportunity" thesis could be sustained on other grounds, Buell's arrival would undermine it completely.

In ordering the army to retire from the enemy's guns on Sunday evening Beauregard was, in part, only recognizing what was already taking place. Reports from regimental and brigade commanders show that some commands were falling back without orders. In the rear areas hordes of men were plundering the Union camps or resting on their arms, tired and hungry; many of them were too exhausted even to cheer when they were told, strangely enough, that they had won a great victory. Many units were scattered and disorganized, and the sun was going down. The Confederate army was "fought out" when Beauregard issued the withdrawal order.

Obviously overconfident, and not aware of Buell's arrival, Beauregard believed that the Union army would retreat during the night, or if it stayed, the Confederates would drive it into the river the next day.[22] Praising the Lord, he dispatched a "victory" telegram to Richmond in which he said: "After a severe battle of ten hours, thanks be to the Almighty, we gained a complete victory, driving the enemy from every position. . . ."[23]

Beauregard was not the only one who was overconfident. A Rebel private was sending a message back home: "The victory was complete and glorious. Beauregard forever!" Corps commanders were coming into Sherman's old tent, which Beauregard had taken for his own use, exuding optimism that victory was theirs, and an attack the next day would destroy the Union army. What they wanted to believe was being

[22] Williams, *Beauregard*, 142.
[23] *OR*, x, part 1, 384.

"confirmed" by a dispatch from Abraham Lincoln's Confederate brother-in-law in northern Alabama, Colonel Ben Hardin Helm, who had reported that Buell's command was not marching toward Pittsburg Landing as first reported, but was instead approaching Decatur. Furthermore, the Confederate commanders apparently did not know that Lew Wallace's division had not fought with Grant on Sunday, although his troops had been observed on their march by some Confederate cavalry.[24]

Probably the Union army could have been beaten on the first day at Shiloh if the Rebel commanders had conducted the battle, particularly the attack plan, with a little more skill and if they had relied a little more on finesse, a little less on muscle. Even as it was, Grant's army was pushed back, driven from position after position, the remnants of two divisions surrendering, always outnumbered, taking heavy losses, almost but never quite broken, and finally occupying a line two and one-half miles behind its original position.

These are the reasons why the Confederates imagined they had success in their grasp. They did not realize that, in effect, the Union force had become stronger as a result of its retreat—ultimately reaching more defensible ground as well as concentrating its troops and artillery along a much shorter line.

Some Union soldiers also were not yet aware that the fortunes of war were shifting in their favor as dusk was gathering in the late afternoon. When McPherson rejoined Grant after helping conduct Wallace's men to the battlefield, he asked the general if he should make preparations to retreat. Grant seemed a bit surprised by his question. "No," he replied, "I propose to attack at daylight and whip them."[25] Sometime later that night Sherman came up to Grant. Grant was standing under a tree, and it was raining. He had experienced at least one close brush with death when a shot struck the metal scabbard of his sword just below the belt and broke it nearly off. Sherman recalled that Grant was holding a lantern and

---

[24] New Orleans *Daily Picayune*, Apr. 8, 1862. Williams, *Beauregard*, 143. *Battles and Leaders*, I, 591.

[25] Catton, *Grant*, 241.

chewing on a cigar. He had his coat collar pulled up around his ears and his hat pulled down over his face to cover him from the rain. Sherman started to ask Grant about retreating but changed his mind at the last second before he spoke. "Well Grant," said Sherman, "we've had the devil's own day, haven't we?" "Yes," replied Grant, "lick 'em tommorow, though."[26]

The Union army held a strong position; it had 7,000 fresh troops on its right wing where Lew Wallace had come up. The steamers continued to ferry Buell's men across the Tennessee, and they were taking position on the army's left. By morning about 17,000 of them would be in line. With more than 24,000 additional men on hand, Grant's confidence was not without justification.

[26] Grant, *Memoirs*, I, 354. Grant said the incident occurred on Monday, but on the basis of other accounts, by Buell and Douglas Putnam, Jr., it was probably Sunday. Sword, *Shiloh*, 350. Interview with Sherman, Washington (D. C.) *Post*, Dec. 30, 1893.

10. *A Night So Long, So Hideous*

THE RAIN CAME SLOWLY at first, then gradually fell harder and harder until it beat against the ground in torrents. Continuing through most of the night, the downpour was accompanied by a cold, chilling wind that swept the battlefield. An intense darkness was broken only by flashes of lightning and the fuses of shells in the sky momentarily illuminating scenes of wasted humanity. Every fifteen minutes, all night long, a gun on each of the Union gunboats roared from the Tennessee River, sending two giant 8-inch shells arching toward the Confederate lines, their red fuses lighting up the starless night for a brief instant before they came screaming down, exploding and scattering fragments of iron in all directions.[1]

The shells were intended primarily to terrorize the Rebels, but many Union soldiers found that the thunderous roar to be expected from the gunboats at such regular intervals made their own night miserable and sleep impossible. A member of the Forty-first Ohio Infantry bitterly described the constant shelling as "one of the . . . stupidities of the war. . . ." And Confederate General Pat Cleburne reported that while some of the shells burst close to his men, he thought the majority were falling among the wounded Union soldiers "who were strewn thickly between my camp and the river. History records few instances of more reckless inhumanity than this."[2]

Many of the wounded, Confederate and Union, were spending an agonizing night—the last night some would ever

---

[1] Barber, *15th Illinois*, 56. Thomas, *14th Iowa*, ch. v. Charles Hubert, *History of the 50th Regiment Illinois Volunteer Infantry* (Kansas City, 1894), 94. Wilbur F. Crummer, *With Grant at Fort Donelson, Shiloh, and Vicksburg* (Oak Park, Ill., 1915), 68. *OR*, x, part 1, 582.

[2] Kimberly and Holloway, *Forty-first Ohio*, 23. *OR*, x, part 1, 582, 583.

know—in the blackness between the lines of the armies. As the flashes of lightning lit the fields and the rolling timberland, they found themselves alone, except for other wounded and the innumerable bodies of the dead.

General W. H. L. Wallace lay that night within the Rebel lines, unattended except that someone during that period covered him with a blanket. His wife had spent the day on the steamboat. While ever conscious of the insistent sounds of battle, she noted the panic-stricken men at the landing who had fled from the struggle and saw the arrival of Buell's reinforcements, and at times she helped care for the wounded who were brought on board. She remembered that one officer, obviously irrational, had drawn his pistol and tried to force the steamboat captain to load his men on board and ferry them across the river. In a few moments, however, he seemed to control himself and put his gun away.

Late in the evening a man from her hometown in Illinois came up to Ann Wallace. She thought he looked worn and depressed. He had been wounded though not seriously. "This is an awful battle," he said. "Yes, but these fresh troops will yet win the day," she replied. He reminded her that she had many relatives in the battle and could not expect that all of them would come through safely. Ann's reply, as she remembered it, was that they had all come safely through the battle of Fort Donelson, and her husband, now a division commander, should be in a comparatively safe position. The friend then repeated his earlier comment, "It is an awful battle." Looking at him carefully, she now knew what he was trying to tell her.

Almost at the same time her brother Cyrus, who had been with her husband when he fell, came in and provided some of the details. He explained how he and another man tried to bring the body back to the landing, but could not because the Rebels were closing in around them. In her grief Ann, who could not possibly sleep, spent most of the night in helping care for the increasing number of wounded arriving on board.[3]

There were others on the battleground that night who, like Wallace, appeared to be dead when they were actually still

[3] Wallace, *Letters*, 197–99.

alive. Such a case was recorded by B. F. Thomas of the Four-teenth Iowa, a veteran of the Hornets' Nest who before his capture in the late afternoon had passed the body of a com-rade lying on his back, apparently the victim of a bullet above the right eye. Thomas reported that he stopped beside the body and fired a shot at the Rebels before moving on. Thomas was sure, as were his companions, that the man was dead. Actually the man was not only alive, but also conscious, though unable to say anything to Thomas. All night he lay there in the rain and was finally found still alive the day after the Confederates retreated to Corinth.[4]

To those who fought over the battlefield the next day, it appeared that in some places several wounded men had crawled up together, perhaps in the hope of gaining some assistance from one another. All had evidently bled to death during the night.

Some of the wounded who were able to move tried to drag themselves to water, a number of them finding a pond which lay north of the peach orchard. Here they quenched their thirst, and here some died, soldiers of both armies, side by side. The little body of water became so colored by the blood of casualties that it came to be known thereafter as "Bloody Pond." A nearby resident who visited the scene after the battle was appalled by the sight of the pond and surrounding area—all strewn with the bodies of soldiers and horses inter-mingled with broken gun carriages, and part of this sickening debris half submerged in blood-tinted water. After looking at the pond itself, he said later, he wanted to see no more of the battlefield and left.[5]

The wounded who were lucky made it back to their lines. A Union soldier on picket duty shortly before midnight was startled by the cracking of twigs in the darkness to his front. With musket ready to fire he listened as the noise came closer and closer, slowly, until there appeared from the darkness a wounded soldier, shot in the leg, hobbling in with the broken ramrod of a cannon for a crutch.[6]

[4] Thomas, *14th Iowa*, ch. IV.
[5] Crummer, *With Grant*, 67. Tom Walker, statement about the "Bloody Pond," SNMP.
[6] Crummer, *With Grant*, 69, 70.

Before the peace was shattered at Shiloh, the small body of water that became known as "Bloody Pond" probably resembled the pond as it appears today, above. Contrasting sharply is the battle sketch below, showing casualties of both sides coloring the water with their blood as they bathe wounds and quench their thirst.

The colonel of the Fiftieth Illinois, with a bullet wound in his right thigh, was not so fortunate. Captured and taken to a Confederate field hospital he received a teaspoonful of alcohol from a surgeon. He then lay exposed to the rain, without care or food, all night and all the next day until the Rebels left him as they retreated. He was finally found by an Ohio regiment.[7]

Soldiers reported that all during the night they could hear the groans and cries of the wounded lying out on the field in the mud and rain. Some called for water, others for relief from their suffering. Many years later, the most distinct memories of Shiloh to one participant were the night sounds of the wounded pleading for water from out on the battlefield.[8]

It was a terrible night. Thousands of men had been wounded, and their pain allowed them little or no rest. Those who had escaped injury were thoroughly exhausted, wet, cold, and often hungry. They were unable to obtain food, and they were too miserable to get adequate rest. One Union officer reported that his men, "lying in the water and mud, were as weary in the morning as they had been the evening before."[9]

Grant, although he could have found dry quarters on one of the boats, spent the night on the battlefield. His first concern was to see that the army was being positioned properly, directing that his own divisions draw up in battle formation on the right, with Buell's two first arriving divisions taking the left as they came off the boats. Grant then tried to steal a little sleep under a large oak tree near the landing, but it was impossible. The rain continued incessantly, and his ankle, which had been hurt a short time before the battle when his horse fell with him, was aching. Around midnight he tried to find shelter in a log cabin up on the bluff where he had maintained his headquarters, but he found that the surgeons had taken it over and were operating on the wounded, in some cases severing arms and legs. The screams were too much for Grant. "The sight

[7] Hubert, *5oth Illinois*, 95, 96, 103.
[8] Crummer, *With Grant*, 69, 70.
[9] Catton, *Grant*, 241.

was more unendurable than encountering the enemy's fire," he said in his *Memoirs*, "and I returned to my tree in the rain."[10]

John A. Cockerill of the Twenty-fourth Ohio was down at the landing. His impressions of that night on the bank of the Tennessee River provide a sober picture of hours that seemed never to end and of depression, discomfort, and frustration. The sixteen-year-old Cockerill had been told that his father was killed earlier in the day. As he stood there on the river-bank, he chanced upon a member of the Seventh Ohio, which his father had commanded, and the two sat down on a bale of hay while Cockerill listened to his comrade's disconcerting story, "in which nearly all his friends and acquaintances figured as corpses." As they sat there, the rain, "a streaming, drenching, semi-tropical downpour," never ceased, said Cockerill, and it continued until far into the next day.[11]

Later Cockerill curled up against the haybale in an attempt to sleep, but the roar of the gunboat cannons seemed almost to lift him from his water-soaked bed. And all night long, continued Cockerill, the transports bringing Buell's men up the river to a landing not far from his resting place "wheezed and groaned, and came and went, with their freight of humanity," disgorging soldiers who marched by him to take their places in the battle line. Their path was churned into knee-deep mud as the men sloshed by with their canteens rattling against bayonet scabbards, the officers urging them to close up ranks and the men grumbling and cursing.

Every now and then an artillery piece would get stuck in the mud, Cockerill wrote, and then "a grand turmoil of half an hour followed, during which time every man found in the neighborhood was impressed to aid in relieving the embargoed gun. The whipping of the horses and the cursing of the drivers" were often mixed with the "soul-shattering" gunboat blasts. "There never was a night so long, so hideous, or so utterly uncomfortable."[12]

To a Confederate soldier, the night "was too shocking, too

[10] Grant, *Memoirs*, I, 349.
[11] Cockerill, "Boy at Shiloh," 370.
[12] *Ibid*.

horrible. God grant that I may never be the partaker in such scenes again. . . . When released from this I shall ever be an advocate of peace."[13] On the other hand, some soldiers, perhaps of a different temperament or because of exhaustion, reported sleeping well that night.

Many of the Confederates were busy plundering the Federal camps they had captured. Bragg's principal aide, David Urquhart, said that more than a third of the army was engaged in such pillaging. Here the hungry soldiers found tea, coffee, cheese, hardtack, bacon, and occasionally liquor. They were also fascinated by Yankee personal possessions left in the camps, letters from home, pictures of girl friends and wives. Not all of the looting was perpetrated by soldiers, however. Civilians who had been trailing the Rebel advance also rushed in to seize their share of the spoils.[14]

Some of the soldiers sat around enjoying the "victory" and comforting each other with the thought that the Federals would flee across the river. The only unfinished business was to bury the dead and care for the wounded. Some had even started back to Corinth, figuring the Union had been whipped and they might as well go home, although some were too "fought out" to move or, like their Federal counterparts under the bluff, too scared to fight any more.

Everywhere behind the Confederate lines was confusion and disorganization. Beauregard's order to withdraw had implied a regrouping for a final blow in the morning, but efforts to reorganize the army were at best only partially successful in the wet, soggy blackness of the night. Hardee was switched from commanding on the left to the right; he would have two of Bragg's brigades under his direction when the fighting was resumed the next morning. Bragg was to take the far left and incorporate one of Polk's divisions in his command. Breckinridge and Polk were to take the right-center and left-center, respectively. The command situation was to be entirely different from the deployment of troops that engaged the Union army during the afternoon of April 6.

Many Confederates apparently made little effort to find

[13] Catton, *Grant*, 224.
[14] *OR*, x, part 1, 467, 469. New Orleans *Daily Picayune*, Apr. 12, 1862.

their regiments, brigades, or divisions. After the fighting had ceased—or after they had finished plundering—they simply slept upon their arms in the first convenient spot they found. Some who did try to locate their units in the darkness and confusion never succeeded.[15]

James Chalmers reported that Cavalry Commander Nathan Bedford Forrest came up to him about midnight and asked first for the headquarters of Beauregard, then of Bragg, Polk, and Hardee. When Chalmers could not provide any of these directions, Forrest then asked where Chalmers' own command was located. Chalmers answered that his troops were sleeping in line before him with their guns by their sides, to which Forrest replied, "You are the first general I have found tonight who knows where his men are!"

An unaccountable action was the decision by General Polk to take Cheatham's entire division out of line and march it back to Hardee's encampment site of the previous night—a distance of approximately three miles. Polk may have feared a flanking movement by the Federals, or misunderstood Beauregard's retirement order, or sought rations for the men—all of these suggestions have been offered in his defense. Whatever the reason, when the Union army attacked the next morning at dawn, Beauregard did not even know where the division was. By the time it was located and then brought to the battle site, the latter about ten-thirty, the fight had already been raging for several hours.[16]

As might be expected from the overconfidence that permeated the Rebel ranks, from private to officer, and from the confusion that existed the night of April 6, the Confederates were caught off guard, both tactically and psychologically, when the Union army carried the fight to them the next morning.[17]

Some warnings were received but given little heed. One

[15] *OR*, x, part 1, 467, *Battles and Leaders*, 1, 591.

[16] *OR*, x, part 1, 410, 411, 440. Johnston, *Life*, 637. Roman, *Beauregard*, 1, 313. *Battles and Leaders*, 1, 591. Jacob Thompson to P. G. T. Beauregard, Apr. 17, 1863, P. G. T. Beauregard Papers, Confederate Records Division, National Archives.

[17] *OR*, x, part 1, 467. Thomas Firth, Reminiscences, Confederate Collection, TSLA.

alert was in fact conveyed by a Union officer. General Prentiss told his Confederate captors that Buell's troops would be on hand by morning to reinforce Grant. Prentiss was sharing a makeshift bed, sandwiched between Beauregard's staff officer, Jacob Thompson, and the Creole's chief of staff, Thomas Jordan, in a tent close to Shiloh Church. Prentiss and Thompson had been acquainted with each other before the war and talked freely. As Jordan remembered it, Prentiss said with a laugh: "You gentlemen have had your way today, but it will be very different tomorrow. You'll see! Buell will effect a junction with Grant tonight, and we'll turn the tables on you in the morning." Jordan said he showed Prentiss the telegram which had come in from Colonel Helm stating that Buell was marching toward Decatur, Alabama. Prentiss then insisted that the dispatch was a mistake, and the Confederates would see in the morning. But neither Thompson nor Jordan believed him.[18]

In the Rebel camp Beauregard and Bragg finally went to sleep in Sherman's old tent. Apparently neither of them expected Buell to arrive in time to aid Grant. In his report of the battle Beauregard said he received another note, sometime after the one which came from Colonel Helm, stating that Buell was moving to join Grant after all but would not be available to assist the Union forces the next day.[19]

Beauregard later had another version of what happened. When it was implied that he had not known of Buell's presence, he maintained that he had realized all along that Buell, and Wallace as well, was reinforcing Grant. In fact, he said it was because he expected to face the fresh troops of Buell and Wallace the next day that he called off the battle on the evening of April 6. If he actually believed that Buell and Wallace would reinforce Grant by morning, he was strangely inactive in preparing to fight such a large force. As the controversy over his actions continued, Beauregard in the late summer of 1862 came up with the most convenient account of

[18] *Battles and Leaders*, I, 602, 603. Thomas Jordon and J. P. Pryor, *Campaigns and Battles of Lieutenant General Nathan Bedford Forrest and His Cavalry* (New Orleans, 1868), 135, 136.
[19] *OR*, x, part 1, 387.

From Indian mounds such as the one above, Confederate scouts spied on enemy reinforcements that had crossed the Tennessee River on steamers during the night following Sunday's battle.

all; he said his memory of what happened was "not very distinct"; he was "so unwell" at the time that he feared his recollection of "certain particulars" might "betray" him.[20]

At least one Confederate officer, however, did know of Buell's presence, for his men had seen Buell's forces arriving. Cavalry Commander Forrest had sent scouts in Union disguise sneaking toward the landing, and from some old Indian mounds close to the river the Rebel observers could see and hear Federal troops marching off the steamers that had ferried them up the Tennessee to the Union camp.

With his scouts' report in hand, Forrest was convinced that the situation was critical. He went in search of officers with the authority to get action. Finally locating Hardee, Forrest told him what his scouts had seen and advised that the Rebels should try to surprise the Union army with a night attack, attempting to drive them into the river before they could recover their balance, or else plan a retreat. If they waited until morning, Forrest said, the Confederates would be "whipped like Hell." Although Hardee did not seem impressed, he told Forrest to find Beauregard and relay the scouting report to him. After wandering about for a while in a futile search for the army's commander, Forrest returned to his camp and sent out his scouts again. The time was then around two o'clock in the morning, and the report of the scouts was the same—Union reinforcements still coming up the river, thousands of them. The anxious Forrest went back to Hardee again, but amazingly, that author of a widely used textbook on military tactics, merely told Forrest to return to his command and "keep up a vigilant, strong picket-line" and "report all hostile movements." The disgusted, frustrated Forrest stomped off and gave up.[21]

It was inconceivable, and yet it all happened: a Confederate corps commander taking a major portion of a division and disappearing from the battlefield; a Union general offering

[20] Thomas Jordan, "The Lost Opportunity at Shiloh," MS in J. F. H. Claiborne Papers, UNC. P. G. T. Beauregard to Thomas Jordan, July 17, 1862, Aug. 8, 1862, Beauregard Papers, LC.

[21] Robert Selph Henry, *"First with the Most" Forrest* (Jackson, Tenn., 1944), 79.

intelligence to Rebel staff officers about Federal reinforcements but being disbelieved; a Confederate corps commander failing to take action after twice receiving reliable information that large numbers of Union reinforcements were at hand; and Beauregard, the commander of the Rebel army, relaxing for the night without taking proper steps to reorganize the army or determine what the enemy was doing.

11. *Glory Cannot Atone*

DAWN WAS GRAYING THE EAST as Grant awoke from his makeshift bed under a large oak tree on April 7 and issued orders to his generals to "advance and recapture our original camps." To the gunboats he sent word to stop their bombardment: the army was going forward. Grant was attacking with seven divisions, a total of 45,000 men pushing out against the Rebels. Commanding his divisions, from left to right, were Nelson, Thomas L. Crittenden, and Alexander McCook of Buell's Army of the Ohio, and Hurlbut, McClernand, Sherman, and Lew Wallace of Grant's Army of the Tennessee. There was to be nothing fancy about the assault. Grant was simply driving straight ahead in an effort to overpower the Confederates. It was a mismatch in numbers, for Beauregard had only 20,000 to 25,000 soldiers available—the lower figure most probably—to stop the Union onslaught.[1]

Inasmuch as the Rebels had broken contact and pulled back all along the line the previous night, except on the western extremity where Preston Pond had not received Beauregard's orders to fall back, the first advance of the Union army was not difficult, encountering little more than scattered resistance from Confederate pickets. Nevertheless the offensive was not as rapid as it might have been if the Federals had been better organized. Although they were more adequately prepared than the Confederates, some of their commands were badly intermingled. Sherman, for example, was attempting to position Stuart's brigade, which had been separated from him all through Sunday's fight, on the left of his command before going forward. And Hurlbut was trying to find a little some-

[1] *OR*, x, part 1, 570.

thing for his men to eat—"a few crackers," as he expressed it—before moving out. About nine o'clock Grant had to personally order him to advance his division in support of McClernand, who had gone forward sometime earlier.[2]

On the Union left Nelson had at first moved out easily against scattered pockets of Confederate resistance, but then, his flank being exposed, he had to stop and wait for Crittenden to form on his right. Upon trying to resume the advance he found the Rebels to his front had concentrated into a stubborn line supported by artillery, stopping his forward progress and, in fact, forcing his division to give ground.[3] Far from being smoothly coordinated, the Union line of advance was sputtering, jerking, and moving forward in very uneven fashion. By eight o'clock, it had virtually ground to a halt all along the front.

The effectiveness of the Confederate resistance was remarkable considering the losses suffered on Sunday and the disorganized condition of the army when the second day of the battle started. Weary, exhausted men struggling to drag themselves awake were shocked and caught off balance; having expected to be the attackers and finish the work begun on Sunday, if indeed the Union army was still on the battlefield, they were surprised to find their enemies advancing upon them in force. Many soldiers were separated from their units, some officers could not even find their commands, and chaos and confusion ruled the sodden and devastated battleground in the early minutes of the fighting.

John K. Jackson, brigadier general commanding the Third Brigade of Withers' Second Division of Bragg's corps, reported that he was unable to locate his command in spite of what he called a "diligent search" for it, and finally, at the request of a staff officer, took command of three new regiments near the road below Shiloh Church and began rallying stragglers. There was more confusion in Withers' division. Colonel Zack C. Deas, commanding the First Brigade after the wounding of Gladden and Adams, had become separated

---

[2] *Ibid.*, 518, 251, 205.
[3] *Ibid.*, 324.

from two of his regiments, the Twenty-first and Twenty-fifth
Alabama, during the latter stages of the battle on April 6. He
did not find them after night came on, and worse yet, had no
idea at daylight on the seventh where even his parent division
was located. He had just sent a captain to hunt for the division
when the Union army advanced. Deas assembled the fragments of his brigade and placed them in action on the left of
R. M. Russell's brigade.[4]

Withers' was not the only Rebel division experiencing such
confusion. Cheatham, as already noted, had taken most of his
Second Division of Polk's corps back to its campsite of the
previous night. But a large portion of one regiment of the
Second Brigade, the Seventh Kentucky, had remained near
the center of the firing line. The regiment's colonel, Charles
Wickliffe, returned to the camp with Cheatham, spent the
night with the division, and consequently was not with his men
at the front when the battle began in the morning. When
Beauregard discovered the Seventh Kentucky near the front
without a commander, he called a staff officer to take charge,
move the men to the firing line, and command them until the
regiment's colonel arrived. A member of that regiment later
claimed that, once under fire, the officer whom Beauregard
had placed in charge was seen no more.[5]

The regiment fought for a while, seemingly without any
commander, and did well. It even went on the attack, led
forward at one point by a company captain, and in conjunction with the regiments on either side, drove the Federals back
for a distance. Finally, Colonel Wickliffe appeared with the
rest of the regiment and continued the fight until he was killed
while leading a charge about noon.[6]

Cheatham was having problems also. His division, already
handicapped by its distance from the combat area, was
further delayed in reaching battle when it attempted to stop
what Polk termed a stampede of men running away from the
front. Additionally, the Second Brigade of Cheatham's unit,

[4] *OR*, x, part 1, 555, 538, 539.
[5] Henry George, "The 7th Kentucky at Shiloh," SNMP.
[6] *OR*, x, part 1, 440–42.

with most of its Seventh Kentucky absent on the firing line, was now looking for the Ninth Tennessee, much of which had become separated from the main force during the night. The brigade commander was just beginning to search for the missing companies of the regiment when a staff officer from Withers arrived with orders to bring his troops forward to reinforce the Confederate line on the extreme right.[7]

Over on the Rebel left, Preston Pond, discovering too late that the main line of the Confederates had fallen back the previous night, found his brigade in a perilous position, alone in the face of a strong force of Federals. He escaped this dilemma with the aid of Captain William Ketchum's Alabama Battery, which came up to protect his right flank while the regiments were drawn off, but Pond's problems continued. His brigade, in one of the battle's most conspicuous examples of command confusion, was marched first here, then there, until it had traveled from one end of the Rebel line to the other—all in response to a succession of five different orders Pond received during the morning. The brigade finally saw action on the extreme left—the same location from which it had started the day.[8]

All along the line, from Beauregard on down the chain of command, the Rebels were doing the only thing left to them: following a sort of "make yourself useful" policy, as they rushed available troops to fill the gaps in the line without regard to command structure. At one point Beauregard himself seized the colors of a regiment and led two brigades in a charge that drove the Union line back at that sector.

Some commanders who had their units well in hand simply did not have enough men available to them. Pat Cleburne reported that his brigade had been reduced from about 2,700 men originally to only 800 on Monday morning. Two of his regiments, the Second Tennessee and the Sixth Mississippi, were absent altogether, virtually wiped out in the fighting of the previous day. Hundreds of his best men were dead or in the hospitals, and, "I blush to add," he wrote, "hundreds of

---

[7] *Ibid.*, 411, 456.
[8] *Ibid.*, 518, 519, 528.

others had run off" either as cowards or as thieves, the latter loaded with plunder from the Yankee camps.[9]

There were others also who deserted their units on Monday morning. Hardee said he placed a regiment in action on the right of the Rebel line and before half its guns had been discharged it broke and fled. Although the general sent one of his staff officers in pursuit to rally the command, the effort was futile, some of the men swearing they would not return to the field. When the officer told them that General Hardee would label them "a pack of cowards," they responded, according to the officer, that they "did not care a damn what [Hardee] might call them."[10]

The rain of the previous night had not helped matters either. In some cases, the ammunition of individual soldiers had become so wet that they could not fire their weapons. The troops were crossing the same ground that had been bitterly contested the previous day, and the battlefield was littered with dead horses, dead and wounded men, and destroyed and abandoned equipment. All this debris of war further impeded the progress of battle.

In spite of these myriad difficulties and a seemingly endless confusion (reflected on page after page of the official reports of the Confederate officers), the Rebels had somehow managed to place enough men in the line to stabilize it by eight o'clock. And most of them, Beauregard said, were exhibiting a "veteran-like steadiness" in the face of exceedingly heavy pressure.[11]

From left to right, the Confederate line was held by units commanded by Pond, Russell, Wood, Gibson, Anderson, Trabue, Martin, Statham, Cleburne, Stewart, Maney, Smith, Moore, and Chalmers. General Hardee was in overall command on the right, Breckinridge in the center, and Bragg on the left. When Polk finally came up, he was given a portion of the line between Breckinridge and Bragg.

By the time the armies confronted each other in force, the Union left, under Nelson and Crittenden, had reached the

[9] *OR*, x, part 1, 583.
[10] *Ibid.*, 570, 571, 572.
[11] *Ibid.*, 546, 387.

area where the troops of Hurlbut, Prentiss, and W. H. L. Wallace had fought on Sunday afternoon. The peach orchard and the ravine where Johnston had died were in front of Nelson, whereas the Hornets' Nest was in front of Crittenden's division. The line was prolonged in the same general northwestern direction by the commands of McCook, Hurlbut (coming up in reserve), McClernand, and Sherman. Sherman's right flank rested in the Jones field, and then Lew Wallace's division, once Pond's Rebel brigade had been forced back, anchored the right flank of the army, continuing almost due west to within about a quarter of a mile of Owl Creek.[12]

On the Union left fighting swirled once again about the Bloody Pond, the peach orchard, and the Sunken Road. The Rebels had two sections of a battery (probably Felix H. Robertson's Florida battery) placed at the southeastern edge of the peach orchard field and a full battery of six guns (the Washington Artillery) about a third of a mile to the west and slightly north, at the eastern end of Davis' wheat field.

The advance of Nelson's division was stopped. His soldiers waited for artillery to be brought up. Since Nelson's batteries had been left at Savannah, General Buell directed two rifled batteries of the Fourth U. S. Artillery (John Mendenhall's guns) to the front immediately. A third section of 12-pound howitzers joined up a little later. Swinging into action just north of the Bloody Pond at the southern end of the Wicker field, these guns alternately engaged the Confederate batteries beyond the peach orchard and those in the wheat field, firing on the latter by watching the smoke of their pieces. Mendenhall dispersed his guns to avoid a concentration of fire from the Rebels, and the Confederate gunners were shifting their pieces for the same reason.[13]

When a lull occurred in the artillery duel, sometime between nine and ten o'clock, Blue skirmishers of the First Kentucky and the Ninth Indiana of Nelson's division charged and drove the Rebel cannoneers from several of their pieces.[14] They were supported, at Nelson's orders, by the

---

[12] *Ibid.*, 293, 355, 335. *Battles and Leaders*, I, 526–30.
[13] *OR*, x, part 1, 373.
[14] *Ibid.*, 293, 294, 348, 342, 350.

Second Kentucky. The Federals managed to seize one of the Confederate guns, but they could hold it only a few minutes in the face of a countercharge by the Louisiana Crescent Regiment. As two more regiments joined the Rebel line the fighting here raged intense, soldiers in some instances battling hand to hand with the bayonet. The colonel of the Second Kentucky reported an awesome slaughter on both sides, and Union brigade commander Sanders Bruce estimated that within the very small compass of the fighting area, 200 of the Confederates could be counted lying dead upon the field.[15]

The Blue line retreated, the Second Kentucky alone having lost nearly two-thirds of its strength, and the struggle seemed to be turning in favor of the Rebels as the Confederate infantry now came charging through the underbrush west of the Wicker field in an effort to silence the Federal artillery.[16]

Mendenhall's guns staggered the oncoming Gray ranks, pouring case shot into their lines and changing to canister as the Rebels closed in. The force of the fire was unbearable, and the Confederates gave ground. A section of William Terrill's Battery H, Fifth U. S. Artillery, was now in position on the left of Mendenhall's guns. Terrill's cannoneers had unlimbered and advanced their four Napoleons west of the Savannah-Hamburg road to command the peach orchard field. The Rebel artillery again opened fire on the Union guns and followed the shelling with infantry advancing against both flanks of Terrill's Napoleons. The fighting was desperate as the First, Second, and Sixth Kentucky, the Ninth Indiana, and the Twenty-fourth and Forty-first Ohio struggled to hold the line.[17]

Three times the Rebels charged and three times they were beaten back. At one point only two men were manning one of Terrill's Napoleons, and another Federal, handling the other gun of the section, stayed at his post although wounded in the head by a musket ball. Only when he was struck in the leg by another missile did he give up and crawl away. An infantry

[15] *OR*, x, part 1, 349, 514, 351, 343, 322.
[16] *Ibid*., 352, 321, 322, 341, 373, 374, 524.
[17] *Ibid*., 343.

sergeant was directed to bring up ammunition for the guns but had hardly begun when he too was shot down.[18]

At last the issue of battle turned against the Rebels when Union brigade commander Colonel William Hazen ordered his drummers to beat the charge. With fixed bayonets the men of his brigade surged forward, driving the Confederates before them for perhaps three-quarters of a mile, at which point they encountered a new Confederate line, this one supported by a battery of artillery. It did not hold, however, as the Blue line pushed forward into the very face of the guns and cut down the cannoneers, one of them stabbed by a bowie knife that had been taken from a captured Texan.[19]

Death had now returned with renewed violence to the battered woods and fields of Shiloh, striking at Blue and Gray, young and old, privates and officers. Major Charles H. Levanway, coming into Savannah the previous day with the Thirty-fourth Illinois, Fifth Brigade of McCook's division, had a strong premonition of death, a premonition that was realized within hours. Sometime before noon on Monday, as he sat astride his mount to the rear of the Thirty-fourth's line, he was struck fatally by a canister shot that destroyed the bone in his neck. An observer described him falling to the ground on his stomach yet with his face grotesquely turned upward.[20]

Another Federal who had been firing from behind a tree stepped out in front of the Fourth Louisiana and waved his hand in token of surrender. But some of the Confederates, either not understanding or not caring, leveled their guns at him and riddled his body with bullets.[21]

On the extreme right of the army a Union regiment found itself pinned down by Rebel fire. Manning Force remembered that suddenly a shell landed on top of a soldier. Terrified, the soldier scrambled to get it off, but instantly it exploded and tore him to pieces.[22]

Such gruesome scenes were accentuated by the macabre

[18] *Ibid.*, 322.
[19] *Ibid.*, 341, 342, 343.
[20] E. W. Payne, *Thirty-Fourth Illinois* (Clinton, Iowa, 1902), 20.
[21] Richardson, "Shiloh."
[22] Force Papers.

residue from Sunday's battle. As Jacob Ammen's troops of
Nelson's division reached an area where heavy fighting had
taken place the previous afternoon, the ground was strewn
with dead and wounded, among whom the Federals were
predominant. A soldier recalled:

> A considerable number of wounded had crawled or been carried
> to one of the ravines, out of range of the fire which swept the
> slopes above. Many had died there, and others were in the last
> agonies as we passed. Their groans and cries were heart-rending.
> One poor fellow begged most piteously to be put out of his misery
> and another kept repeating, "O God, have mercy! O God, O God!"
> until we passed out of hearing. The gory corpses lying all about
> us, in every imaginable attitude, and slain by an inconceivable
> variety of wounds, were shocking to behold, but they made no
> sign and claimed no recognition; their sufferings were over.[23]

There were other reminders of Sunday's butchery as once
again foolish orders sometimes contributed to the devasta-
tion. Pat Cleburne, fighting against Buell's army in the area
just south of the Sunken Road, received a command from
Breckinridge to move forward in conjunction with the latter's
frontal attack on the Federals. Although Cleburne protested
that he was without support on his left and would be destroyed if he tried to attack, he was told to obey the order
immediately, that it was a command from General Bragg.
Cleburne moved forward only to find himself in a wooded
valley, while an artillery duel, which he thought was the
fiercest of the day, raged over the heads of his troops. "Here,"
he reported, "I had some men killed by limbs cut from the
trees by our own artillery." But the Rebel artillery was over-
matched by the enemy's rifled guns, and when the Confederate batteries ceased firing, Cleburne tried to move forward
again. This time, he said, "There was a very thick undergrowth . . . of young trees, which prevented my men from
seeing any distance, yet offered them no protection from the
storm of bullets . . . that swept through it. I could not see what

[23] E. Hannaford, *The Story of a Regiment: A History of the Campaigns, and
Associations in the Field of the Sixth Regiment Ohio Volunteer Infantry* (Cincinnati,
1868), 572–73.

was going on to my right or left, but my men were dropping all around before the fire of an unseen foe. . . . My brigade was repulsed and almost completely routed in this unfortunate attack. As far as I know the Fifteenth Arkansas was the only regiment rallied anywhere near the scene of disaster."[24]

By noon the Confederate line had been forced back to a position along the Hamburg-Purdy road, but not until soldiers had sometimes fought back and forth over the same ground several times in what seemed to be the bloodiest fighting of the day. In fact Sherman wrote of "the severest artillery fire I ever heard" taking place on this day in this area. Beauregard described "the unceasing, withering fire of the enemy" as the Union "drove forward line after line of fresh troops," and Polk described the fighting here as "desperately contested."[25]

The reports of Rebel officers such as Beauregard, Polk, Cheatham, Wood, and Thompson leave no doubt about where the greatest pressure was coming from. The Confederate left and center were then receiving the brunt of the Union attack as Wallace, Sherman, McClernand, Hurlbut and McCook were all converging in the general direction of Shiloh Church.

It was around this time, shortly before noon, that a Confederate brigade, commanded by S. A. M. Wood, made a determined counterattack against the Federals about a half mile north and to the east of Shiloh Church. The brigade, estimated by its commander to have numbered not over 650 men, charged across a large pond of water, now known as Water Oaks Pond, which in some places was waist-deep. Major John H. Kelly, of the Ninth Arkansas Battalion, was described as displaying conspicuous courage during the advance. Dashing through the pond, he sat on horseback in the open ground under extremely heavy fire and rallied his men in line as they moved forward. Crossing the pond the brigade then charged through an open field and, for a moment, drove the Union soldiers back in disorder. The victory was short-lived, how-

---

[24] *OR*, x, part 1, 583, 584.
[25] *Ibid.*, 251, 388.

ever, for the Federals soon rallied on the Rebel left and poured a cross fire into Wood's brigade that compelled it to retire, seeking cover in the edge of a woods.[26]

This Union counterattack was perhaps symbolic of the entire fight on April 7. The Rebels, time and again, demonstrated determination and selfless courage, but the Federal army possessed too much sheer power for the Confederates to do more than blunt its advance momentarily. Here and there a Rebel regiment would break and retreat as the pressure became unbearable. Then those regiments alongside it would be compelled to give ground, or be outflanked. General Wood's official report conveys well the desperate fighting of the last hours of April 7.

Two or three times, he wrote, the regiment next to his brigade on the left broke and fell back. Finally, when Wood tried to steady that unit, he was told by the regiment's colonel that the soldiers were worn out and scattered in the bushes and could not be rallied again. Nevertheless, with the assistance of some staff officers Wood managed to gather the regiment, form the troops in line, and lead them to the fight once more. Yet upon returning to his own command, Wood found all except two of his field officers wounded, and those two were on foot, their horses killed. Then, looking to his left, the command which he had just rallied was disintegrating once more. There seemed to be no alternative to retiring his own brigade. Similar scenes were occurring all along the jagged Confederate line.[27]

The Rebel losses were swelling, and the stream of stragglers was becoming more and more difficult to restrain. Beauregard was observing the action from his headquarters at Shiloh Church. It was about two-thirty in the afternoon. Thomas Jordan recalled that he said to the Creole: "General, do you not think our troops are very much in the condition of a lump of sugar, thoroughly soaked with water, but yet preserving its original shape, though ready to dissolve? Would it not be judicious to get away with what we have?" Quietly and simply

[26] *OR*, x, part 1, 594, 595.
[27] *Ibid.*, 594.

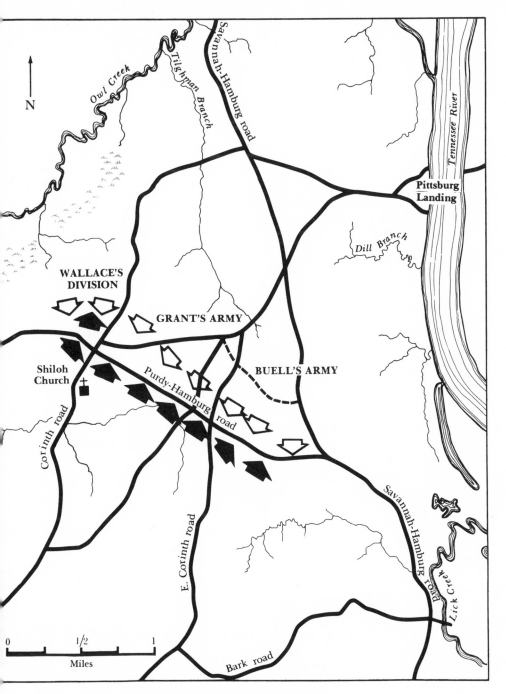

Map 12. The Union Advance, Noon, April 7, 1862.

Beauregard replied: "I intend to withdraw in a few moments."[28]

Dispatching his aides with orders to the corps commanders to begin the retreat, Beauregard directed Jordan to collect as many of the broken organizations as he could—both infantry and artillery—and post them in the best defensive positions he could locate. He must then hold his ground until the entire army could pass to the rear. Jordan gathered up about 2,000 infantry, together with a dozen or more cannon, and placed them on an elevated ridge just to the south and in view of Shiloh Church. Here they stayed until the last of the army, Breckinridge's troops, filed past sometime after four o'clock, at which time they too fell in line and began the weary tramp back toward the campsites of two nights earlier and then on to Corinth.[29]

There had been intermittent showers all through the day. Now, as the night before, the rain came down, slow and sporadic at first, then constant. Both sides of the road were becoming littered with equipment thrown away by the exhausted soldiers as they attempted to lighten their loads. The hard jolting wagons were filled with wounded, as one of them said, "piled in like bags of grain" upon one another. Some of the wounded had lain in the rain all the night before. Some of them had lost arms or legs or had been otherwise mutilated. Most of the Confederates had had enough of the glory of war. So too, apparently, had the Union army. At least they made no effort whatsoever to pursue the Rebels until Tuesday morning. And then Sherman moved out toward Corinth with two brigades, and the Fourth Illinois Cavalry, supported by Brigadier General Thomas J. Wood's division of Buell's army.

It was not much of a pursuit, and one of the many criticisms later leveled at Grant was that he did not vigorously press the enemy after the battle. The criticism seems to be justified. Although much of Grant's battered army was apparently in no better shape to pursue the Rebels than the Rebels were to continue fighting, many of Buell's units, as well as Lew Wal-

[28] *Battles and Leaders*, I, 603.
[29] *Ibid.*

lace's division, were in condition to pursue. Nevertheless, Sherman's move toward Corinth was intended merely to make sure the Confederates did not remain in the battle area.

Sherman's command had not progressed very far before it found the Rebels. At a place called the Fallen Timbers, where a skirmish had taken place on the afternoon of April 4, Nathan Bedford Forrest, commanding about 350 cavalrymen, was drawn up on a ridge to protect the rear of Beauregard's army. Sherman sent out a regiment of skirmishers in front, posted cavalry on his flanks, aligned the rest of one brigade in attack formation, and moved toward the ridge. Forrest was outnumbered five or six to one, but the Union soldiers did not know that, for they could not see beyond the ridge. And Forrest knew that they did not know.

As the Federal skirmishers began picking their path through the Fallen Timbers, and became somewhat disorganized and momentarily preoccupied, Forrest seemed to sense it was time to act. Shouting to his men to "Charge!" he led the way as the cavalry thundered toward Sherman's men. Some of the Union skirmishers panicked and fled; others were blasted by shotguns and pistols as the Rebel horsemen rode them down. The fury of the charge also turned back the Fourth Illinois Cavalry, and Forrest, seemingly carried away by the exhilaration of combat, was waving his sword and shouting "Charge! Charge!" as he kept after them. His men, seeing the strong front of the oncoming brigade, were not following, however, and Forrest was galloping, alone, directly into the ranks of the main Federal force.

He should have been killed. Federal infantry swarmed all about him trying to shoot him or drag him from his horse. The horse was kicking and rearing. Forrest was slashing right and left. Even when a soldier managed to place his gun up against Forrest's hip and pull the trigger, the blast lifting the commander high in his saddle and the bullet lodging against his spine, the action did not unhorse him or stop him. Turning his horse around and clearing a path with his saber, Forrest plowed back in the direction from which he came. As he was emerging from the mass of Blue infantry he reached down, grabbed an enemy soldier by the collar, swung the man onto the horse, and used him as a shield as he galloped away. Once out of range of the Union fire, Forrest flung the man to the ground and rode on up the ridge to the point where his command was waiting in amazement. Sherman, too, was amazed, as well as disgusted. But that was neither the first nor the last time that "that Devil Forrest," as Sherman came to call him, cheated death, though perhaps never more spectacularly than at the Fallen Timbers.[30]

The Union "pursuit" of the Rebels was over. Sherman gathered up his wounded, buried the dead, and turned toward his headquarters at Shiloh. The battle of Shiloh was all over—all over except for the burying of the dead, the suffering of the wounded, and the anguish of those back home who would soon learn of their loved ones lost in battle.

Ann Wallace was with her husband at the Cherry mansion in Savannah. About ten o'clock on Monday morning her spirit had been lifted as news came that Will had been found on the battlefield, still breathing. She had rushed to the adjoining boat where they had brought him. He was wet and cold, his face flushed, and Ann was stunned by the sight of the wound in his head. She clasped his hand and, although those standing around doubted it, was convinced that he immediately recognized her, if only for a moment. He was removed to Savannah where Ann stayed with him constantly. He spoke to her a few times briefly, and her hopes for his recovery grew brighter for a while. But then it gradually became obvious that his condition was growing worse, that he was mortally wounded. He died on Thursday night. She later wrote how thankful she was that he had not died on the battlefield and that she was able to be with him during those final hours.[31]

Another soldier, a young Confederate by the name of Will Pope, was also dying of the wounds he had received at Shiloh. Pleadingly he questioned a companion, Johnny Green: "Johnny, if a boy dies for his country the glory is his forever isn't it?"[32]

[30] Henry, *"First with the Most,"* 80, 81. R. S. Henry, ed., *As They Saw Forrest* (Jackson, Tenn., 1956), 39, 40.

[31] Wallace, *Letters,* 199, 200.

[32] Kirwan, *Johnny Green,* 37.

Mass graves—trenches—became the final resting place for most of the Confederate dead. In the sketch above, Federal troops are shown engaged in this onerous detail, and below is one of the burial trenches as it appears today.

The Federal army was forming burial details and digging mass graves into which they were stacking the bodies in rows, one on top of another. To those assigned to the task, and to others who traveled the battleground shortly after the guns were silenced, the stench of the dead was almost unbearable. Equally repugnant were some of the scenes that assaulted the eyes. Where fire had taken hold in the leaves and grass of the Hornets' Nest, for instance, observers recorded the shock of seeing corpses from which flames had burned away the facial flesh and exposed grinning skulls. Others who died on the battlefield seemed to be at peace, as with the big Northerner, still gripping his musket, and the young Rebel, revolver in hand, who had shot each other at virtually point-blank range. Now they lay together, almost in a death embrace, with neither face showing any expression of pain or anger.[33]

There were many scenes of pathos. Lying in a ravine was the rigid body of a bugler of the Fifty-fifth Illinois. He was found leaning against a tree. Someone had apparently cut away his bugle because only the cord was left around his neck, but his extended hand still held an open letter which he must have been reading at the time of his death. It was a letter from his wife.[34]

One Federal officer, returning to his old tent on Prentiss' campground, discovered the dead body of a Rebel soldier along with a mortally wounded Union private. Raising the youth's head to enable him to sip water from a canteen the officer watched while the lad's life ebbed away. The young man struggled to utter one last sentence: "Tell mother where you found me," he said, "on the front line."[35]

Walking over the battlefield in those days immediately after Shiloh was James A. Garfield. Wandering out beyond the Union lines with his pickets, he came upon a group of tents in which there were about thirty wounded Rebels, attended by a surgeon and a few aides. He found dead men lying in among the wounded living. Sight and smell, he said, were appalling.

[33] Richardson, "Shiloh." Kirwan, *Johnny Green*, 33.
[34] Crooker, *55th Illinois*, 124.
[35] Hickenlooper, "Battle of Shiloh," 430, 431.

It was soon after this that he was moved to write, in a letter sent back home, "The horrible sights that I have witnessed on this field I can never describe. No blaze of glory, that flashes around the magnificent triumphs of war, can ever atone for the unwritten and unutterable horrors of the scene of carnage."[36]

[36] Garfield to wife, April 21, 1862, Garfield Papers.

12. *Never Smile Again*

THE BATTERED CONFEDERATE ARMY finally struggled back to Corinth in the pouring rain. Upon reaching the small northeast Mississippi town, the army set up makeshift hospitals at every likely location—in schools, churches, hotels, even homes. Still there was not enough room for all the wounded. Numbering more than 8,000, they were in some cases simply stretched out in the halls or on porches and sidewalks. Neither were there enough doctors and nurses, and of the doctors available some were not qualified. Also facing a shortage of medical supplies, those attending the sick and wounded were soon worn out, from frustration as well as lack of rest. Little wonder that many of the amputations, performed in such huge numbers in the temporary hospitals of Corinth, resulted in death. Furthermore, with an inadequate water supply, which was soon contaminated by refuse, a typhoid fever epidemic and mass dysentery plagued the town. Opium, which was considered an invaluable remedy for dysentery as well as an effective pain-killer, and morphine were dispensed to the men who seemed to be suffering the most. The supply was inadequate, however, for the surgeons also depended heavily on opiates for the men on whom they were operating.

A nurse later wrote that the foul air from the mass of human beings made her so sick initially that she felt she could not go on. She wondered, too, if there would be any end to the tales of horror being related about the battle and, more poignantly, any respite from the sight of men dying all around her, some of whom she had come to know quite well. She told of trying to cheer a young man she had been attending for several days who had learned that his arm was to be amputated. He said he knew that he would die, and he would not be comforted. A few hours after the amputation he was dead. She shuddered, she added, as she inadvertently passed the amputating area later and saw the man's lifeless arm resting in a bloody tub with its hand hanging over the edge.[1]

Back at Shiloh the battlefield presented an equally macabre spectacle. Five hundred or more dead horses lay scattered among the dead and wounded soldiers, the latter largely unattended by the overtaxed surgeons. The stench of dead bodies, turning black and swollen, penetrated the air. The horse carcasses were removed as soon as possible by burning, but burial details for the human casualties worked for days to clear the area, sometimes digging regular graves, at other times preparing huge trenches into which several hundred dead Confederates would be placed. Often the Union dead would be buried by companies, all of one company in one grave. Occasionally, little more than a few shovelfuls of dirt were tossed over a dead body. A soldier recalled passing such a makeshift grave a few days later. An inert arm extended from the fresh earth toward the sky, the hand with stiff open fingers as if groping for something. As he stared in disbelief, another soldier walked over and, attempting a crude joke, placed a piece of hardtack in the empty hand. "That fellow," he said, "is not going off hungry if I can help it."[2]

General Beauregard sought permission of General Grant "to send a mounted party to the battlefield of Shiloh, for the purpose of giving decent interment to my dead." Grant refused the request, replying that because of the warmth of the weather he thought it advisable to have all the dead, of both armies, buried immediately and that he had already mustered large details for the purpose.[3]

In many cases relatives were coming to claim the bodies of their dead kinfolk. Among these was Samuel Stokes Rembert III, who drove a team of horses and a wagon from his farm in Shelby County, north of Memphis, to Shiloh. Somehow he found the body of his eldest son, Andrew Rembert, a private

---

[1] Jones, *Heroines of Dixie*, 110–17.
[2] Ephraim A. Wilson, *Memoirs of the War* (Cleveland, 1893), 112, 113.
[3] Simon, *Papers of Grant*, v, 30.

Grant estimated that 500 dead horses were left on the battlefield when the fighting ceased. Union troops are shown here burning the carcasses as part of their job in clearing the area.

in the Confederate army. Andrew's body was brought back and buried on the homeplace. Years later Andrew's brother Sam erected a monument to his memory. That monument, still a striking sight today, is in the form of a kneeling angel and stands 11 or 12 feet in height. But more startling than the white angel suddenly looming up in the midst of a forested area is the bitter epitaph, which reads: "Three Generations of Remberts. To my dear parents and loving sisters and my noble, gentle, brilliant and brave brother, killed for defending home against the most envious lot of cut throats that ever cursed the face of this earth."[4]

The battle of Shiloh was over, but it was a long time before such feelings of bitterness subsided. It was also a while before the South as a whole recognized Shiloh as a defeat. Under the pen name "Agate," Whitelaw Reid's account for his Cincinnati paper describing the Union army as surprised and fearfully cut up was carried in many Northern newspapers and filtered back to the South, reinforcing the initial Southern impression of triumph. Several other newspaper correspondents penned exaggerated stories of Union disaster. Beauregard's announcement of victory in his communiqué to Richmond on the night of April 6 had the Confederate capital soon celebrating what it believed to be a great triumph. He never retracted the statement. In fact, two days after the battle he wrote Earl Van Dorn to hurry up so they could whip the Union army again! The Creole went on to say that the Federals were hurt so badly they could not even take the field. Perhaps anticipating that the Rebels' withdrawal to Corinth might seem puzzling in view of the smashing victory he claimed, he explained that the retreat was part of his strategic planning. Only "untoward events" had saved the Union army from annihilation.[5] Beauregard continued to write of Shiloh as a victory even after he had been compelled to evacuate Corinth and thus had lost the strategic Memphis and Charleston Railroad.

Gradually the truth became evident to many in the South, and for the first time in his career Beauregard found himself

[4] Memphis *Press-Scimitar*, July 14, 1967.
[5] *OR*, x, part 1, 397.

being widely criticized and even ridiculed. His claim that Shiloh was a victory came to seem ludicrous—as it was. Actually, Shiloh was a decisive defeat for the South in the struggle for the Western Confederacy. As such it was also one of the decisive battles of the war. The great Confederate offensive to reclaim Tennessee, protect the Mississippi Valley, and restore the balance of power in the West had failed. When the Rebels had done all the damage they could do, a powerful Union army still held its position on the flank of the line of the Mississippi and within a few miles of the railroads at Corinth. As many of those who fought at Shiloh predicted, the battle, together with the fall of Island Number Ten which surrendered a few hours after the guns of Shiloh were silent, opened the way to the final splitting of the Confederacy, both along the Mississippi and along the line of the Memphis and Charleston Railroad. This is why Sherman said that the victory at Shiloh was "one of the most important that has ever occurred on this continent" and Grant wrote that "in importance of results, but few such [battles] have taken place in the history of the world."[6]

Unfortunately for the Confederacy, Robert E. Lee, serving as President Davis' general supervisor of military operations, recognized too late the issue at stake in the West. It was only after Shiloh, when Beauregard's army lay depleted and suffering at Corinth, hopelessly outnumbered by Union forces, that Lee was wiring Atlantic Coast commanders to send reinforcements west at any cost, warning them: "If the Mississippi Valley is lost, the Atlantic States would be ruined."[7] His evaluation was accurate, even though belated. To no small degree the fate of the Confederacy was dependent on what happened on the Mississippi, but the hour of opportunity had already passed.

If the Union army were to be stopped, it had to be halted at Shiloh—before Buell could join with Grant. The Confederates sacrificed the heart of their army in this attempt, and it

---

[6] Sherman, *Report of the Proceedings of the Society of the Army of the Tennessee at the 14th Annual Meeting* (Cincinnati, 1881). *OR*, x, part 1, 111, 112.
[7] *OR*, vi, 432.

almost succeeded. When they failed, however, and the broken Rebels went trudging back to Corinth, Shiloh became symbolic of a huge floodgate unhinged. The Rebels had tried with all their might to slam it shut, but when they failed, the pressure of the Federal onslaught mounted steadily and rapidly. Never did the South have a better opportunity to reverse the trend and save the Western Confederacy.

The subsequent action of the next few weeks was mild in comparison to the bloodletting at Shiloh. General Halleck arrived at Pittsburg Landing on April 11 and took over the army. Grant was named second in command, but his troops were placed under another, and there seemed to be nothing for him to do. Humiliated by the demotion, and probably disturbed by his blunders at Shiloh, he again considered leaving the army. Halleck spent about three weeks getting organized and bringing up reinforcements; then he moved toward Corinth. By that time he commanded an army of 100,000 men and more than 200 guns. Beauregard, even after Van Dorn with his reinforcements finally arrived, could not have mustered half that number.

Despite his superior force, Halleck, who was wary and cautious by nature, spent many days organizing and then marched southward very carefully. When his army moved, pickets and scouts were deployed at both its front and flanks. He was determined not to repeat Grant's mistake. When Halleck arrived in front of the Rebel lines at the Corinth approaches and began a careful investment of the Confederate position, Beauregard had no choice but to evacuate and move south. Although he knew he could not fight off the Union army, he did succeed in escaping with his forces intact by employing a clever ruse: Beauregard arranged for railroad locomotives to come chugging noisily into town at intervals, each trip accompanied by loud cheering—a maneuver that convinced the Federal troops on the left under John Pope that the Rebels were being reinforced. Only when the last departing Confederates blew up the supplies that could not be moved did the Union army realize what had been happening. On May 30, Halleck's army pushed forward into an empty town, a fitting climax, or aftermath, to a campaign that was marked by confusion from beginning to end.

While the final events at Corinth may have seemed strangely lacking in drama, the South's fate was being sealed. The Memphis and Charleston Railroad, the one line directly connecting the Mississippi River with Virginia, was broken. Fort Pillow on the Mississippi was outflanked. So was Memphis, and both, with the enemy now moving closer, were soon to fall just as Columbus, Kentucky, did after the loss of Fort Henry and Fort Donelson. Another few hundred miles of the Mississippi would be in Federal hands—in fact, as far as the neighborhood of Vicksburg. At the other end of the great river the wealthiest and largest of Southern cities, the strategic mart of ocean and river commerce, New Orleans, stripped of its seasoned defenders for the concentration at Corinth which preceded the battle of Shiloh, had already fallen to the Federals, capitulating before the end of April. Now the Crescent City would serve as a secondary base for the attempt to complete the opening of the Mississippi. Vicksburg would hold out for more than a year, but when the Rebels failed at Shiloh the entire valley was placed in a more precarious position. And without the valley the Confederacy would be split asunder, its heartland vulnerable to piecemeal strangulation by an adversary that controlled the waters to the east, south, and west. Shiloh was the key to the railroad and a major step toward control of the valley.

Speculation about "what might have been" is a game played by many students of Civil War battles, and it sometimes borders on fantasy. At the battle of Shiloh, however, the possibilities for a totally different outcome were so real that they bear repeating.

The Rebels were in fact so close to victory on April 6 that one marvels that the Union army was able to escape disaster. Early in the fighting on that Sunday morning, the Southerners possessed a numerical advantage of probably 5,000 men, the element of surprise was all on their side, and they boasted superior momentum. The encampments of the Union army lacked any tactical formation, green troops manned the advance camps, and only about 1,500 men protected the critical left flank and route to Pittsburg Landing. Yet the Rebels squandered their opportunity. The high command was confused, apparently unable to decide whether to drive the enemy back to Pittsburg Landing or away from it. A derivative of this confusion, in which lack of imagination surely played a part, was the army's expenditure of too many men and too much time in assaulting the Hornets' Nest while ignoring an immediate opportunity to break through the weak Union left flank nearer the river. And compounding the confusion was the Rebel army's inefficient attack formation, in which one corps advanced in front of another instead of side by side.

Although victory at Shiloh was clearly within reach of the Rebels for a few hours that morning, what might have happened following a Union defeat is pure conjecture. Had Grant's army been smashed, Buell, who was never known as aggressive, probably would have retreated to Nashville, speeded that way by rumors prevalent in the Union army that the Rebels were 60,000, 80,000, or even 100,000 strong. And his position at Nashville could have been made untenable. More certainly, Grant's fate would have been sealed and probably the career of Sherman ruined also.

Grant, already under fire from Halleck during the course of the battle, would have been discredited, especially so when news spread of how the army was surprised while its commander was residing in a mansion nine miles down the river. As it was, he encountered troubles enough in victory. From the Northwest, the section which had taken such heavy casualties at Shiloh, came accusations that he was incompetent and lazy and a drunkard. Some went so far as to seriously contend that his inept conduct of the battle indicated that he was party to a sinister conspiracy to prolong the war for political purposes.[8] He was denounced in Congress. Lincoln was urged to remove him.

Among the soldiers who fought under Grant at Shiloh was a bitterness that lingered long after the battle. Their choice

[8] Horn, *Army of Tennessee*, 122.

phrases of criticism, such as "imbecile character," "blundering stupidity," "criminal carelessness," abound in letters, diaries, and memoirs.[9] One of these veterans, writing a quarter of a century later, spoke of the "odiousness" of Grant's presence, claimed that the general was drunk, and said further, "From that time until now I have charged Grant with the responsibility of having uselessly slaughtered at least half of the men that were killed and wounded in that battle; so universal was the disapprobation felt by the army that he was passed as a dog and hissed by his men."[10]

The colonel of the Union Forty-fourth Indiana probably spoke for much of the army when he declared that the general opinion of the regiment was that the Rebel surprise attack on April 6 was "the result of gross carelessness and an insufficient system of picketing."[11]

It is doubtful also that Sherman's career could have survived a Union defeat. A beating would have provided a perfect climate for revival of earlier rumors that Sherman was crazy. And criticism of his failure to provide proper outposting against surprise and of his adamant refusal to credit any possibility of a Confederate attack could only have flourished.

In fact, just as with Grant, the criticism of Sherman was severe, even in victory. Colonel Thomas Worthington, one of Sherman's regimental commanders, published such derogatory remarks about the general that Sherman court-martialed him and managed to have him dismissed from the army. But Sherman could not then, and never did, succeed in proving that he was not surprised at Shiloh. Years later, when Sherman published his memoirs, arguing therein that he was not surprised by the Rebel attack, H. V. Boynton, Washington correspondent of the Cincinnati *Gazette*, wrote a book caustically entitled *Sherman's Historical Raid: The Memoirs in Light of the Record*. Boynton demonstrated how Sherman had con-

---

[9] Throne, "Letters," 257, 258. James M. Merrill, *William Tecumseh Sherman* (Chicago, 1971), 202.

[10] Louis Elseffer Papers, MSS Division, LC. Foote, *Civil War*, I, 372.

[11] Rerick, *Forty Fourth Indiana*, 60.

tradicted himself, and he thoroughly exploded the general's argument.[12]

Actually, Sherman apparently, and understandably, really preferred not to say much at all about his part at Shiloh. When the Congressional Joint Committee on the Conduct of the War requested a summation of his military career during the conflict, he chose to pass hurriedly over everything prior to the Atlanta campaign. To do otherwise, he pleaded, would consume an inordinate amount of time.[13]

There were many, even among Sherman's friends, who never saw any reasonable excuse for his conduct before the battle of Shiloh. One Federal soldier well summarized the common feeling when he said that there was "one cloud on [Sherman's] horizon; one blot on his escutcheon—he was surprised at Shiloh."[14]

General Buell also found himself immersed in controversy about Shiloh. Both his role in possibly saving the Union army from disaster, discussed in an earlier chapter, and his slowness in joining up with Grant received widespread attention. While Buell did take a long time in marching from Nashville to Savannah (particularly in crossing the Duck River at Columbia), and as a general principle such dalliance should not be tolerated, there is no evidence to support the more sinister charge that he hoped Grant would be defeated. He did not know of Grant's vulnerability at Pittsburg Landing, and there were no messages from Grant or Halleck urging Buell to hurry. He was also a man of high character, which further mitigates against the charge that he desired to see Grant beaten. After the battle, relations between the two were strained, but they did not have problems before.

These and other controversies over Shiloh, which are manifested throughout this book, went on for years. They in-

[12] Thomas Worthington, Court Martial Proceedings, Aug. 1862, General Services Administration, National Archives. Boynton, *Sherman's Raid*, 25-43.

[13] Supplemental Report of the Joint Committee on the Conduct of the War, 2 vols. (Washington, D. C., 1866), I, 3-6.

[14] Alfred T. Andreas, "The 'Ifs and Buts' of Shiloh," *Military Essays and Recollections*, Military Order of the Loyal Legions of the United States, Illinois Commandery, vol. 1 (1891), 123.

volved a great number of people on both sides of the conflict and produced reams of paper filled with intense and sustained argument, until Shiloh has become one of the war's most controversial battles. It all contributed to a mass of confusion which has partly obscured the vast significance of the campaign itself. History records a Union victory, however. With that victory the Rebels lost a potential psychological advantage, as well as the opportunity to reclaim much of Tennessee and perhaps undo much of what the Union army had accomplished in the West during the winter and early spring campaign. In the defeat at Shiloh, the Southerners surrendered their chance to stop a decisive Union drive. The words of the New Orleans writer George Washington Cable captured both the significance of that action and the emotion of the day when he said: "The South never smiled again after Shiloh."

Organization of the Union Army
AT THE BATTLE OF SHILOH, TENN., APRIL 6–7, 1862.

REPRINTED FROM *War of the Rebellion: A Compilation of the Official Records of the Union and Confederate Armies*

ARMY OF THE TENNESSEE

Maj. Gen. U. S. Grant, Commanding.

FIRST DIVISION

Maj. Gen. John A. McClernand.

First Brigade.

Col. Abraham M. Hare,[a] 11th Iowa
Col. Marcellus M. Crocker, 13th Iowa.

8th Illinois: Capt. James M. Ashmore.[a]
Capt. William H. Harvey.[b]
Capt. Robert H. Sturgess.
18th Illinois: Maj. Samuel Eaton.[a]
Capt. Daniel H. Brush.[a]
Capt. William J. Dillon.[b]
Capt. Jabez J. Anderson.
11th Iowa, Lieut. Col. William Hall.[a]
13th Iowa, Col. Marcellus M. Crocker.

Second Brigade.

Col. C. Carroll Marsh, 20th Illinois.

11th Illinois: Lieut. Col. Thomas E. G. Ransom.[a]
Maj. Garrett Nevins.[a]
Capt. Lloyd D. Waddell.
Maj. Garrett Nevins.

---

[a]Wounded.   [b]Killed.

20th Illinois: Lieut. Col. Evan Richards.[a]
Capt. Orton Frisbie.
45th Illinois, Col. John E. Smith
48th Illinois: Col. Isham N. Haynie.[a]
Maj. Manning Mayfield.

Third Brigade.

Col. Julius Raith,[c] 43d Illinois.
Lieut. Col. Enos P. Wood, 17th Illinois.

17th Illinois: Lieut. Col. Enos P. Wood.
Maj. Francis M. Smith.
29th Illinois, Lieut. Col. Charles M. Ferrell.
43d Illinois, Lieut. Col. Adolph Engelmann.
49th Illinois, Lieut. Col. Phineas Pease.[a]

Unattached.

Dresser's Battery (D), 2d Illinois Light Artillery, Capt. James P. Timony.
McAllister's Battery (D), 1st Illinois Light Artillery, Capt. Edward McAllister.[a]
Schwartz's Battery (E), 2d Illinois Light Artillery, Lieut. George L. Nispel.
Burrows' Battery, 14th [Battery] Ohio Light Artillery, Capt. Jerome B. Burrows.[a]
1st Battalion, 4th Illinois Cavalry, Lieut. Col. William McCullough.
Carmichael's Company Illinois Cavalry, Capt. Eagleton Carmichael.
Stewart's Company Illinois Cavalry, Lieut. Ezra King.

SECOND DIVISION.

Brig. Gen. William H. L. Wallace.[c]
Col. James M. Tuttle, 2d Iowa.

First Brigade.

Col. James M. Tuttle.

2d Iowa, Lt. Col. James Baker.

---

[a]Wounded.   [c]Mortally wounded.

7th Iowa, Lt. Col. James C. Parrott.
12th Iowa: Col. Joseph J. Woods.[b]
　　　Capt. Samuel R. Edgington.[c]
14th Iowa, Col. Wm. T. Shaw.[c]

Second Brigade

Brig. Gen. John McArthur.[d]
Col. Thomas Morton, 81st Ohio.

9th Illinois, Col. August Mersy.
12th Illinois: Lieut. Col. Augustus L. Chetlain.
　　　Capt. James R. Hugunin.
13th Missouri, Col. Crafts J. Wright.
14th Missouri, Col. B. S. Compton.
81st Ohio, Col. Thomas Morton.

Third Brigade.

Col. Thomas W. Sweeny,[d] 52d Illinois.
Col. Silas D. Baldwin, 57th Illinois.
8th Iowa, Col. James L. Geddes.[b]
7th Illinois, Maj. Richard Rowett.
50th Illinois, Col. Moses M. Bane.[d]
52d Illinois: Maj. Henry Stark.
　　　Capt. Edwin A. Bowen.
57th Illinois: Col. Silas D. Baldwin.
　　　Capt. Gustav A. Busse.
58th Illinois, Col. Wm. F. Lynch.[c]

Artillery.

Willard's Battery (A), 1st Illinois Light Artillery, Lieut. Peter P. Wood.
Maj. J. S. Cavender's Battalion Missouri Artillery:
　Richardson's Battery (D), 1st Missouri Light Artillery, Capt. Henry Richardson.
　Welker's Battery (H), 1st Missouri Light Artillery, Capt. Frederick Welker.
　Stone's Battery (K), 1st Missouri Light Artillery, Capt. George H. Stone.

---

[b]Wounded and captured.　　　[c]Captured.　　　[d]Wounded.

Cavalry.

Company A, 2d Illinois Cavalry, Capt. John R. Hotaling.
Company B, 2d Illinois Cavalry, Capt. Thomas J. Larison.
Company C, 2d United States Cavalry, ⎫
Company I, 4th United States Cavalry, ⎰ Lieut. James Powell.

THIRD DIVISION.

Maj. Gen. Lew. Wallace.

First Brigade.

Col. Morgan L. Smith, 8th Missouri.

11th Indiana, Col. George F. McGinnis.
24th Indiana, Col. Alvin P. Hovey.
8th Missouri, Lieut. Col. James Peckham.

Second Brigade.

Col. John M. Thayer, 1st Nebraska.

23d Indiana, Col. William L. Sanderson.
1st Nebraska, Lieut. Col. William D. McCord.
58th Ohio, Col. Valentine Bausenwein.
68th Ohio, Col. Samuel H. Steadman.[a]

Third Brigade.

Col. Charles Whittlesey, 20th Ohio.

20th Ohio, Lieut. Col. Manning F. Force.
56th Ohio, Col. Peter Kinney.[a]
76th Ohio, Col. Charles R. Woods.
78th Ohio, Col. Mortimer D. Leggett.

Artillery.

Thompson's Battery, 9th [Battery] Indiana Light Artillery, Lieut. George R. Brown.

---

[a]Not engaged at Shiloh; remained at Crump's Landing.

Buell's [Independent] Battery (I), Missouri Light Artillery, Lieut.
Charles H. Thurber.

Cavalry.

3d Battalion, 11th Illinois Cavalry, Maj. James F. Johnson.[a]
3d Battalion, 5th Ohio Cavalry, Maj. Charles S. Hayes.[a]

FOURTH DIVISION.

Brig. Gen. Stephen A. Hurlbut.

First Brigade.

Col. Nelson G. Williams,[b] 3d Iowa.
Col. Isaac C. Pugh, 41st Illinois.

28th Illinois, Col. Amory K. Johnson.
32nd Illinois, Col. John Logan.[b]
41st Illinois: Col. Isaac C. Pugh.
           Lieut. Col. Ansel Tupper.[d]
           Maj. John Warner.
           Capt. John H. Nale.
3d Iowa: Maj. William M. Stone.[c]
           Lieut. George W. Crosley.

Second Brigade.

Col. James C. Veatch, 25th Indiana

14th Illinois, Col. Cyrus Hall.
15th Illinois: Lieut. Col. Edward F. W. Ellis.[d]
           Capt. Louis D. Kelley.
           Lieut. Col. William Cam, 14th Illinois.
46th Illinois: Col. John A. Davis.[b]
           Lieut. Col. John J. Jones.
25th Indiana: Lieut. Col. William H. Morgan.[b]
           Maj. John W. Foster.

Third Brigade.

Brig. Gen. Jacob G. Lauman.

---

[a]Not engaged at Shiloh; remained at Crump's Landing.
[b]Wounded.   [c]Captured.   [d]Killed.

31st Indiana: Col. Charles Cruft.[b]
Lieut. Col. John Osborn.
44th Indiana, Col. Hugh B. Reed.
17th Kentucky, Col. John H. McHenry, jr.
25th Kentucky: Lieut. Col. Benjamin H. Bristow.
Maj. William B. Wall.[b]
Capt. B. T. Underwood.
Col. John H. McHenry, jr.,
17th Kentucky.

Artillery.

Battery [B], 1st Michigan Light Artillery, Lieut. Cuthbert W. Laing.
Mann's [Independent] Battery (C), Missouri Light Artillery, Lieut.
Edward Brotzmann.
Myers's Battery, 13th [Battery] Ohio Light Artillery, Capt. John B.
Myers.

Cavalry.

1st and 2d Battalions 5th Ohio Cavalry, Col. William H. H. Taylor.

FIFTH DIVISION.

Brig. Gen. William T. Sherman.[b]

First Brigade.

Col. John A. McDowell,[c] 6th Iowa.

40th Illinois: Col. Stephen G. Hicks.[b]
Lieut. Col. James W. Boothe.
6th Iowa: Capt. John Williams.[b]
Capt. Madison M. Walden.
46th Ohio: Col. Thomas Worthington.

Second Brigade.

Col. David Stuart,[b] 55th Illinois
Lieut. Col. Oscar Malmborg,[d] 55th Illinois.
Col. T. Kilby Smith, 54th Ohio.

---

[b]Wounded.   [c]Disabled.   [d]Temporarily commanding.

55th Illinois, Lieut. Col. Oscar Malmborg.
54th Ohio: Col. T. Kilby Smith.
          Lieut. Col. James A. Farden.
71st Ohio: Col. Rodney Mason.

Third Brigade.

Col. Jesse Hildebrand, 77th Ohio.

53d Ohio: Col. Jesse J. Appler.
          Lieut. Col. Robert A. Fulton.
57th Ohio, Lieut. Col. Americus V. Rice.
77th Ohio: Lieut. Col. Wills De Hass.
          Maj. Benjamin D. Fearing.

Fourth Brigade.

Col. Ralph P. Buckland, 72d Ohio.

48th Ohio: Col. Peter J. Sullivan.[a]
          Lieut. Col. Job R. Parker.
70th Ohio, Col. Joseph R. Cockerill.
72d Ohio, Lieut. Col. Herman Canfield.[b]
          Col. Ralph P. Buckland.

Artillery.

Maj. Ezra Taylor, Chief of Artillery.

Taylor's Battery (B), 1st Illinois Light Artillery, Capt. Samuel E. Barrett.
Waterhouse's Battery (E), 1st Illinois Light Artillery:
Capt. Allen C. Waterhouse.[a]
Lieut. Abial R. Abbott.[a]
Lieut. John A. Fitch.
Morton Battery, 6th [Battery] Indiana Light Artillery, Capt. Frederick Behr.[b]

Cavalry.

2d and 3d Battalions 4th Illinois Cavalry, Col. T. Lyle Dickey.
Thielemann's two companies Illinois Cavalry, Capt. Christian Thielemann.

---

[a]Wounded.   [b]Killed.

SIXTH DIVISION.

Brig. Gen. Benjamin M. Prentiss.[e]

First Brigade.

Col. Everett Peabody,[d] 25th Missouri.

12th Michigan, Col. Francis Quinn.
21st Missouri: Col. David Moore.[b]
Lieut. Col. H. M. Woodyard.
25th Missouri: Lieut. Col. Robert T. Van Horn.
16th Wisconsin, Col. Benjamin Allen.[b]

Second Brigade.

Col. Madison Miller,[e] 18th Missouri.

61st Illinois, Col. Jacob Fry.
18th Missouri, Lieut. Col. Isaac V. Pratt.[e]
18th Wisconsin Col. James S. Alban.[d]

Not Brigaded.

16th Iowa:[a] Col. Alexander Chambers.[b]
Lieut. Col. Addison H. Sanders.
15th Iowa,[a] Col. Hugh T. Reid.[b]
23d Missouri:[c] Col. Jacob T. Tindall.[d]
Lieut. Col. Quin Morton.[e]

Artillery.

Hickenlooper's Battery, 5th [Battery] Ohio Light Artillery, Capt. Andrew Hickenlooper.
Munch's Battery, 1st [Battery] Minnesota Light Artillery: Capt. Emil Munch.[b]
Lieut. William Pfaender.

Cavalry.

1st and 2d Battalions, 11th Illinois Cavalry,
Col. Robert G. Ingersoll.

---

[a]15th and 16th Iowa were on right in an independent command.
[b]Wounded.   [c]Arrived on field about 9 o'clock, April 6.
[d]Killed.   [e]Captured.

Unassigned Troops.

15th Michigan,[f] Col. John M. Oliver.
14th Wisconsin,[g] Col. David E. Wood.
Battery H, 1st Illinois Light Artillery, Capt. Axel Silfversparre.
Battery I, 1st Illinois Light Artillery, Capt. Edward Bouton.
Battery B, 2d Illinois [Light] Artillery, siege guns, Capt. Relly Madison.
Battery F, 2d Illinois Light Artillery, Capt. John W. Powell.[b]
8th Battery, Ohio Light Artillery, Capt. Louis Markgraf.

ARMY OF THE OHIO.

Maj. Gen. Don Carlos Buell, Commanding.

SECOND DIVISION.

Brig. Gen. Alexander McD. McCook.

Fourth Brigade.

Brig. Gen. Lovell H. Rousseau.

6th Indiana, Col. Thomas T. Crittenden.
5th Kentucky, Col. Harvey M. Buckley.
1st Ohio, Col. Benjamin F. Smith.
1st Battalion, 15th United States,
  Capt. Peter T. Swain,
1st Battalion, 16th United States,   } Maj. John H. King.
  Capt. Edwin F. Townsend,
1st Battalion, 19th United States,
  Maj. Stephen D. Carpenter,

Fifth Brigade.

Col. Edward N. Kirk,[b] 34th Illinois.

34th Illinois: Maj. Charles N. Levanway.[d]
Capt. Hiram W. Bristol.

---

[b]Wounded.   [d]Killed.
[f]Temporarily attached Monday to 4th Brigade, Army of the Ohio.
[g]Temporarily attached Monday to 14th Brigade, Army of the Ohio.

29th Indiana, Lieut. Col. David M. Dunn.
30th Indiana: Col. Sion S. Bass.[a]
Lieut. Col. Joseph B. Dodge.
77th Pennsylvania, Col. Frederick S. Stumbaugh.

Sixth Brigade.

Col. William H. Gibson, 49th Ohio.

32d Indiana, Col. August Willich.
39th Indiana, Col. Thomas J. Harrison.
15th Ohio, Maj. William Wallace.
49th Ohio, Lieut. Col. Albert M. Blackman.

Artillery.

Terrill's Battery (H), 5th United States [Light] Artillery,
Capt. William R. Terrill.

FOURTH DIVISION.

Brig. Gen. William Nelson.

Tenth Brigade.

Col. Jacob Ammen, 24th Ohio.

36th Indiana, Col. William Grose.
6th Ohio, Lieut. Col. Nicholas L. Anderson.
24th Ohio, Lieut. Col. Frederick C. Jones.

Nineteenth Brigade.

Col. William B. Hazen, 41st Ohio.

9th Indiana, Col. Gideon C. Moody.
6th Kentucky, Col. Walter C. Whitaker.
41st Ohio, Lieut. Col. George S. Mygatt.

Twenty-second Brigade.

Col. Sanders D. Bruce, 20th Kentucky.

---

[a]Mortally wounded.

1st Kentucky, Col. David A. Enyart.
2d Kentucky, Col. Thomas D. Sedgewick.
20th Kentucky, Lieut. Col. Charles S. Hanson.

FIFTH DIVISION.

Brig. Gen. Thomas L. Crittenden.

Eleventh Brigade.

Brig. Gen. Jeremiah T. Boyle.

9th Kentucky, Col. Benjamin C. Grider.
13th Kentucky, Col. Edward H. Hobson.
19th Ohio, Col. Samuel Beatty.
59th Ohio, Col. James P. Fyffe.

Fourteenth Brigade.

Col. William Sooy Smith, 13th Ohio.

11th Kentucky, Col. Pierce B. Hawkins.
26th Kentucky, Lieut. Col. Cicero Maxwell.
13th Ohio, Lieut. Col. Joseph G. Hawkins.

Artillery.

Bartlett's Battery (G), 1st Ohio Light Artillery, Capt. Joseph Bartlett.
Mendenhall's batteries (H and M), 4th United States [Light] Artillery, Capt. John Mendenhall.

SIXTH DIVISION.[a]

Brig. Gen. Thomas J. Wood.

Twentieth Brigade.

Brig. Gen. James A. Garfield.

13th Michigan, Col. Michael Shoemaker.

---

[a]This division arrived upon the field about 2 o'clock on Monday. Wagner's brigade reached the front and became engaged, the 57th Indiana losing 4 men wounded.

64th Ohio, Col. John Ferguson.
65th Ohio, Col. Charles G. Harker.

Twenty-first Brigade.

Col. George D. Wagner, 15th Indiana.

15th Indiana, Lieut. Col. Gustavus A. Wood.
40th Indiana, Col. John W. Blake.
57th Indiana, Col. Cyrus C. Hines.
24th Kentucky, Col. Lewis B. Grigsby.

Commanding and Staff Officers.

DEPARTMENT OF MISSISSIPPI.

Maj. Gen. H. W. Halleck, commanding.

Brig. Gen. Geo. W. Cullum, Chief of Staff.

Capt. N. H. McLean, assistant adjutant-general.

Capt. J. C. Kelton, assistant adjutant-general.

Capt. P. M. Preston, assistant adjutant-general.

Col. Richard D. Cutts, aid-de-camp.

Capt. C. B. Throckmorton, aid-de-camp.

Lieut. J. T. Price, aid-de-camp.

Lieut. D. C. Wagner, aid-de-camp.

Lieut. A. Backer, aid-de-camp.

Brig. Gen. W. Scott Ketchum, Inspector-General.

Brig. Gen. A. J. Smith, Chief of Cavalry.

Col. J. V. D. DuBois, Chief of Artillery.

Col. George Thom, Chief of Engineers.

Lieut. Col. J. B. McPherson, assistant chief of engineers.

Col. J. C. McKibbin, Judge-Advocate.

Maj. Robert Allen, Chief Quartermaster.

Maj. T. J. Haines, Chief Commissary of Subsistence.

Surg. J. J. B. Wright, Medical Director.

ARMY OF THE TENNESSEE.

Maj. Gen. U. S. Grant, commanding.

Col. J. D. Webster, Chief of Staff.

Capt. J. A. Rawlins, assistant adjutant-general.

Capt. W. S. Hillyer, aid-de-camp.

Capt. W. R. Rowley, aid-de-camp.

Capt. C. B. Lagow, aid-de-camp.

Lieut. Col. J. B. McPherson, Chief of Engineers.

Lieut. W. L. B. Jenney, assistant chief of engineers.

Lieut. Wm. Kossak, assistant chief of engineers.

Capt. J. P. Hawkins, Chief Commissary of Subsistence.

Surg. Henry S. Hewitt, Medical Director.

Col. G. G. Pride, volunteer aid.

FIRST DIVISION

Maj. Gen. John A. McClernand, commanding.

Maj. Adolph Schwartz,[a] 2d Illinois Artillery, chief of staff.

Maj. M. Brayman, acting assistant adjutant-general.

Capt. Warren Stewart,[a] Illinois Cavalry, aid-de-camp.

Lieut. Henry C. Freeman,[a] aid-de-camp.

Lieut. Jos. E. Hitt, 4th Illinois Cavalry, aid-de-camp.

Lieut. A. B. Hall, 4th Illinois Cavalry aid-de-camp.

Lieut. S. R. Tresilian, assistant engineer.

Lieut. Erastus S. Jones, ordnance officer

First Brigade

Col. Abraham M. Hare,[a] 11th Iowa, commanding.

Lieut. and Adjt. Cornelius Cadle, jr., 11th Iowa, acting assistant adjutant-general.

Lieut. Samuel Caldwell, 8th Illinois, volunteer aid.

Second Brigade.

Col. C. C. Marsh, 20th Illinois, commanding.

Lieut. E. P. Boas, acting assistant adjutant-general.

---

[a]Wounded.

Adjt. J. E. Thompson,[b] 20th Illinois, aid-de-camp.

Capt. G. W. Kennard, acting assistant quartermaster.

Surg. Christopher Goodbrake, brigade surgeon.

Third Brigade.

Col. Julius Raith,[b] 43d Illinois, commanding

Lieut. Abraham H. Ryan, acting assistant adjutant-general.

---

[b]Killed.

Organization of the Confederate Army

AT THE BATTLE OF SHILOH, TENN., APRIL 6–7, 1862.

REPRINTED FROM *War of the Rebellion: A Compilation of the Official Records of the Union and Confederate Armies*

ARMY OF THE MISSISSIPPI.

Gen. Albert Sidney Johnston.[b]
Gen. P. G. T. Beauregard.

FIRST ARMY CORPS.

Maj. Gen. Leonidas Polk.

FIRST DIVISION.

Brig. Gen. Charles Clark.[c]
Brig. Gen. Alexander P. Stewart.

First Brigade.

Col. Robert M. Russell, 12th Tennessee.

11th Louisiana: Col. Samuel F. Marks.[c]
　　　　　　　　Lieut. Col. Robert H. Barrow.
12th Tennessee: Lieut. Col. Tyree H. Bell.
　　　　　　　　Maj. Robert P. Caldwell.
13th Tennessee, Col. Alfred J. Vaughan, jr.
22d Tennessee, Col. Thomas J. Freeman.[c]
[Bankhead's] Tennessee Battery, Capt. Smith P. Bankhead.

Second Brigade.

Brig. Gen. Alexander P. Stewart.

---

[b]Killed.　　　　　[c]Wounded.

13th Arkansas: Lieut. Col. A. D. Grayson.[a]
Maj. James A. McNeely.[b]
Col. James C. Tappan.
4th Tennessee: Col. Rufus P. Neely.
Lieut. Col. Otho F. Strahl.
5th Tennessee, Lieut. Col. Calvin D. Venable.
33d Tennessee, Col. Alexander W. Campbell.[b]
[Stanford's] Mississippi Battery, Capt. Thomas J. Stanford.

SECOND DIVISION.

Maj. Gen. Benjamin F. Cheatham.[b]

First Brigade.

Brig. Gen. Bushrod R. Johnson.[b]
Col. Preston Smith, 154th Tennessee.[b]

Blythe's Mississippi: Col. A. K. Blythe.[a]
Lieut. Col. David L. Herron.[a]
Maj. James Moore.
2d Tennessee, Col. J. Knox Walker.
15th Tennessee: Lieut. Col. Robert C. Tyler.[b]
Maj. John F. Hearn.
154th Tennessee (senior): Col. Preston Smith.
Lieut. Col. Marcus J. Wright.[b]
[Polk's] Tennessee Battery, Capt. Marshall T. Polk.[b]

Second Brigade.

Col. William H. Stephens, 6th Tennessee.
Col. George Maney, 1st Tennessee.

7th Kentucky: Col. Charles Wickliffe.[c]
Lieut. Col. William D. Lannom.
1st Tennessee (Battalion): Col. George Maney.
Maj. Hume R. Feild.
6th Tennessee, Lieut. Col. Timothy P. Jones.
9th Tennessee, Col. Henry L. Douglass.
[Smith's] Mississippi Battery, Capt. Melancthon Smith.

---

[a]Killed.   [b]Wounded.   [c]Mortally wounded.

Cavalry.

1st Mississippi, Col. Andrew J. Lindsay.
Mississippi and Alabama Battalion, Lieut. Col. Richard H. Brewer.

Unattached.

47th Tennessee, Col. Munson R. Hill.[d]

SECOND ARMY CORPS.

Maj. Gen. Braxton Bragg.
Escort.
Company Alabama Cavalry, Capt. Robert W. Smith.

FIRST DIVISION.

Brig. Gen. Daniel Ruggles.

First Brigade.

Col. Randall L. Gibson, 13th Louisiana.

1st Arkansas, Col. James F. Fagan.
4th Louisiana: Col. Henry W. Allen.[a]
            Lieut. Col. Samuel E. Hunter.
13th Louisiana: Maj. Anatole P. Avegno.[b]
            Capt. Stephen O'Leary.[a]
            Capt. Edgar M. Dubroca.
19th Louisiana: Col. Benjamin L. Hodge.
            Lieut. Col. James M. Hollingsworth.
Vaiden, Mississippi Battery [Light Artillery], Capt. S. C. Bain.

Second Brigade.

Brig. Gen. Patton Anderson.

1st Florida Battalion: Maj. Thaddeus A. McDonell.[a]
            Capt. W. G. Poole.
            Capt. W. Capers Bird.
17th Louisiana, Lieut. Col. Charles Jones.[a]

---

[a]Wounded.   [b]Mortally wounded.   [d]Arrived on field April 7.

20th Louisiana, Col. August Reichard.
Confederate Guards Response Battalion, Maj. Franklin H. Clack.
9th Texas, Col. Wright A. Stanley.
Washington (Louisiana) Artillery, Fifth Company,
Capt. W. Irving Hodgson.

Third Brigade.

Col. Preston Pond, jr. 16th Louisiana.

16th Louisiana, Maj. Daniel Gober.
18th Louisiana: Col. Alfred Mouton.[a]
Lieut. Col. Alfred Roman.
Crescent (Louisiana) Regiment, Col. Marshall J. Smith.
Orleans Guard (Louisiana) Battalion, Maj. Leon Querouze.[a]
38th Tennessee, Col. Robert F. Looney.
Ketchum's Alabama Battery, Company A, Alabama State Artillery,
Capt. William H. Ketchum.

Cavalry.

Alabama Battalion (5 companies—Jenkins, Cox, Robins, Tomlinson, and Smith), Capt. Thomas F. Jenkins.

SECOND DIVISION.

Brig. Gen. Jones M. Withers.

First Brigade.

Brig. Gen. Adley H. Gladden.[b]
Col. Daniel W. Adams,[a] 1st Louisiana.
Col. Zach C. Deas,[a] 22d Alabama.

21st Alabama: Lieut. Col. Stewart W. Cayce.
Maj. Frederick Stewart.
22d Alabama: Col. Zach C. Deas.
Lieut. Col. John C. Marrast.
25th Alabama: Col. John Q. Loomis.[a]
Maj. George D. Johnston.
26th Alabama: Lieut. Col. John G. Coltart.[a]
Lieut. Col. William D. Chadick.

---

[a]Wounded.   [b]Mortally wounded.

1st Louisiana: Col. Daniel W. Adams.
Maj. Fred H. Farrar, jr.
Robertson's, Florida, Battery, Capt. Felix H. Robertson.

Second Brigade.

Brig. Gen. James R. Chalmers.

5th Mississippi, Col. Albert E. Fant.
7th Mississippi, Lieut. Col. Hamilton Mayson.
9th Mississippi, Lieut. Col. William A. Rankin.[b]
10th Mississippi, Col. Robert A. Smith.
52d Tennessee, Col. Benjamin J. Lea.
Gage's Alabama Battery, Capt. Charles P. Gage.

Third Brigade.

Brig. Gen. John K. Jackson.

17th Alabama, Lieut. Col. Robert C. Fariss.
18th Alabama, Col. Eli S. Shorter.
19th Alabama, Col. Joseph Wheeler.
2d Texas: Col. John C. Moore.
Lieut. Col. William P. Rogers.
Maj. Hal. G. Runnels.
Girardey's Georgia Battery (Washington Artillery),
Capt. Isadore P. Girardey.

Cavalry.

Clanton's Alabama Regiment, Col. James H. Clanton.[a]

THIRD ARMY CORPS.

Maj. Gen. William J. Hardee.[a]

First Brigade.

Brig. Gen. Thomas C. Hindman.[c][d]
Col. R. G. Shaver, 7th Arkansas.[d]

---

[a]Wounded.   [b]Mortally wounded.
[c]Commanding his own and 3rd Brigade.   [d]Disabled.

2d Arkansas: Col. Daniel C. Govan.
Maj. Reuben F. Harvey.
6th Arkansas: Col. Alexander T. Hawthorn.
7th Arkansas: Col. John M. Dean.[d]
Maj. James T. Martin.
3d Confederate, Col. John S. Marmaduke.
Warren Light Artillery, Capt. Charles Swett.
Pillow Flying Artillery, or Miller's Tennessee Battery,
Capt. —— Miller.

Second Brigade.

Brig. Gen. Patrick R. Cleburne.

15th Arkansas, Lieut. Col. Archibald K. Patton.[d]
6th Mississippi: Col. John J. Thornton.[a]
Capt. W. A. Harper.
2d Tennessee: Col. William B. Bate.[a]
Lieut. Col. David L. Goodall.
5th (35th) Tennessee, Col. Benjamin J. Hill.
23d Tennessee: Lieut. Col. James F. Neill.[a]
Maj. Robert Cantrell.
24th Tennessee, Lieut. Col. Thomas H. Peebles.

(Shoup's Batallion.)

Trigg's (Austin) Arkansas, Battery, Capt. John T. Trigg.
Helena Arkansas Light Artillery, Capt. J. H. Calvert.
Hubbard's Arkansas Battery, Capt. George T. Hubbard.

Third Brigade.

Brig. Gen. Sterling A. M. Wood.[b]
Col. William K. Patterson, 8th Arkansas, temporarily.

16th Alabama, Lieut. Col. John W. Harris.
8th Arkansas, Col. William K. Patterson.
9th (14th) Arkansas (battalion) Maj. John H. Kelly.
3d Mississippi Battalion, Maj. Aaron B. Hardcastle.
27th Tennessee: Col. Christopher H. Williams.[d]
Maj. Samuel T. Love.[d]
44th Tennessee, Col. Coleman A. McDaniel.

---

[a]Wounded.   [b]Disabled.   [d]Killed.

55th Tennessee, Col. James L. McKoin.
Jefferson Mississippi Flying Artillery: Capt. William L. Harper.[a]
Lieut. Put Darden.
Georgia Dragoons, Capt. Isaac W. Avery.

RESERVE CORPS.

Brig. Gen. John C. Breckinridge.

First Brigade.

Col. Robert P. Trabue, 4th Kentucky.

(Clifton's) 4th Alabama Battalion, Maj. James M. Clifton.
31st Alabama, Lieut. Col. Montgomery Gilbreath.
3d Kentucky, Lieut. Col. Benjamin Anderson.[a]
4th Kentucky, Lieut. Col. Andrew R. Hynes.[a]
5th Kentucky, Col. Thomas H. Hunt.
6th Kentucky, Col. Joseph H. Lewis.
Crews's Tennessee Battalion, Lieut. Col. James M. Crews.
Cobb's Kentucky Battery, Capt. Robert Cobb.
Byrne's [Kentucky] Battery, Capt. Edward P. Byrne.
Morgan's Squadron, Kentucky Cavalry, Capt. John H. Morgan.

Second Brigade.

Brig. Gen. John S. Bowen.[a]
Col. John D. Martin.

9th Arkansas, Col. Isaac L. Dunlop.
10th Arkansas, Col. Thomas D. Merrick.
2d Confederate: Col. John D. Martin.
Maj. Thomas H. Mangum.
1st Missouri, Col. Lucius L. Rich.
Pettus Mississippi Flying Artillery, Capt. Alfred Hudson.
Watson Louisiana Flying Artillery, Capt. Daniel Belthoover.
Thompson's Company, Kentucky Cavalry, Capt. Phil. B. Thompson.

Third Brigade.

Col. Winfield S. Statham, 15th Mississippi.

---

[a]Wounded.

15th Mississippi, Maj. William F. Brantly.
22d Mississippi, Col. Frank Schaller.[a]
19th Tennessee, Col. David H. Cummings.
20th Tennessee, Col. Joel A. Battle.[b]
28th Tennessee, Lt. Col. Uriah T. Brown.
45th Tennessee, Lieut. Col. Ephraim F. Lytle.
Rutledge's Tennessee Battery, Capt. Arthur M. Rutledge.

Unattached.

Forrest's Regiment Tennessee Cavalry, Col. Nathan B. Forrest.[a]
Wharton's Texas Regiment Cavalry, Col. John A. Wharton.[a]
Wirt Adams' Mississippi Regiment Cavalry, Col. Wirt Adams.
McClung's Tennessee Battery, Capt. Hugh L. W. McClung.
Roberts' Arkansas Battery, Capt. Franklin Roberts.

---

[a]Wounded.   [b]Captured.

Bibliography

PRIMARY MATERIALS

Records

Official Records of the Union and Confederate Navies in the War of the Rebellion. 22 vols. Washington, D. C., 1908.

Supplemental Report of the Joint Committee on the Conduct of the War. 2 vols. Washington, D. C., 1866.

War of the Rebellion: A Compilation of the Official Records of the Union and Confederate Armies. 129 vols. Washington, D. C., 1880–1901.

Worthington, Thomas. Court Martial Proceedings, Aug. 1862. General Services Administration, National Archives and Records Service, Washington, D. C.

Memoirs, Diaries, Reminiscences, Papers

Ammen, Jacob. "Diary of the March to and Battle at Pittsburg Landing." *War of the Rebellion: A Compilation of the Official Records of the Union and Confederate Armies.* 129 vols. Washington, D. C., 1880–1901.

Andreas, Alfred T., "The 'Ifs and Buts' of Shiloh." *Military Essays and Recollections.* Military Order of the Loyal Legions of the United States, Illinois Commandery, vol. 1, 1891.

Billings, John D. *Hardtack and Coffee or The Unwritten Story of Army Life.* Boston, 1887.

Buell, Clarence C., and Robert U. Johnson, eds. *Battles and Leaders of the Civil War.* 4 vols. New York, 1887–88.

Chestnut, Mary B. *A Diary from Dixie.* Ed. Ben Ames Williams. Boston, 1905.

Cockerill, John A. "A Boy at Shiloh." *Under Both Flags.* Chicago, 1896.

Confederate Veteran. 40 vols. Nashville, 1893–1932.

Crooker, L. B. "Battle of Shiloh." *Manual of the Panorama of the Battle of Shiloh*. Chicago, 1885.

Crummer, Wilbur F. *With Grant at Fort Donelson, Shiloh, and Vicksburg*. Oak Park, Ill., 1915.

Grant, Ulysses S. *Personal Memoirs of U. S. Grant*. 2 vols. New York, 1885.

Hickenlooper, Andrew. "The Battle of Shiloh." *Sketches of War History, 1861–1865*. Military Order of the Loyal Legion of the United States, Ohio Commandery, vol. 5, 1903.

Howe, M. S. DeWolfe, ed. *Home Letters of General Sherman*. New York, 1909.

Jones, Katharine M., ed. *Heroines of Dixie*. New York, 1955.

Lawrence, Elijah C. "Stuart's Brigade at Shiloh." Read before the Commandery of the State of Massachusetts, Military Order of the Loyal Legion of the United States. Boston, 1900.

Mason, George. "Shiloh." *Military Essays and Recollections*, Military Order of the Loyal Legion of the United States, Illinois Commandery, vol. 1, 1891.

Miller, Madison. Diary, 1862. Missouri Historical Society, St. Louis.

Morton, Charles A. "A Boy at Shiloh," Military Order of the Loyal Legion of the U. S., N.Y. Commandery. New York, 1907.

Olney, Warren. "The Battle of Shiloh, with Some Personal Reminiscences." Albert Sidney Johnston—William Preston Johnston Collection, MSS Division, Howard-Tilton Memorial Library, Tulane Univ., New Orleans.

Overby, Garrett Turman. Diary. In possession of Mrs. Ann Beasley Johnson, Franklin, Tenn.

Parker, Nathan. Diary. Univ. of Kentucky, Lexington.

Preston, William. Diary. War Department Collection of Confederate Records, National Archives.

Richardson, Frank L. "Shiloh." July, 1877. Albert Sidney Johnston—William Preston Johnston Collection, MSS Division, Howard-Tilton Memorial Library, Tulane Univ., New Orleans.

Robertson, John. *Michigan in the War*. Lansing, Mich., 1882.

Shea, John G. *The American Nation*. New York, 1862.

Sherman, William T. *Memoirs of General W. T. Sherman*. 2 vols. New York, 1875.

———. *Report of the Proceedings of the Society of the Army of the Tennessee at the 14th Annual Meeting*. Cincinnati, 1881.

Simon, John Y., ed. *The Papers of Ulysses S. Grant*. 5 vols. Carbondale, Ill., 1973.

Stanley, Henry Morton. *The Autobiography of Henry Morton Stanley.*
    Ed. Dorothy Stanley. New York, 1937.
The Southern Bivouac. 5 vols. Louisville, 1882–87.
Thirteen Months in the Rebel Army: By an Impressed New Yorker. New
    York, 1862.
Todd, Oliphant M. Diary. MSS Division, Library of Congress.
Wallace, Isabel. *Life and Letters of General W. H. L. Wallace.* Chicago,
    1909.
Wallace, Lew. *An Autobiography.* 2 vols. New York, 1906.
Wheeler, Joseph. "The Battle of Shiloh." *Southern Historical Society
    Papers* 24, 1895.
Wilson, Ephraim A. *Memoirs of the War.* Cleveland, 1893.

Unit Histories

Anders, Leslie. *The 18th Missouri.* Indianapolis, 1968.
Barber, Lucius W. *Army Memoirs of Co. "D" 15th Illinois Volunteer
    Infantry.* Chicago, 1894.
Belknap, W. W. *History of the 15th Iowa Veteran Infantry.* Keokuk,
    Iowa, 1887.
Bell, John T. *Tramps and Triumphs of the Second Iowa Infantry.* Omaha,
    Neb., 1886.
Bouton, Edward. *Events of the Civil War.* n.d.
Crooker, Lucien B., and Committee. *The Story of the 55th Regiment
    Illinois Volunteer Infantry in the Civil War 1861–1865.* Clinton,
    Mass., 1887.
Daggett, George H. "Thrilling Moments," *Glimpses of the Nation's
    Struggle: A Series of Papers Read before the Minnesota Commandery,
    Military Order of the Loyal Legion of the U. S.* St. Paul and Min-
    neapolis, 1889–1909.
Downing, Alexander. *Downing's War Diary.* Des Moines, 1916.
Duke, Basil W. *Morgan's Cavalry.* New York, 1906.
Duke, John K. *History of the 53rd Ohio Volunteer Infantry.* Portsmouth,
    Ohio, 1900.
Eisenschiml, Otto, and Ralph Newman, eds. *Eyewitness: The Civil War
    as We Lived It.* New York, 1956.
Force, Manning. *From Fort Henry to Corinth.* New York, 1862.
George, Henry. *History of the 3rd, 7th, 8th, and 12th Kentucky, C. S. A.*
    Louisville, 1911.
Hannaford, E. *The Story of a Regiment: A History of the Campaigns, and
    Associations in the Field of the Sixth Regiment Ohio Volunteer Infantry.*
    Cincinnati, 1868.

Hubert, Charles. *History of the 50th Regiment Illinois Volunteer Infantry*. Kansas City, 1894.

Kimberly, Robert L., and Ephraim S. Holloway. *The Forty-first Ohio Veteran Volunteer Infantry*. Cleveland, 1897.

Kiner, F. F. *14th Iowa Infantry*. Lancaster, 1863.

Kirwan, A. D., ed. *Johnny Green of the Orphan Brigade: The Journal of a Confederate Soldier*. Lexington, 1956.

Kremer, W. P. *Sixth Iowa Infantry*. Rutledge, N. J., n.d.

Neal, W. A. *An Illustrated History of the Missouri Engineer and the 25th Infantry Regiment*. Chicago, 1889.

Payne, E. W. *Thirty-Fourth Illinois*. Clinton, Iowa, 1902.

Rerick, John H. *The Forty Fourth Indiana Volunteer Infantry*. LaGrange, Ind., 1880.

Smith, J. T. *The Thirty First Indiana*. Cincinnati, 1900.

Stillwell, Leander. *The Story of a Common Soldier of Army Life in the Civil War, 1861–1865*. n.p., 1920.

Thomas, B. F. *14th Iowa Volunteer Infantry*. n.p., 1907.

Thompson, E. Porter. *History of the First Kentucky Brigade*. Cincinnati, 1868.

Watkins, Samuel R. *"Co. Aytch," Maury Grays, 1st Tennessee Regiment*. Jackson, Tenn., 1952.

Wilkie, Franc B. *Pen and Powder*. Boston, 1888.

Wright, Charles W. *A Corporal's Story: Experiences in the Ranks of Company C, 81st Ohio Volunteer Infantry*. Philadelphia, 1887.

Wright, Henry H. *History of the Sixth Iowa Infantry*. Iowa City, 1923.

Manuscripts

P. G. T. Beauregard Papers. Duke Univ. Library, Durham, N. C. Confederate Records Division, National Archives.

Braxton Bragg Papers. William P. Palmer Collection, Western Reserve Historical Society, Cleveland. William K. Bixby Collection, Missouri Historical Society, St. Louis.

Irvin A. Buck Papers. Southern Historical Collection, Univ. of North Carolina, Chapel Hill.

J. F. H. Claiborne Papers. Southern Historical Collection, Univ. of North Carolina, Chapel Hill.

Louis Elseffer Papers. MSS Division, Library of Congress.

Manning F. Force Papers. Library of Congress.

James A. Garfield Papers. Library of Congress.

Jeremy F. Gilmer Papers. Southern Historical Collection, Univ. of North Carolina, Chapel Hill.

James I. Hall Papers. Southern Historical Collection, Univ. of North
    Carolina, Chapel Hill.
Albert Sidney Johnston—P. G. T. Beauregard Correspondence.
    Manuscripts Division, Howard-Tilton Memorial Library, Tulane
    Univ., New Orleans.
Albert Sidney Johnston and William Preston Johnston Papers, Mrs.
    Mason Barrett Collection, MSS Division, Howard-Tilton Memorial
    Library, Tulane Univ., New Orleans.
Shiloh National Military Park Library.
    Franklin Bailey Letters.
    Henry George, "The 7th Kentucky at Shiloh."
    R. F. Learned Letters.
    D. W. Reed Letters.
    John Ruckerman Letters.
    William Skinner Letters.
    Tom Walker, statement about the "Bloody Pond."
Tennessee State Library and Archives, Nashville.
    Confederate Collection.
        George T. Blakemore Diary.
        Henry M. Doak Memoirs.
        Thomas Firth Reminiscences.
        John Johnston Diary.
        W. E. Yeatman Memoirs.
Wilkinson, B. F. Letter, Apr. 16, 1862. Department of Archives and
    MSS, Louisiana State Univ., Baton Rouge.

Newspapers

Chicago *Times*.
Cincinnati *Daily Enquirer*.
Louisville *Journal*.
McNairy County (Tenn.) *Independent*.
Memphis *Daily Avalanche*.
Memphis *Press-Scimitar*.
Nashville *Banner of Peace*.
Nashville *Daily Union*.
New Orleans *Daily Picayune*.
New Orleans *Crescent*.
New York *Times*.
Richmond *Enquirer*.
Washington *National Tribune*.
Washington *Post*.

SECONDARY MATERIALS

Books and Papers

Baldock, Jeremiah. *Soldiers and Citizens' Album of Biographical Records.* Vol. 1—Wisconsin. Chicago, 1888.

Boynton, H. V. *Sherman's Historical Raid: The Memoirs in the Light of the Record.* Cincinnati, 1875.

Catton, Bruce. *Grant Moves South.* Boston, 1960.

_____. *Terrible Swift Sword.* Boston, 1963.

_____. *This Hallowed Ground.* New York, 1956.

Commager, Henry Steele, ed. *The Blue and the Gray.* New York, 1950.

Connelly, Thomas L. *Army of the Heartland.* Baton Rouge, 1967.

_____, and Archer Jones. *The Politics of Command: Factions and Ideas in Confederate Strategy.* Baton Rouge, 1973.

Davidson, Donald. *The Tennessee: The New River, Civil War to TVA.* New York, 1948.

Dosch, Donald F. "The Hornets' Nest." Unpublished paper, Shiloh National Military Park Library.

Eaton, Clement. *A History of the Southern Confederacy.* New York, 1954.

Eisenschiml, Otto. *The Story of Shiloh.* Chicago, 1946.

Foote, Shelby. *The Civil War: A Narrative.* New York, 1958.

_____. *Shiloh.* New York, 1952.

Fuller, Claude E., and Richard D. Steuart. *Firearms of the Confederacy.* Huntington, W. Va., 1944.

Hedley, F. Y. *Marching through Georgia.* Chicago, 1890.

Henry, Robert Selph. *"First with the Most" Forrest.* Jackson, Tenn., 1944.

_____. The Story of the Confederacy. Indianapolis, 1931.

_____, ed. *As They Saw Forrest.* Jackson, Tenn., 1956.

Hollister, John J. *Shiloh on Your Own.* n.p., 1973.

Horn, Stanley F. *The Army of Tennessee: A Military History.* New York, 1941.

_____, ed. *Tennessee's War, 1861–1865, Described by Participants.* Nashville, 1965.

Howard, Samuel M. *The Illustrated Comprehensive History of the Great Battle of Shiloh.* Gettysburg, S. D., 1921.

Hughes, Nathaniel C., Jr. *General William J. Hardee: Old Reliable.* Baton Rouge, 1965.

Johnston, William Preston. *The Life of General Albert Sidney Johnston.* New York, 1878.

Jordan, Thomas, and J. P. Pryor. *Campaigns and Battles of Lieutenant General Nathan Bedford Forrest and His Cavalry*. New Orleans, 1868.

Kay, William, "The Sunken Road." Unpublished Paper, Shiloh National Military Park Library.

Killebrew, J. B. *Middle Tennessee as an Iron Centre*. Nashville, 1879.

Lesley, J. P. *Iron Manufacturer's Guide to the Furnaces, Forges and Rolling Mills of the United States*. New York, 1859.

Lewis, Lloyd. *Sherman: Fighting Prophet*. New York, 1932.

Liddell-Hart, Basil Henry. *Sherman, Soldier, Realist, American*. New York, 1929.

Livermore, Thomas L. *Numbers and Losses in the Civil War in America, 1861–1865*. Boston, 1900.

McKee, Irving, *"Ben-Hur" Wallace: The Life of General Lew Wallace*. Berkeley, 1947.

McWhiney, Grady. *Braxton Bragg and Confederate Defeat*. 2 vols. New York, 1969.

Merrill, James M. *William Tecumseh Sherman*. Chicago, 1971.

Nevins, Allan. *The War for the Union*. 4 vols. New York, 1960.

Parks, Joseph H. *General Leonidas Polk, C. S. A.: The Fighting Bishop*. Baton Rouge, 1962.

Pitts, Charles F. *Chaplains in Gray: The Confederate Chaplain's Story*. Nashville, 1957.

Purdue, Howell and Elizabeth. *Pat Cleburne, Confederate General: A Definitive Biography*. Hillsboro, Tex., 1973.

Reed, David W. *Shiloh: Campaign and Battle*. Contained in John Obreiter, *History of the 77th Pennsylvania Volunteers*. Harrisburg, 1905.

————. *The Battle of Shiloh and the Organizations Engaged*. Washington, D. C., 1903.

Rich, Joseph W. *The Battle of Shiloh*. Iowa City, 1911.

Roland, Charles P. *Albert Sidney Johnston: Soldier of Three Republics*. Austin, Tex., 1964.

Roman, Alfred. *The Military Operations of General Beauregard in the War Between the States, 1861 to 1865*. 2 vols. New York, 1884.

Seitz, Don C. *Braxton Bragg: General of the Confederacy*. Columbia, S.C., 1924.

Soldiers and Citizens' Album of Biographical Records, vol. 1—Wisconsin. Chicago, 1888.

Strode, Hudson. *Jefferson Davis: Confederate President*. New York, 1959.

Sword, Wiley. *Shiloh: Bloody April*. New York, 1974.

Tucker, Glenn. *Chickamauga: Bloody Battle in the West.* Indianapolis, 1961.

Williams, Kenneth P. *Lincoln Finds a General.* 5 vols. New York, 1952.

Williams, T. Harry. *P. G. T. Beauregard: Napoleon in Gray.* Baton Rouge, 1954.

Periodicals

Connelly, Thomas L. "The Johnston Mystique." *Civil War Times Illustrated*, Feb. 1967.

Eisenschiml, Otto. "Shiloh—The Blunders and the Blame." *Civil War Times Illustrated*, Apr. 1963.

Lewis, Lloyd. "Rivers of Blood." *American Mercury*, May 1931.

Stillwell, Leander. "In the Ranks at Shiloh." *Journal of the Illinois Historical Society*, 1922.

Thompson, William R., ed. "From Shiloh to Port Gibson," by William Candace Thompson. *Civil War Times Illustrated*, Oct. 1964.

Throne, Mildred, ed. "Letters from Shiloh." *Iowa Journal of History*, vol. 52, 1954.

Wallace, Harold Lew. "Lew Wallace's March to Shiloh Revisited." *Indiana Magazine of History*, vol. 59, Mar. 1963.

Wiley, Bell I. "Johnny Reb and Billy Yank at Shiloh." *West Tennessee Historical Society Papers*, 1972.

Index